Cambridge 1994

An Introduction to Phonology

Learning About Language

General Editors:
Geoffrey Leech and Mick Short, Lancaster
University

Already published:

Analysing Sentences
Noel Burton-Roberts

Patterns of Spoken English
Gerald Knowles

Words and Their Meaning
Howard Jackson

An Introduction to Phonology
Francis Katamba

Grammar and Meaning
Howard Jackson

An Introduction to Sociolinguistics
Janet Holmes

Realms of Meaning
An Introduction to Semantics
Th. R. Hofmann

An Introduction to Semantics
Danny D. Steinberg

An Introduction to Spoken Interaction
Anna-Brita Stenström

An Introduction to Phonology

Francis Katamba

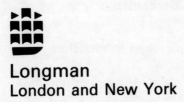

Longman
London and New York

Longman Group UK Limited,
Longman House, Burnt Mill, Harlow,
Essex CM20 2JE, England
and Associated Companies throughout the world.

*Published in the United States of America
by Longman Inc., New York*

© Longman Group UK Limited 1989

First published 1989
Sixth impression 1993

British Library Cataloguing in Publication Data
Katamba, Francis
   An introduction to phonology
   1. Phonology
   I. Title
   414

   ISBN 0-582-29150-X

Library of Congress Cataloging-in-Publication Data
Katamba, Francis, 1947–
   An introduction to phonology/Francis Katamba.
      p.   cm. — (Learning about language)
   Bibliography: p.
   Includes indexes.
   ISBN 0–582–29150–X
   1. Grammar, Comparative and general – Phonology.   I. Title.
II. Series.
P217.K33   1989
414–dc 19   88–28149
                         CIP

Set in Linotron 202 11/12 pt Bembo

Printed in Malaysia by CL

Contents

Preface

This book is a hands-on introduction to PHONOLOGY for the absolute novice. Probably the best way to learn about phonology, i.e. to learn how speech sounds are used to convey meaning, is to *do* phonological analysis and confront theoretical issues as they get thrown up by the data.

With this in mind, this book has been written not only with exercises at the end of each chapter, but also with in-text problems and tasks which are separated from the discussion by a line drawn across the page. You should always attempt these problems before reading on. They are an integral part of the discussion. Suggested answers are included within each chapter. Answers to end of chapter exercises will be found at the end of the book.

Some remarks on presentation: technical terms are commented on and highlighted using capital letters when they are introduced for the first time or when it is important to emphasise them. The common convention of using an asterisk to indicate impossible or wrong forms is also observed (e.g. *tleg* is 'starred' to show that it is not a possible word in English). Examples discussed in the text are written in italics.

The model of phonology which I introduce you to is called GENERATIVE PHONOLOGY. It was given its first full and authoritative statement in Chomsky and Halle's 1968 book *The Sound Pattern of English*. As we shall see, since then it has moved on in various directions. In the next few paragraphs the objectives of this theory are explained.

Generative phonology is part of the theory of language called GENERATIVE GRAMMAR which has been developed by Chomsky and his collaborators. The basic goal of generative grammar is to explore and understand the nature of linguistic knowledge. It seeks answers to questions like: what does knowing a language entail? How is linguistic knowledge acquired by infants? Are there any properties of language that are universal, i.e. is there such a thing as 'Universal Grammar'?

Chomsky believes that the answer to the last question, which he thinks holds the key to the other questions, is 'yes' and goes on to argue that Universal Grammar has a biological basis. Biologically determined characteristics of the brain pre-dispose humans to acquire grammars with certain properties. But this raises further questions: what are the properties of Universal Grammar? In attempting to answer this question, generative linguists have developed principles and posited rules of the kind we shall explore. They form part of their model of Universal Grammar.

Like other linguists, generative linguists know that some aspects of language are not universal. But still they raise the question whether some non-universal properties of language fall into certain well defined parameters. Are there any pre-set limits within which differences between languages occur? If the answer is 'yes' what are these limits and why do they exist? These are some of the main issues which this book addresses.

Besides being concerned with general patterns of language structure, linguistic theory must provide us with the tools for describing those idiosyncratic properties which are peculiar to a particular language. For instance, linguistic theory should enable us to write a grammar for English showing that the final *f* consonant of *chief* is pronounced *f* when the plural -*s* ending is present but the final *f* of *thief* is pronounced *v* when the same plural ending is present.

The grammar of a language can be regarded as a model of the COMPETENCE (i.e. inexplicit knowledge of rules) that underlies a native speaker's overt linguistic PERFORMANCE as a speaker–hearer. We need to distinguish between the knowledge speakers have and the manner in which they put that knowledge to use in concrete situations as, sometimes, there is a difference between what one knows to be correct and what one actually says. This may be due to a number of factors such as slips of the tongue or memory lapses. Linguistics is primarily concerned with linguistic competence (knowledge) rather than performance (use). This book is primarily concerned with PHONOLOGICAL COMPETENCE.

Interestingly, knowing a language, say English, is not merely a matter of learning by rote a very large number of sentences. Native speakers of a language can always produce and understand completely new sentences which they have not previously encountered. No list, however long, could contain all the potential sentences of a language. Therefore a grammar of a language cannot be simply a list of words and sentences of that language. In view of this, Chomsky proposes that a grammar of a language should be a generative algebraic system of formal, explicit rules that enumerates a non-finite number of well-formed sentences and assigns to each one of them a correct analysis of its structure.

The motivation for using rules to account for the fact that there is no limit to the number of possible sentences that a language can contain is obvious: speakers produce and understand sentences using rules. They do not merely memorise long lists of sentences. However, the reasons for assuming that there are rules which underlie speakers' knowledge of the sound system of their language are perhaps less obvious, given the fact that a language only uses a finite set of sounds to form words.

Just a little reflection is enough to show that the sound system is also rule governed. Determine which of the following nonsense words (which you are probably seeing for the first time) is a possible English word: *tpat, lsender, bintlement* and *zvetsin*. You no doubt have chosen *bintlement* as the only potential English word. This is because you **know** that the consonant sequences *tp, ls* and *zv* which occur in the other 'words' are not permitted at the beginning of an English word. On the other hand, all the sequences of sounds in *bintlement* are allowed by the rules of English phonology. You might indeed be tempted to look up *bintlement* in a good English dictionary – but not the other nonsense words.

The implicit knowledge of linguistic rules that speakers have is probably modular. Generative linguists have proposed that it can be represented using a model with a number of components which represent semantic knowledge, syntactic knowledge, knowledge of sound structure, and so on.

Over the years, various proposals have been made regarding the precise organisation and content of a generative grammar. You are not expected to have any prior knowledge of these theories. Nothing is presupposed. Essential aspects of the theory will be introduced, where necessary.

The diagram below shows the place of phonology in the general theory of language which we shall be using:

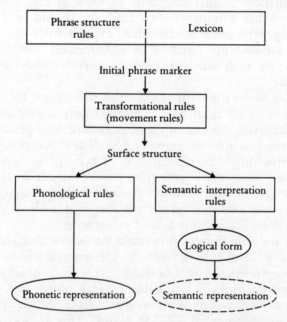

A Generative Grammar Model of Language (Based on Lightfoot 1982)

The SYNTACTIC COMPONENT consists of the base sub-component and the transformational rules. The PHRASE STRUCTURE (PS) rules and the LEXICON found in the base sub-component of the grammar generate the INITIAL PHRASE MARKER (DEEP STRUCTURE) of a sentence. The lexicon lists the words of the language, together with their syntactic and phonological properties and the PS rules define the constituent structure (i.e. the structure of noun phrases, verb phrases etc.) and how they interact with each other. The initial phrase marker enters the transformational component where it may be modified by various transformational rules which move around constituents. This is done to relate sentences like *Money is what I need* and *What I need is money.* The output of the syntactic component is the SURFACE STRUCTURE.

Surface structures are the input to rules of LOGICAL FORM and SEMANTIC INTERPRETATION. The rules of logical form explain, for example, why *to pay* in the sentence *Jane ordered Bill to pay* is understood to mean that *Bill* is the one that was expected to pay while in *Jane promised Bill to pay* it is *Jane* who is expected to pay.

Rules of semantic interpretation are used, for instance to account for logical relations like entailment. A sentence like '*The Mayor of Lancaster switched on the Christmas lights last year*' entails that **there were** *Christmas lights last year.* It would be contradictory to utter that sentence and continue '*but there were no Christmas lights last year because of budget cuts*'.

PHONOLOGICAL RULES also apply to the surface structure and assign it a PHONETIC REPRESEN-TATION (i.e. show how it is pronounced). It is this final aspect of the grammar that we are mainly concerned with in this book.

This book is a simple, practical introduction to phonology within the model of generative phonology as it has evolved during the last twenty years or so. While in the early years the emphasis was on making explicit the relationship between underlying and surface phonological representations by investigating the nature of formal phonological rules, the ways in which rules interact and the distance between underlying and surface representations in phonology, lately the focus has shifted to scrutinising the nature of phonological representations themselves and the relationship between phonology and other components of the grammar.

This shift in focus is reflected in the contents of this book. After a brief introduction to articulatory phonetics, the opening chapters deal with distinctiveness, 'naturalness', the relationship between levels of phonological representation and rule interaction. These were the main issues explored in the 1960s and 1970s.

However, the latter part of the book is devoted to topics of current interest. One major trend in generative phonology today involves several 'non-linear' approaches to the nature of phonological representations. It is being developed through an examination of the nature of sound 'segments', syllable, tone, stress, and intonation in numerous languages. The other major current trend focuses on the relationship between phonology and other components of the grammar such as the lexicon, morphology and syntax. These two trends are complementary.

The exclusive concentration on generative phonology should not be taken as evidence of a belief on my part that nothing of value has been said about phonology in the other frameworks. Occasionally the contributions of other schools are mentioned in a footnote. But I have restricted the exposition to generative phonology for two reasons. In my experience, for the beginning student it is more bewildering than enlightening to be presented with several competing theoretical positions, with their different theoretical concepts, analytical techniques and nomenclature. There is virtue in introducing students initially to one coherent theoretical approach. The question that then arises is: which approach?

I have chosen to introduce you to generative phonology. This is not merely a matter of my personal taste. Generative phonology is currently the dominant model of phonology. It is the model to come to grips with, if eventually you wish to read the current descriptive and theoretical phonological literature. Much of it is written in some version of this framework.

However, should you wish to survey other past and present trends in phonology there are many books which you can turn to. If you wish to acquaint yourself with the history of phonology you can read excellent historical studies like Fischer–Jørgensen (1975) and the more recent Anderson (1985). If you want an eclectic, 'unbiased' introduction to phonological concepts and their philosophical underpinnings you can turn to Lass (1984).

This book has developed from phonology courses that

I have taught over the years at the University of Nairobi, Kenya and at the University of Lancaster. I am grateful to the generations of students who were subjected to earlier drafts of the book for the feedback I got from them.

In writing this book I have benefited immensely from the help of Professor Geoffrey Sampson. Very special thanks also go to my editors and colleagues Mr. Mick Short and Professor Geoffrey Leech whose critical comments and suggestions have made this a better book than it would otherwise have been. Those others who over the years have taught me directly or indirectly something about phonology deserve a special mention. Their scholarship is reflected in the theory presented here as well as in the data from the dozens of languages cited. And finally, I am grateful for the encouragement of my wife Janet during the long gestation of this book.

21 March 1988

Acknowledgements

We are grateful to the following for permission to reproduce copyright material:

Cambridge University Press for extracts from *NGIYAMBA* (1980) by T. Donaldson & from 'Kimatumbi phrasal phonology' by D. Odden *Phonology Yearbook 4* (1987); Harper & Row Inc for an adaptation based on pp 302–329 from *The Sound Pattern of English* by Noam Chomsky & Morris Halle (Copyright © 1968 by Noam Chomsky & Morris Halle); the Editor, Professor Larry M. Hyman for an adaptation of pp 112–115 'Noun tonology in Kombe' by B. Elimelech in *Studies on Bantu Tonology* SCOPIL 3 (1976). International Phonetic Association for a table from p. 10 of *Principles of the International Phonetic Association* 1949/84; the author, P. Kiparsky for a figure from 'From cyclic phonology to lexical phonology' in *The Structure of Phonological Representations* Part 1 (1982) by Van der Hulst & Smith; MIT Press for a figure from p. 39 of *The Language Lottery* by D. Lightfoot. Copyright © 1983 MIT Press.

CHAPTER 1

Introduction to phonetics

1.1 Introduction

The purpose of this book is to introduce you to the study of PHONOLOGY. Phonology is the branch of linguistics which investigates the ways in which sounds are used systematically in different languages to form words and utterances.

In order to understand phonology, one must have a grasp of the basic concepts of PHONETICS, the study of the inventory of all SPEECH SOUNDS which humans are capable of producing. The term speech sound has been used advisedly since not all noises which we are capable of producing with our vocal apparatus are employed in speech: we can all snore; we can all cough and hiccup; we can all sneeze and we can all gnash our teeth. However, no linguist, has yet discovered a community that has a language in which noises produced by any one of these mechanisms are used to form words. It is almost certain that no such speech community exists. One reason for this is the fact that there are obvious disadvantages in letting communication depend on involuntary noises like hiccups which speakers cannot start and stop at will. Other methods like the gnashing of teeth may be easy to control, but have their drawbacks – the wear and tear which gnashing of teeth would entail must have ruled out that method. I am using these examples to underscore the point that speech sounds form a small subset of all the noises which humans can produce with their vocal apparatus. It is this subset that phoneticians focus on.

The study of speech sounds can be approached from

various angles. These are reflected by the three major branches of phonetics:

(a) ACOUSTIC PHONETICS: the study of the physical properties of speech sounds using laboratory instruments;
(b) AUDITORY PHONETICS: the study of speech perception;
(c) ARTICULATORY PHONETICS: the study of speech production.

1.2 The production of speech

It is articulatory phonetics that we shall concentrate on here because it is the branch of phonetics on which most phonological theories have been based in the past.

1.2.1 The production of consonants

Speech sounds are produced by interfering in some way with a body of moving air. Phoneticians use the term AIR-STREAM MECHANISM to describe a body of moving air used in speech production. It is important to describe how the air is set in motion and the direction in which it travels because that makes a difference in the sound produced. The commonest airstream mechanism used in the world's languages (and the only one found in English) is the PULMONIC EGRESSIVE mechanism. When this mechanism is employed, air is expelled from the lungs, up the windpipe and gets out through the mouth, or through the nose, or through both.

There exist other airstream mechanisms, but we shall postpone discussion of these until Chapter 3. We shall provisionally assume that all speech sounds are made with air pushed from the lungs up the WIND PIPE (also called the TRACHEA, more technically). Continuing its outward journey, the air reaches the LARYNX (or voice box – that cartilaginous membrane at the top of the windpipe which is called the Adam's apple in everyday language). Once in the larynx, the air must pass through the GLOTTIS. This is the space between the vocal cords. If the vocal cords are apart, i.e. if the glottis is open, the air escapes unimpeded. Sounds produced in this way are said to be VOICELESS.

If, on the other hand, the vocal cords are very close together, the air will blow them apart as it forces its way through. In doing so, it will make them vibrate, producing a VOICED sound.

You can perform a little experiment to determine for yourself whether a given sound is voiced or voiceless. Say [ffff] and then [vvvv] with two fingers held firmly on your larynx. Repeat this four times. What do you observe?

Now say [ffffvvvvffffvvvv] this time with your index fingers in your ears. What do you observe?

In the first experiment, you should be able to feel your fingers vibrating slightly when you say [vvvv] but not when you say [ffff]. And in the second experiment, you should be able to hear a low buzzing noise in your head when you produce [vvvv], but not when you produce [ffff]. The noise that causes the vibration in your larynx which you feel with your fingers as well as the low buzzing sound which you feel when you have fingers in your ears is called VOICING.

Voicing is linguistically important. The difference between voiced and voiceless sounds is functional. In many languages, English included, as you can see in [1.1], there are many consonants which come in pairs, with the two sounds in question differing in voicing:

[1.1] A   B
       pull   bull
       ten   den
       cot   got
       fast   vast
       sink   zinc
       chew   Jew

The initial consonant of the words in column A is voiceless while the initial consonant of the words in column B is voiced.

Find five more words which begin with voiceless and voiced consonants respectively.

[1.2]

The Organs of Speech

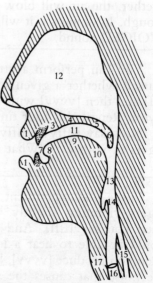

1	lips
2	teeth
3	alveolar ridge
4	(hard) palate
5	velum
6	uvula
7	tongue tip
8	tongue blade
9	front of the tongue
10	back of the tongue
11	mouth cavity
12	nose cavity
13	pharynx
14	epiglottis
15	oesophagus
16	glottis
17	larynx

The term VOCAL TRACT is used to refer to the air passages which the air enters on leaving the larynx. As you can see in the figure in [1.2], the vocal tract has two parts: the ORAL TRACT, which is the air passage offered by the mouth and the NASAL TRACT, which is the air passage provided by the nose.

Consonants are produced by obstructing in some way the flow of air through the vocal tract. We can identify the PLACE (or POINT) where the obstruction takes place, and the organs involved. The parts of the oral tract such as the tongue and lips which can be used to form speech sounds are called ARTICULATORS. A list of places of articulation is given in [1.3] together with the phonetic symbols representing some of the sounds made at each place.

As you read through [1.3] you should say aloud the words in the illustrative examples and observe how you use the articulators to produce each sound. Next, you should find examples of your own of each sound. The examples can come from any language you know. If you are uncertain about the terminology, consult [1.2].

[1.3] Places of articulation

place	articulators	examples	
BILABIAL	both lips	[p] *peat*	[b] *beat*
			[m] *meat*
LABIO-DENTAL	lower lip and upper front teeth	[f] *fine*	[v] *vine*
DENTAL	tongue tip and upper front teeth	[θ] *thigh*	[ð] *thy*
ALVEOLAR	tongue tip or blade and the alveolar ridge	[t] *tip*	[d] *dip*
		[s] *sip*	[z] *zip*
		[l] *lip*	[r] *rip*
			[n] *nip*
RETRO-FLEX	tongue tip curled back past the alveolar ridge	[ʈ] *raft*	(in American English)
		[ɳ] *pina*	'lake' (in Wangkatja (Australia))
PALATO-ALVEOLAR	blade of the tongue rising towards the alveolar ridge and the front of the hard palate	[ʃ] *sheep*	[ʒ] *genre*
		[tʃ] *cheap*	[dʒ] *jeep*
PALATAL	front of the tongue and the hard palate	[j] *yes*	[ç] *ich* 'I' (German)
		[ɲ] *agneau*	'lamb' (French)
VELAR	back of the tongue and the velum	[k] *cot*	[g] *got*
			[ŋ] *song*
LABIO-VELAR	simultaneously using both lips and raising the back of the tongue towards the velum	[w] *win*	
		[kp] *kpakpa* 'field' (Yoruba (Nigeria))	
GLOTTAL	vocal cords	[h] *hot*	
		[ʔ] *better* (in many varieties of nonstandard British English, e.g. Cockney)	

Besides describing the place where the obstruction occurs in the production of a consonant, it is also essential to consider the MANNER OF ARTICULATION, i.e. the nature and extent of the obstruction involved because sounds made at the same place of articulation – and which are both voiced or voiceless, as the case may be – can still differ depending on the manner in which the airstream is modified. Take these words, which all begin with VOICED ALVEOLAR consonants: *dine, nine, line* and *Rhine*. Not only do they sound different, they also mean different things. The difference lies in the manner of articulation of their initial consonants.

In [1.4] below a brief survey of manners of articulation is given, together with English examples.

[1.4] STOP: The articulators come together and completely cut off the flow of air momentarily, then they separate abruptly. Examples: *pin bin tin din kilt gilt*.

Stops like [p b t d k g] which are made with the pulmonic egressive airstream mechanism (as the speaker breathes out through the mouth) are called PLOSIVES. Sounds like [m n], as we shall see presently, are also stops but they are not plosives; they differ from plosives in that they are formed by completely blocking off the airstream in the mouth while at the same time allowing it to escape through the nose.

AFFRICATE: In the production of an affricate, first the articulators come together and completely cut off the flow of air, just as they do in a stop; then they separate gradually.

Examples: *chain   Jane*
[tʃ]   [dʒ]

Say the following words very carefully
char jar
Describe as accurately as you can the ways in which the articulators are used to obstruct the flow of air in the first sound of each word. Which one of the affricates is voiced?

FRICATIVE: the articulators are brought very close together leaving only a very narrow channel through which the air squeezes on its way out, producing turbulence in the process. Examples: [f v θ ð s z ʃ ʒ]

Say the following words and listen for the turbulence of the initial consonant:
fan van thin then sink zinc shrill genre

APPROXIMANT: the articulators are brought near each other but a large enough gap is left between them for air to escape without causing turbulence.
Examples: [r l w j] as in *read lead weed* and *yield* respectively.
NASAL: Nasal sounds are produced with air escaping through the nose; the velum is lowered to allow access to the nasal tract. Examples [m n ŋ]
The final sounds in all these words are nasal: *sum sun sung.*
On the other hand, to produce ORAL sounds like [p t k b d g s z] the VELUM is raised right up against the back wall of the PHARYNX, cutting off access to the nasal cavity and making air escape through the mouth only (see [1.2]).
LATERAL: to produce a lateral, the air is obstructed by the tongue at a point along the centre of the mouth but the sides of the tongue are left low so that air is allowed to escape over one or both sides of the tongue.
Example: [l]
If you say the following words slowly and carefully, you will be able to observe how the air escapes over the sides of the tongue in the last [l] sound:
> *peddle paddle   huddle*
> *kettle battle   cattle*

Examine the examples in [1.4] above once again. State the place of articulation of each consonant and also determine whether it is voiced or voiceless.

Next find three more words exemplifying each manner of articulation that has been described. Take your examples from any language which you know.

Summary

The production of consonants involves four major parameters which can be varied independently of each other to create different kinds of consonant. The four parameters are:

(a) THE AIRSTREAM MECHANISM
    This refers to the way in which the moving body of air that provides the power for speech production is generated and the direction in which it moves.

(b) THE STATE OF THE GLOTTIS
    Voiceless sounds are produced when there is a wide open glottis, with a big space between the vocal cords; voiced sounds are produced when the vocal cords are close together so that the air has to force its way through them, making them vibrate in the process.

(c) THE PLACE OF ARTICULATION
    This refers to the place in the vocal tract where the airstream is obstructed in the production of a consonant.

(d) THE MANNER OF ARTICULATION
    This refers to the way in which the airstream is interfered with in producing a consonant.

1.3 The production of vowels

Vowels are more difficult to describe accurately than consonants. This is largely because there is no noticeable obstruction in the vocal tract during their production. It is not easy to feel exactly where vowels are made. Moreover, in many cases, sounds perceived by hearers as the 'same vowel' may be produced using a number of substantially different articulatory gestures. The only reliable way of observing vowel production is using x-ray photography. But this is not only expensive, it is also dangerous and could not be carried out each time one wanted to describe a particular vowel (even if willing subjects eager to allow themselves to be exposed to radiation in the noble cause of phonetic inquiry could be found).

The account in this chapter will be restricted to vowels which occur in English but much of what is said is generalizable to many other languages. As we noted above, many of the parameters described above which are used in the description of consonants have not been found applicable to vowels. Vowels are typically voiced, but they have no place or manner of articulation. Traditionally, for the description of vowels a different set of concepts has been found necessary.

Say the words in [1.5] carefully. Observe in a mirror the position of the highest point of your tongue and your lower jaw.

[1.5] [i] seek [u] pool
  [ɪ] sick [ʊ] pull
  [e] set [ɒ] pot
  [æ] sat [ɑ] part

Now repeat the exercise, just uttering the vowel sounds on their own. Again observe the position of your tongue and jaw.

In each column your tongue is high when you say the vowel in the first word on the list and gets progressively lower as you work your way through the list. If you watch yourself in a mirror, you will observe that there is a correlation between tongue height and jaw opening: when the tongue is high, the jaw is not lowered but when the tongue is low the jaw is also low and your mouth is wide open.

Vowels produced with the highest point of the hump in the tongue close to the roof of the mouth are said to be HIGH and those produced with the highest point of the hump in the tongue barely rising above the floor of the mouth are said to be LOW; the intermediate position is referred to as MID.

Up to now, we have considered the vertical axis in locating the highest point of the tongue. That is not enough. It is also necessary to determine the location of the highest point on the horizontal axis: the highest point of the tongue may be at the front, in the centre or at the back of the mouth. Depending on the location of the highest point of the tongue, vowels may be regarded as FRONT, CENTRAL or BACK.

Say the words in [1.6] slowly a number of times and observe the position of your tongue in each case:

[1.6] [e] shed   [ə] should [1]   [ɒ] shod

When you say the vowel [e] your tongue is in the front, palatal region; when you say [ə] your tongue is in the centre of the mouth; when you say [ɒ] your tongue shifts to the back of the mouth. That this is the case will be clear if you utter the vowels on their own one after the other.

Finally, the quality of a vowel is affected by the shape of the lips. For simplicity's sake, phoneticians assume that lips can assume only two positions: they are either ROUNDED or UNROUNDED – intermediate positions are ignored. Lip rounding results in an elongated resonating chamber while lip SPREADING or UNROUNDING (the position the lips assume if you put on that fixed grin when the voice behind the camera tells you to smile or say 'cheese') does not. Just as the notes which can be produced by different wind instruments partly depend on the shape of the instrument, the QUALITY of a vowel sound partly depends on the shape of the resonating chamber in the vocal tract resulting from adjustments in lip position.

Get a mirror and once again observe your lips as you say the words in [1.7]. You will be able to verify that in each case the first word in each pair is said with spread (unrounded) lips while the second is produced with the lips rounded:

[1.7] [i] see   [u] sue
      [i] tea   [u] two

[e] fen   [ɔ] fought
[æ] lag   [ɒ] log

The various articulatory parameters are not entirely independent of each other. Note, for instance, that there is a systematic correlation between lip rounding and tongue height. For a rounded vowel, the higher the tongue is, the greater the degree of lip rounding.

The phonetic properties of vowels surveyed in this section are conventionally represented in this diagram:

[1.8]

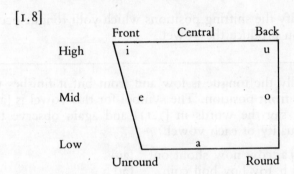

As [1.8] shows, typically front vowels are unrounded and back vowels are rounded.

The parameters high, mid and low enable one to distinguish three degrees of vowel height as you can see in [1.8]. But this is not always sufficient. There are languages which make a four way distinction on this parameter. Many phoneticians use the terms CLOSE, HALF-CLOSE, HALF-OPEN and OPEN to reflect this:

[1.9]   Front   Central   Back

Close   i   u

Half-close   e   o

Half-open   ε   ɔ

Open   a

All the vowels which have been described so far are MONOPHTHONGS i.e. vowels whose quality remains virtually unchanged throughout their duration. In addition to such vowels some languages (English included) also have DIPHTHONGS, i.e. vowels whose quality changes during their production.

Say the following words, concentrating on the vowel sound:

[1.10] pie   buy   my   guy   cry   tie
       die   sigh shy high lie   five

Identify the shifting positions which your tongue occupies as you produce the vowel.

Initially the tongue is low and front but it finishes up in a high, front position. The symbol for this vowel is [aɪ].

Now say the words in [1.11] and again observe the shifting quality of each vowel:

[1.11] a. cow now shout out [aʊ]
       b. toy boy boil coin [ɔɪ]
       c. wait pay weight hay [eɪ]
       d. air fare wear chair [eə]

In [1.12] you can see the changing quality of the diphthongs exemplified above:

[1.12]

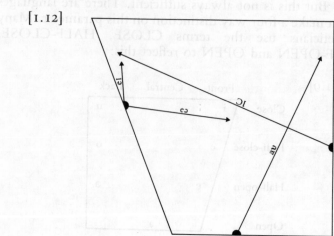

The primary aim of this chapter has been to introduce you to the basic concepts of articulatory phonetics so that you can understand the nature of speech production. The secondary aim is to introduce standard symbols for phonetic transcription largely through familiar English data.[2]

For a complete list of phonetic symbols see the **International Phonetic Alphabet** in the chart in [1.13]. You do not need to learn all the symbols in the chart right away. The chart is provided so that you can refer back to it whenever you encounter unfamiliar phonetic symbols in the course of reading this book.

[1.13]

Consonants	Bilabial.	Labiodental.	Dental and Alveolar.	Retroflex.	Palato-alveolar.	Alveolo-palatal.	Palatal.	Velar.	Uvular.	Pharyngal.	Glottal.
Plosive . . .	p b		t d	ʈ ɖ			c ɟ	k g	q ɢ		ʔ
Nasal . . .	m	ɱ	n	ɳ			ɲ	ŋ	N		
Lateral . . .			l	ɭ			ʎ				
,, fricative .			ɬ ɮ								
Rolled . . .			r						R		
Flapped . .			ɾ	ɽ					R		
Rolled fricative .			ɼ								
Fricative . .	ɸ β	f v	θð|sz|ɹ	ʂ ʐ	ʃ ʒ	ɕ ʑ	ç j	x ɣ	χ ʁ	ħ ʕ	h ɦ
Frictionless Continuants and Semi-vowels . .	w|ɥ	ʋ	ɹ				j (ɥ)	(w) ɣ	ʁ		

Vowels	Rounded			Front Centr. Back		
Close . . .	(y ʉ u)			i y ɨ ʉ ɯ u		
Half-close . .	(ø o)			e ø ɤ o		
				ə		
Half-open . .	(œ ɔ)			ɛ œ ʌ ɔ		
				ɐ		
				æ		
Open . . .	(ɒ)			a ɑ ɒ		

Exercises

1. Write a one-page summary of this chapter. Your summary should include the following points:
(a) the domain of phonetics
(b) the three main branches of phonetics
(c) the description of speech sounds
    (i) The four parameters used to describe consonants are:
      (a)
      (b)
      (c)
      (d)
    (ii) The three parameters used to describe vowels are:
      (a)
      (b)
      (c)
    (iii) The two major types of vowel sounds are:
      (a)
      (b)

2.(a) Write down the appropriate phonetic symbol for each one of the sounds described below.
 (b) Give an example of a word containing the sound you have written down. Use examples from any language which you know. Underline the relevant sound.
    (i) alveolar lateral
    (ii) voiceless alveolar fricative
    (iii) alveolar nasal
    (iv) voiceless glottal fricative
    (v) voiced bilabial stop
    (vi) voiceless bilabial stop
    (vii) velar nasal
    (viii) voiced dental fricative
    (ix) voiceless alveo-palatal fricative
    (x) voiced alveo-palatal affricate

3. Circle each sound in the following words which matches the description given. Follow the example given in (i).
    (i) a high front vowel
      f ⟨ee⟩ t fell pat wet full p ⟨ea⟩ t
    (ii) a low front vowel
      what bad cat saw these eggs

(iii) a high back vowel
women suit pool fool blood flood
(iv) a front vowel
weed word when hat card hit
(v) a back vowel
hut call guard sell soot mist
(vi) a central vowel
skin her winter pertain doctor sir
(vii) a rounded vowel
her good dumb ball pod cart
(viii) a high vowel
we do see ten pan bin
(ix) a mid vowel
send card keys school hall you
(x) a low vowel
man moon art cup knot teeth
(xi) a diphthong
why he may boy tar house bird

Notes

1. Say 'should' as you would in a casual conversation when uttering a sentence like 'John should go' where there is no emphasis on *should*.

2. For a general introduction to phonetics I refer you to one of a number of textbooks such as Abercrombie (1967), Ladefoged (1982) or Knowles (1987).

Chapter 2
The phoneme

2.1 Segments of sound

As we hinted in the opening chapter, and are going to see in detail in this and subsequent chapters, in purely physical terms, any utterance is a continuum: articulatorily, it is a continuous flow of gestures that blend with each other; acoustically, it is a continuously fluctuating wave of sound. Yet, for several reasons, from a **functional** point of view, the fiction of discrete speech segments with which the last chapter ended is worth clinging to.

Firstly, an ALPHABETIC WRITING SYSTEM, with discrete letters written in a line one behind the other, seems to be capable of representing the sound system of any language in a non-arbitrary way. Indeed, native speakers, if they are literate in an alphabetic writing system, can usually determine without any difficulty, the 'distinct' sounds which a word consists of. Of course, to this you might reply that the idea of SEGMENTS is perhaps not inherent in the nature of the spoken language but is rather something inculcated by an alphabetic writing system – if people see words in terms of segments, that is simply attributable to the conditioning they have been subjected to by alphabetic writing. You might argue that it would not be surprising if it turned out that illiterate people or literate speakers of languages like Chinese and the American Indian language Cherokee, which have non-alphabetic writing systems, do not view speech in terms of segments.

The Chinese writing system represents the WORD in its entirety. Thus the CHARACTER 日 represents the word 'sun' and the character 人 represents the word 'man'. This is analogous to way in which mathematical symbols like ≥

< etc. represent entire concepts or words which are pronounced differently in different languages. Turning to Cherokee writing we observe that each symbol represents an entire syllable. For instance, f, A, Ᏻ respectively represent the syllables *ga, go,* and *gu.*

By itself, alphabetic writing is not sufficient proof of the reality of sound segments. More persuasive evidence needs to be found. One source of such evidence is SPEECH ERRORS. Quite often, speech errors occur in which sounds are transposed in words, as though they were discrete items. Have we not all heard spoonerisms where word initial consonants are switched from one word to another, resulting in forms like *polley trusher* and *sork pausages* when the speaker really means to say *trolley pusher* and *pork sausages*?

Pause for a moment and list at least three more spoonerisms. Describe the transposition of sounds that takes place in each one of your examples.

Admittedly, spoonerisms are an aberration (the Rev. W.A. Spooner would not have become so famous if swopping consonants between words was the norm). What makes spoonerisms interesting is the way in which they clearly illustrate the treatment of speech sounds by speakers as discrete segments which can be shunted from one word to another.

The same kind of segmentalization of speech sounds is also manifested in normal spoken language – albeit usually in a less extreme form. There are numerous phonological operations (as you will discover as you work your way through the book) which re-arrange, add or delete individual consonant and vowel segments of a word rather than some larger pieces such as syllables. For instance, many non-standard varieties of British English have a rule which 'drops aitches' at the beginning of a word. The effect of this rule is to make words like *at* and *hat* sound exactly the same. Rules which drop sound 'segments' exist in languages regardless of whether they have an alphabetic writing system. Similarly, rules which insert segments exist in languages regardless of whether they have an alphabetic writing system. I have in mind rules like the one which optionally inserts [r] between vowels within a word as in *draw(r)ing* (for *drawing*) or across a word boundary as in *the idea (r) is* (for *the idea is*).

The upshot of this discussion is that one important aspect of linguistic knowledge is the knowledge of the functional phonological units which occur in one's language – the knowledge of the segments which can be arranged in different patterns to form words. This knowledge is for the most part unconscious (just in the same way that knowledge of how to build boats which can float when fully laden has been in the minds of boat builders from time immemorial – long before they had any explicit understanding of the principles of physics involved). Most speakers of English do not spend half the day wondering whether to 'drop an aitch' in a word like *hat* or 'swallow a t' in a word like *better*. But that does not mean that they do not **know** the rules which govern the sound pattern of their language. Phonology attempts to make explicit the nature of the knowledge that underlies their subconscious linguistic behaviour.

2.1.1 Distinctiveness: phonemes and allophones

A useful approach to the problem of how segments of sound are used in speech is to consider sounds from a FUNCTIONAL point of view, to talk not in terms of individual physical sounds, but of FAMILIES of sounds which count as the same in the language in question. Such a family of sounds is called a PHONEME.[1] Members of the same phoneme family, i.e. the various physically distinct sounds which count as executions of a given phoneme are called the ALLOPHONES (or VARIANTS) of that phoneme. A phoneme is conventionally represented by a letter symbol between slant lines. Thus, in English, the infinitely physically diverse voiceless stops that can be made with contact between the tongue and the palate are grouped into two phonemes labelled /t/ and /k/, each of which has a range of allophones which differ slightly from each other.

Which phoneme a particular sound heard in speech belongs to entirely depends on the language in which it occurs. In some languages, such as Slavonic ones, some of the physically attested sounds which in English would be regarded as somewhat off-target renderings of /t/ or /k/ would instead be members of a third, separate phoneme /c/, to which English has nothing corresponding.

Sounds are grouped together as members of the same phoneme when the very real physical differences between them happen to be functionally immaterial with respect to the language being described.

Utter the following words slowly: *car keys*. You will notice that in *car*, the back of the tongue touches the part of the soft palate near the uvula (see the figure in [1.2] on page 4), at the very back of the roof of your mouth, but in *key*, it is the more front part of the soft palate near the hard palate that the tongue makes contact with. The two varieties of 'k' are physically different. But they are not functionally different in English. They cannot be used to distinguish word meaning. Rather, they are allophones of the same /k/ phoneme and which one is used on a given occasion depends on what the neighbouring sounds happen to be.

The two 'k' sounds are in COMPLEMENTARY DISTRIBUTION. When two sounds are in complementary distribution, they are barred from occurring in identical environments: there is a rigid division of labour, as it were, so that one sound appears in certain contexts and the other in some different, clearly defined contexts. Thus, in our example, the very back allophone (variant) [k] of the phoneme /k/ found in *car* (allophones are written in square brackets) occurs before back vowels and the fronted [k̟], as in *key* occurs before front vowels (the + diacritic under a consonant indicates fronting). Another example of complementary distribution in English should make the point clearer. The phoneme /t/ has several allophones. It is possible to predict the allophone that speakers produce in a given word if you know the sounds that are adjacent to it.

Say the words: *tea, too* and *eighth*. You will notice that the alveolar allophone [t] in *tea* [ti] is made with the lips spread but that in *too* [tʷu] is made with pursed or rounded lips (a little, raised 'w' is used to show lip rounding). However, in [eit̪θ] 'eighth' the allophone of /t/ is dental,

[t̪] [.] is the diacritic mark for dental sounds) not alveolar
– in anticipation of the dental fricative [θ] which follows,
the tip of the tongue is positioned against the upper front
teeth.

It is worth stressing that the relationship between a
family of sounds is not like that between members of a
human family. The phoneme is an abstraction. What actually occur are the allophones – to be precise PHONES i.e.
sounds which can be grouped together as allophones of a
particular phoneme. We hear a range of physically different
sounds in English, such as those described above, which we
recognise as being functionally non-distinct. We use the
theoretical construct of PHONEME to mean that functionally speaking, a given set of sounds never contrast with
each other although they may contrast with other sounds
outside that set.

All sounds used in a language belong to some
phoneme. Some phonemes have numerous allophones
others may have a less diverse membership. Since we need
some label to identify a phoneme, the obvious and usual
thing to do is to represent the phoneme using the phonetic
symbol for one of its allophones. Accordingly, for
simplicity the phoneme that includes [t] and [t̪] and [tʷ] is
labelled /t/; it could equally well be labelled /tʷ/ or, for
that matter an arbitrary number like /13/. But, although in
principle there is no significance in the label given to a
phoneme, it would be perverse to make a determined effort
to avoid mnemonic labels: /t/ is preferable to /13/ as the
label for the English phoneme which we are discussing.

Some phonemes such as English /m/ have a dominant
family member which occurs in almost all contexts. In such
cases the selection of the symbol of that allophone to
represent the phoneme is uncontroversial. Other phonemes
such as /t/ have no clearly dominant family member and
the choice of the symbol of one of the allophones to
represent the phoneme is not as easily justified. Nevertheless, in neither case should the sound chosen to represent
the family be equated with the family itself.

The family metaphor is also useful in highlighting
another principle of phoneme theory: namely, the

PHONETIC SIMILARITY OF ALLOPHONES of the same phoneme. The phoneme is a suitable label for a group of sounds which are phonetically alike and which show certain typical patterns of distribution. This principle is intended to prevent the lumping together as allophones of the same phoneme; sounds which appear to be in complementary distribution but have no phonetic similarity. A classic example of this is provided by [ŋ] and [h] in English. At first sight, these two sounds appear to be in complementary distribution, with [h] occurring syllable initially followed by a vowel (as in *hat* and *ahead*) and [ŋ] occurring in consonant clusters and syllable finally (as in *longer* and *long*). But because they lack phonetic similarity, [h] and [ŋ] cannot be grouped together as allophones of the same phoneme.

What are the articulatory differences which disqualify [h] and [ŋ] from counting as allophones of the same phoneme? Take into account the following articulatory parameters: place of articulation, manner of articulation and the state of the glottis.

Recall from Chapter 1 that [h] is a voiceless glottal fricative and [ŋ] a voiced velar nasal.

   There is an alternative approach to the phoneme which highlights the linguistic function of phonemes in DISTINGUISHING (or CONTRASTING) word meaning rather than their physical phonetic characteristics. The key notion in this approach is CONTRAST or DISTINCTIVENESS. On this view, the phoneme is a minimal sound unit which is capable of contrasting word meaning. As we noted above, although in reality there is an infinite amount of variation in the sounds produced by speakers of a given language, not all these phonetic differences are pertinent. Some objectively noticeable variation in the production of sounds is not used to convey semantic differences. Consider the words in [2.1]:

   [2.1] tip ~ dip   bet ~ bed   pat ~ pad
         bit ~ bid   mate ~ made   white ~ wide

The words in each pair have different meanings and this difference is signalled by the difference between [t] and [d]. When two sounds can be used to distinguish word meanings in a particular language they are said to be separate phonemes. On the basis of [2.1] we can say that in English /t/ and /d/ are separate phonemes.

Supply examples of English words with different meanings which only differ in that where one word has [l] the other has [r], all the other sounds being exactly the same. Are [l] and [r] separate phonemes in English?

2.2 Identifying phonemes

In this section I shall outline the basic procedures which are used to identify the phonemes, i.e. the functionally significant segments of a language.

2.2.1 The minimal pair test

When two words are identical in all respects, except for one segment, they are referred to as a MINIMAL PAIR. The pairs in [2.1] are minimal pairs (and so should be the pairs illustrating the contrast between [r] and [l] which you have written down). The MINIMAL PAIR TEST (i.e. the method of determining that a single sound difference distinguishes the meanings of two words) is a key principle of phonemic analysis. Sounds are classified as separate phonemes if they are responsible for a difference in meaning in a minimal pair.

Another way of saying this is to state that sounds are separate phonemes if they CONTRAST IN IDENTICAL ENVIRONMENTS, i.e. if either sound can occur in a given context and the choice of one or the other does alter the meaning of a word. The forms in [2.2] show minimal pairs in which [r] and [l], [m] and [n] and [k] and [g] contrast in identical environments and are therefore distinct phonemes:

[2.2] read ~ lead   rice ~ lice   room ~ loom
mow ~ know   mice ~ nice   seen ~ seem
buck ~ bug   cot ~ got   card ~ guard

Before you read on, list as many minimal pairs as you can think of which show that [b] and [m], [s] and [z] and [i] and [e] are separate phonemes in English or some other language which you know. To start you off, here are some minimal pairs which show that [b] and [m] contrast word meaning in English: *bat* ~ *mat*, *bet* ~ *met*, *meat* ~ *beat*, *robe* ~ *roam*, *cub* ~ *come*.

2.2.2 Contrast in analogous environments

Sometimes it is not possible to find minimal pairs contrasting each single phoneme. In such circumstances, the phonologist has to settle for something less rigorous: CONTRAST IN ANALOGOUS ENVIRONMENTS. Using this principle, sounds are isolated as belonging to separate phonemes if they occur in phonetically very similar, though not identical environments provided that the differences between them cannot be reasonably attributed to the influence of neighbouring sounds (see Chapter 5). Admittedly, there are bound to be occasional differences of opinion between phonologists as to what constitutes adequate similarity to justify labelling environments as 'analogous'. Phonological analysis is not an exact science. Here, I shall avoid getting bogged down in controversies and simply illustrate the principle of contrast in analogous environments with an example from Ewe, a Ghanaian language.

We can regard /f/ and /v/ as separate phonemes in Ewe because they contrast in analogous environments in words like [evlo] 'he is evil' and [ẽflẽ] 'he split off' ([ẽ] symbolises a nasalised [e] vowel). The difference between nasalised [ẽ] on the one hand and oral [e] and [o] on the other cannot be the reason for the difference between voiceless [f] and voiced [v] since nasal [ẽ] as well as oral [e] and [o] are all voiced and should not affect in different ways the voicing of neighbouring sounds.

2.2.3 Suspicious pairs

Since, as we observed above, only those sounds which show considerable phonetic similarity can be grouped together as allophones of the same phoneme, it would be pointless to comb through the entire phonological system of a language in search of minimal pairs and examples of contrast in analogous environments. A practising phonologist can normally safely assume that sounds like [n] and [x] or [l] and [p] which show no phonetic resemblance are distinct phonemes. As a rule, methods for determining whether or not sounds belong to the same phoneme are only employed where SUSPICIOUS PAIRS have been identified, that is to say, pairs of words containing sounds which only differ slightly and which can plausibly be members of the same phoneme.

A few examples should clarify this point. If you look back at the data in [2.2] which were used to illustrate the minimal pair test, you will notice that the sounds in each pair are quite similar and could conceivably be allophones of the same phoneme: [r] and [l] are both voiced alveolar approximants, the main difference between them being the fact that [l] is lateral and [r] is not; [m] and [n] are both voiced nasal stops, only differing in place of articulation – the former is labial and the latter alveolar; [k] and [g] are both velar stops – the only difference between them is that [k] is voiceless while [g] is voiced. Likewise, in the Ewe example, the contrast in analogous environments test is worth attempting because [f] and [v] are both labiodental fricatives, only distinguished by voicing: they could easily be allophones of the same phoneme.

2.2.4 Recapitulation

While admitting that the tacit 'theory' of clear-cut speech-sound distinctions implied by the nature of our alphabet script is physically quite wrong, nevertheless we have gone on to argue that functionally it is largely right: a phonemic transcription will indeed treat a language as containing a small number of discretely-different unitary sounds, even though the phonetician knows that it does not. Many of the physical details of a sound are functionally irrelevant within a given language. Hence sounds that are physically different may be regarded as functionally the same in a particular language. For example, speakers of English who are not linguists are unlikely to be aware of the variety of allophones of /t/ which we noted above; they are only likely to be interested in knowing whether a word contains /t/ as opposed to some other phoneme – they will only want to know whether the word uttered by their interlocutor is *cart* or *card, tin* or *thin* etc.

Furthermore, as we shall see presently, functionally it makes sense to think of the changes in the various phonetic variables which make up a sound as happening in an abrupt and synchronised fashion, even though physically they are gradual and they overlap each other. That is to say, although in a word like *inn*, it is true that the soft palate will begin to be lowered before the tongue makes contact with the alveolar ridge, there is no functional significance in the fact that the latter part of [ɪ] in *inn* will be progressively nasalised while the [ɪ] of *if* is wholly oral. The English-speaking hearer will not perceive the difference between the two [ɪ]'s. To such a hearer *inn* consists of just two sharply-separated sounds: oral [ɪ] followed by nasal [n]. In view of this, psychologically we are justified in thinking of speech as segmented along the time dimension, even though physically the segments blend into one another – the situation is very much analogous to that of cursive handwriting.

2.3 Phonological symmetry

There remains one aspect of the 'tacit alphabet theory' of speech-sound which has not yet been justified even in functional or psychological terms, and which indeed cannot be so justified. I refer here to the way that alphabetic transcription (traditional orthography and phonemic transcription alike) treats successive segments of speech-sound as single atomic elements, transcribed with one symbol each, rather than as bundles of simultaneous elements, each element being a value of a particular phonetic variable. That is: let us forget for a moment that the [n] of *inn* overlaps the [ɪ], and pretend instead that there is a sharp division between the [ɪ] part of the word and the [n] part; it still remains true that an utterance of [n] is not one unitary action, but the simultaneous realisation of a range of separate phonetic properties. These include: a tongue/palate contact belonging to the family that count as 'alveolar' rather than 'palatal', 'stop' rather than 'fricative' closure, voice, a lowered soft palate that results in a sound that is nasal rather than oral (see [1.4]); and, if we are thinking about dissimilarities not only with other English phonemes but with non-English sounds as well, we would need to add 'pulmonic egressive airstream' and perhaps other features of sound. Clearly, speech sounds are not indivisible atoms.

However, for convenience in reading and writing, it is advantageous to use a code which represents a whole bundle of such phonetic properties using a single symbol, rather than having to represent a word like *inn* in a two-dimensional notation, with a table showing articulatory parameters as in [2.3]:

[2.3]

	Segment 1: [ɪ]	Segment 2: [n]
vocal cords:	vibrating	vibrating
soft palate:	up	down
place of articulation:	(not applicable)	alveolar
manner of articulation:	(not applicable)	stop
degree of aperture:	close etc.	(not applicable)

This aspect of alphabetic writing is only a matter of practical convenience and long tradition, and there seems to be no good theoretical justification for it; functionally as well as physically, sounds are 'bundles of phonetic properties' rather than unitary lumps.

One reason for saying that the internal structure of phonemes is in all probability relevant to the way in which they function phonologically has to do with the tendency to SYMMETRY found in the phonological systems of numerous languages.

Consider vowel systems, for instance. It is possible to classify vowel systems into two common categories: TRIANGULAR and QUADRANGULAR systems. They may be very basic, or more elaborate as you can see in [2.4]

[2.4]

	Front unrounded	Back rounded	Front unrounded	Back rounded	Front unrounded	Back rounded
Close	i	u	i	u	i	u
Half-close			e	o	e	o
Half-open					ɛ	ɔ
Open	a		a		a	

(e.g. Arabic, Aleut Eskimo (Alaska) Dyirbal (Australia))	(e.g. Spanish, Czech, Burmese, Swahili)	(e.g. Italian, Kikuyu (Kenya) Efik (Nigeria))

and [2.5] which illustrate triangular and quadrangular vowel systems respectively.

About the simplest system of vowel phonemes commonly found (it occurs in Aleut Eskimo and Arabic, for instance) has just three members. Many other languages, such as Spanish, Czech, Burmese, and Swahili, distinguish three degrees of aperture and have a five-member vowel system. Yet others, like Italian, Kikuyu and Efik have four degrees of aperture and a seven-member vowel system. All these systems are triangular: there is a lone low (open) vowel and at least one pair of non-low vowels.

Azerbaijani, British Columbian French, Persian and English exemplify (with different embellishments) the other common type, namely a quadrangular vowel system which may be represented as [2.5]:

[2.5]

	Front unrounded	Back rounded
Close	i	u
Half-close	e	o
Open	a	ɒ/ɑ

(rounded/unrounded respectively)

Asymmetrical systems are logically possible but occur less commonly than symmetrical ones. Thus, for instance, four-member vowel systems such as those in [2.6] seem to be rare in comparison with the symmetrical ones.

[2.6] (a). i   u   (b). i

   e

                              ə
                              ɐ
        a   a
(Cocopa (Arizona, USA))   (Marshalese,
                              (Marshall Islands))

Likewise, consonant systems also tend to be symmetrical. If we consider just stop consonants, for simplicity, English has:

[2.7]   bilabial alveolar velar
voiceless   p   t   k
voiced   b   d   g

while Czech has:

[2.8]   bilabial alveolar palatal velar
voiceless   p   t   c   k
voiced   b   d   j   g

A system like that of Siriono, a Bolivian language, which has holes in the pattern is less common. In Siriono there are no voiced alveolar, velar and palatalised velar stops corresponding to voiceless stops at these places of articulation.

[2.9]   bilabial alveolar palatalized velar
                                   velar
voiceless   p   t   kʲ   k
voiced   b

If a language uses a particular phonetic property (such as 'back' or 'stop' or 'voiced') at all, rather than use it to make a one off contrast, it will normally exploit it fully by employing it to form several phonemes. Consequently phonological systems tend to be symmetrical. Hence, symmetry is an outward sign of the underlying dimension of contrast in phonology.

Another common factor encouraging phonological symmetry has to do with permissible combinations of phonetic properties in particular languages. In the vowel systems surveyed above, all the vowels were either front and unrounded (spread) or back and rounded. In all the languages in our examples front vowels must be unrounded and back vowels (with the exception of [ɑ]) must be rounded. The prohibition of the combination of roundedness with frontness and backness with unroundedness in vowels is by no means universal. There exist languages such as French and Swedish in which it is permissible for front vowels to be rounded and other languages such as Ivatan, spoken in the Philippines, and Vietnamese in which back vowels may be unrounded.

Thus, in French, the vowel in words like *tu, vu* and *lu* which is represented by the phonetic symbol [y] is both front and round. And again, as you can see in [2.10], this combination of frontness and roundedness is not restricted to the close vowel [y] but is also found with other degrees of aperture (other than fully open – the reason for this gap being that the physical distinctions between spread and rounded lip-position are very slight for fully-open vowels, so that lip rounding is seldom used contrastively for such vowels in most languages):

[2.10] Unrounded   Rounded
         Front   Front   Back
       i (as in *six*)   y (as in *tu*)   u (as in *fou*)
       e (as in *été*)   ø (as in *peu*)   o (as in *peau*)
       ɛ (as in *père*)   œ (as in *œuf*)   ɔ (as in *monopole*)

In [2.10] I have not shown the degree of aperture. Before you proceed, rank the vowels on a scale indicating the relative height of the highest point of the tongue during the production of each one of these vowels. You may use [2.11] to check your answer.

I do not mean to exaggerate the extent to which languages exhibit PHONOLOGICAL SYMMETRY, it is only a tendency, and often a chart of phonemes will include one or two gaps which spoil the symmetrical pattern. For instance, among the consonants listed above for Czech, /g/ is quite marginal, being found only in words borrowed from other languages; in this case, one might be tempted to argue that it was the existence of this gap in an otherwise balanced pattern that enabled words containing [g] to be borrowed into Czech without this sound having to be modified in the way that foreign sounds that do not exist in the borrowing language are normally modified.

This account might look plausible for Czech, but it would not do in those situations where asymmetry is unrelieved, even by borrowing. Thus, while French permits front rounded vowels although they are unusual, Vietnamese forbids them but permits back spread (unrounded) ones which are no less unusual. Interestingly, there are only two back unrounded vowels in Vietnamese where symmetry would lead one to expect three:

[2.11]		Unrounded		Rounded
		Front	Back	Back
Close		i	ɯ	u
Half-close		e		o
Half-open Open		ɛ	Ⓐ	ɔ
Open			a	

There 'ought' to be a phoneme /ʌ/ (I have filled it in and circled it in the chart), but in fact, Vietnamese has no such phoneme, not even in borrowed words.

Such counter-examples notwithstanding, the importance of phonological symmetry as a tendency rather than an absolute rule is very well established. Yet, if phonemes were regarded as unitary, indivisible atoms, with their internal phonetic make-up irrelevant to their functioning, this tendency would seem quite inexplicable. If a language, say English, were to possess twenty-four consonant phonemes, one would suppose that any selection of twenty-four consonant sounds would do as well as any other, and it would be a remarkable coincidence if the twenty-four actually used in the language manifested any particular symmetrical patterning. It would be even more remarkable if the types of symmetrical patterns accidentally stumbled upon by one language, say English, just happened to be the same as those stumbled upon by numerous unrelated languages. As we have seen, this is indeed the case: the symmetrical patterns found in the phonological systems of the languages of the world appear to come from a very restricted range.

If, on the other hand, instead of regarding phonemes as indivisible, atomic entities we think of phonemes and the phonemic symbols that represent them as merely a shorthand way of indicating bundles of distinctive phonetic features, then the apparently mysterious recurrence of the same parameters in phonological symmetry can be explained. Members of a language-community have to learn to produce and perceive the psychological 'target-value' of various phonetic dimensions which their language uses to distinguish word meanings: for instance, the Arabic speaker has to learn to make two distinctions on the dimension of vowel aperture and the Spanish speaker three.[2] For a language to be phonologically symmetrical, with simple rules for combining phonetic properties, is a way of optimizing the use of phonetic parameters; it is a way of getting a relatively small number of different bundles of phonetic properties to do the job of distinguishing word meanings.

Referring to the **International Phonetic Alphabet** in [1.13] on page 13, study the following consonant systems and write down your answers to the questions that follow:

[2.12] (a) b n x t f g z
     (b) p ŋ t x d m k g b ɣ n f v s z

Which of these two systems is symmetrical? What advantages has the symmetrical system got over the asymmetrical one?

I hope you chose the system in [2.12b] as the symmetrical one. There, every stop has a corresponding fricative, every voiced oral stop has a corresponding nasal one, and every voiced stop and fricative has a corresponding voiceless one:

[2.13]	labial		alveolar		velar	
	voiced	voiceless	voiced	voiceless	voiced	voiceless
stop	b	p	d	t	g	k
fricative	v	f	z	s	ɣ	x
nasal	m		n		ŋ	

The system in [2.12a] is the asymmetrical one. As [2.14] shows it is riddled with holes:

[2.14]	labial		alveolar		velar	
	voiced	voiceless	voiced	voiceless	voiced	voiceless
stop	b			t	g	
fricative		f	z			x
nasal			n			

The consonant inventory in [2.14] is extremely un-economical, using, as it does, three places of articulation, three manners of articulation and two values of the voicing variable (eight phonetic parameters in all) to define a mere seven consonants. On the other hand, the consonant inventory in [2.13] represents a much better use of resources: a consonant system with fifteen sounds is created using the same eight parameters.

Furthermore, you should note that while the asymmetrical inventory can be defined only by imposing complicated regulations to ensure that only segments with permissible combinations of phonetic properties are generated (e.g. in [2.14] only the labial and velar stops, the alveolar fricative and nasal can be voiced), no such *ad hoc* restrictive statements are needed for the symmetrical system.

One probable consequence of this is that a symmetrical system is easier to learn than an asymmetrical one – even when, as in our example the latter contains fewer elements. Predictably, for the most part phonological systems tend to be symmetrical, using in an optimum way phonological properties such as *voice, alveolar* and *fricative* which speech-sounds are made up of.

As we have already noted, it is unusual, but not unheard of, for a language to have an asymmetrical conso-nant system like the one in [2.14]. An example is given below in [2.15] of such a skewed consonant system in Palauan, a Filipino language:

[2.15]*Palauan consonants*

		t	k	ʔ
b				
	ð	s		
m			ŋ	
	l			
	r			

We shall conclude this chapter by emphasising the point that while the practical convenience of alphabetic tran-scription is so great that it is used much of the time even in the theoretical study of phonology, we should nonethe-less bear in mind the fact that such a transcription is no more than a practically convenient short-cut. What is 'really' happening in phonology is happening in terms of separate phonetic properties, not of 'unitary sounds'. It is these phonetic properties rather than phonemes that are the basic building blocks of phonology. Before we delve any deeper into phonology we shall explore the nature of these phonetic and phonological properties. That is the subject of the next chapter.

Exercises

1. The pairs of consonants listed below are separate phonemes in English. Provide minimal pairs showing how these sounds contrast word meaning.

		word initially		word finally	
/p b/	e.g.	$p$at	$b$at	cu$p$	cu$b$
/b m/					
/t s/					
/z s/					
/p t/					
/d n/					
/k g/					
/s ʃ/					
/tʃ z/					
/tʃ dʒ/					
/l d/					

2. In French, the following pairs of sounds are in COMPLEMENTARY DISTRIBUTION: [m m̥], [l l̥], [r r̥]. Study the data below and identify the phonetic context in which the voiced and voiceless member of each pair occurs. State the rule that governs the distribution of each sound.

materniṭe	'maternity'
mekɔnɛtr̥	'to fail to recognise'
maṭinal	'morning (adj.)'
preṭã:dr	'to claim as a right'
prezãṭabl	'presentable'
mɛtr̥	'to put'
tɔrdr̥	'to wring'
rãṭabl	'profit-earning'
il	'island'
ɛl	'she'

pœpl̩	'people'
tãpl̩	'temple'
ɔ:kl̩	'uncle'
t̪abl	'table'
rym	'cold (with a running nose)'
rymat̪ism̩	'rheumatism'
film	'film'
rɔ̃fle	'to snore'
kɑsabl	'breakable'
rali	'race-meeting'
ʃɛ:r	'fare, living'
ʃifʳ	'number, figure'
limit̪e	'limited'
mɛ:r	'mother'
pɛrs	'Persian'
ɛtʳ	'to be'
ekri:r	'to write'
t̪ɛrm	'term'
li:r	'to read'
lɛvr	'lip'

Notes

1. There exists a very rich literature on the phoneme. Key
    works include Bloomfield (1926, 1933), Sapir (1925,
    1933), Jones (1931), Bloch (1941), Pike (1947), Hockett
    (1955) and Trubetzkoy (1939). Standard textbooks like
    Hyman (1975: 59–98) and Sommerstein (1977: 16–53)
    also contain good introduction to the literature. To
    those who want a more detailed account of the devel-
    opment of phoneme theory (and phonological theory
    in general), I recommend Fischer–Jørgensen (1975) and
    Anderson (1985).

2. This view is held by those who regard the phoneme
    as a psychological entity. Badouin de Courtenay is
    probably the best known holder of this view. He
    defined the phoneme as 'a mental reality, as the inten-
    tion of the speaker or the impression of the hearer or
    both' (Twaddell 1953: 56) (see page 67 below).

CHAPTER 3
Distinctive features

3.1 Why are features needed?

We saw at the end of Chapter 2 that phonological systems
tend to be symmetrical and that a limited number of
phonetic parameters, taken from a fairly small universal set
recur in a variety of combinations in different languages. It
makes sense to look beyond the phoneme and focus on
those basic phonological ingredients, called DISTINCTIVE
FEATURES, which phonemes are made of.

Besides introducing you to distinctive features, this
chapter will also serve as a restatement in a slightly different
form of the principles of phonetics which were outlined in
the first chapter. There is nothing mysterious about the fact
that there is a relatively small inventory of phonetic features
from which languages select different combinations to
construct their individual phoneme systems. As all members
of the human race are endowed with very similar articulatory and auditory capabilities, it is only to be expected that
they will only be able to produce and utilise speech sounds
built up from the set which is pre-determined by their
biological endowment.

The position presented in this chapter regarding
distinctive features has not always been accepted by all
students of phonology. At one time some scholars, like
Bloomfield (1926), would not agree with the claim that the
phoneme is not the most basic phonological element.
Bloomfield thought that there were no phonologically
relevant particles more elementary than the phoneme,
although he was aware that on purely phonetic grounds the
phoneme can be decomposed into more basic particles.

The belief that the phoneme is the atomic, basic

building block of phonology is untenable, not only because of the arguments which have already been advanced concerning symmetry, but also for other reasons which I explore below.

Firstly, even a cursory inspection of the phonology of any language will reveal that the phonological behaviour of phonemes is largely determined by the phonetic features which they are made up of. Consider the behaviour of /r/ in English. It undergoes partial devoicing when immediately preceded by voiceless stops but not when it is preceded by voiced ones:

[3.1] pray   [pr̥eɪ]   brain   [breɪn]
      train   [tr̥eɪn]   drain   [dreɪn]
      crane   [kr̥eɪn]   grain   [greɪn]

If you look at it in terms of the implementation of distinct articulatory gestures, it is clear that the signal to start voicing is delayed until well after the beginning of the /r/ due to imprecise adjustment of the articulatory apparatus in the transition from one sound to the next. Looking at sounds in terms of the individual parameters which they consist of allows an insightful expression of ASSIMILATION PROCESSES, i.e. phonological processes whereby one sound changes to become more like some other sound in its environment (see Chapter 5). By highlighting each articulatory parameter and singling out the sub-phonemic particles (i.e. distinctive features) which phonemes are made up of, this approach is capable of treating assimilation insightfully as an instance of SPREADING of distinctive features.

Examine the American English data in columns A and B in [3.2] and suggest reasons why a distinctive feature approach to these data is preferable to an indivisible, atomic phoneme approach:

[3.2]	A			B		
	/pad/	[pæd]	'pad'	/pan/	[pæ̃n]	'pan'
	/pas/	[pæs]	'pass'	/pam/	[pæ̃m]	'Pam'
	/pak/	[pæk]	'pack'	/paŋ/	[pæ̃ŋ]	'pang'

When solving [3.2], you will have discovered that if you treat phonemes as unanalysable entities, you have no straightforward way of showing that the vowel only assimilates the property of nasality from the following consonant if that consonant is nasal as in [3.2B]. The SPREADING of nasality to the preceding vowel is due to the premature, anticipatory lowering of the velum, as the vowel is being produced, to let air escape through the nose during the articulation of the nasal consonant. Distinctive features thus facilitate the statement of assimilation processes by highlighting the various separate gestures involved in the production of speech. No equally natural way of stating assimilation processes is available if phonemes are treated as unanalysable units.

An added advantage of the feature approach is that it enables us to highlight the internal structure of a sound. When we do that, it soon becomes obvious that **phonological segments have internal structure**. Sounds are not bundles of unordered, unstructured phonetic properties. A simple example like [3.3] shows that distinctive features can be arranged one before another within a single phoneme:

[3.3]

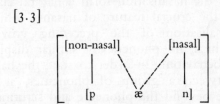

Whereas [p] is wholly oral and [n] is wholly nasal, the vowel [æ] occurring between them is oral to begin with but subsequently becomes nasalised in anticipation of the following nasal consonant. The properties NASAL and NON-NASAL occur together in sequence in the same phoneme.

Similar evidence of internal structure is to be found in diphthongs. In words like *way* [weɪ] and *why* [waɪ] the vowel sound has two distinct vowel qualities, a fact which is reflected in this case in the way in which the two phases of the sound are transcribed. The same point can be made about affricates like [ts], [dz], [tʃ] and [dʒ]. They are composite consonants starting with a stop phase and ending with a fricative phase. In many languages, affricates behave in part as though they were stops and in part as though they were fricatives. Thus we can see that the phoneme is not an indivisible phonological unit.

If we revisit the American English example above, a further reason for the espousal of a feature approach should become apparent: distinctive features bring out the fact that, in general, phonological rules apply to NATURAL CLASSES of sounds i.e. sounds which share certain phonetic properties. Thus, it would be bizarre for any language to have a rule nasalising vowels before the following assortment of consonants: [d s k t h]. This is a ragbag of sounds which are phonetically very different from each other and which all lack the crucial property of being **nasal** which is passed on to an adjacent vowel during nasalisation. The chances of such an arbitrary nasalisation rule existing in any language are extremely remote. On the other hand, a rule which nasalises vowels in the neighbourhood of nasal consonants (as in [3.2]) is phonetically plausible and is found in numerous languages. The nasal consonants [m n ŋ] which condition the nasalisation form a natural class and they all contain the crucial feature of nasality which triggers off the nasalisation of the preceding vowel. Normally, sounds which are phonetically similar display similar phonological behaviour. In order to state the basis of the similarity between a group of phonemes, it is necessary to penetrate beyond the phoneme and scrutinise the phonetic features which they share.

3.2 Jakobsonian features

Current distinctive feature theory has its roots in the work of the Russian scholars Trubetzkoy and Jakobson who were based in Prague between the wars. When the Nazis occupied Czechoslovakia, Jakobson fled to New York and later moved to Harvard where he introduced some of the ideas of the 'Prague School' to the Americans.

The key publications are Trubetzkoy (1939) and Jakobson, Fant and Halle (1952). Trubetzkoy was mainly interested in devising a system of classifying the phonemic

OPPOSITIONS (i.e. contrasts) in the use of common phonological parameters like voicing and aspiration. His approach was TYPOLOGICAL, i.e. concerned with the classification and comparison of the sound systems of different languages in order to show that there is a limited number of ways in which phoneme inventories can be organised. He regarded the exploration of the constraints on the structuring of phonoloigcal systems as one of the tasks of the phonologist

To take one example, Polish and English have only two bilabial stops, namely /p/ and /b/; the two sounds are almost identical except for the fact that the latter has the additional property or 'mark' of being voiced. It can therefore be referred to as being MARKED while the former, which lacks that additonal property, can be said to be UNMARKED. Note that the question of MARKEDNESS only arises when two sounds are in a two-way opposition. In the case of a multi-dimensional opposition like the place of articulation contrast between /p t k/, where no one sound is in any sense more basic than the others, the question of markedness does not arise.

Significantly, if in a particular language a phonemic contrast is NEUTRALISED or SUSPENDED, i.e. if a phonemic contrast generally observed is not found in a given environment, it is invariably a two-way opposition that is involved and normally it is the unmarked member of such an opposition that occurs in the PLACE OF NEUTRALISATION. Thus, in Polish /k/ and /g/ are distinct phonemes and contrast between vowels in minimal pairs like [roɡi] 'horns' and [soki] 'juices'. But, in word-final position, [k] and [g] do not contrast. There, the opposition between them is neutralised or suspended and only the voiceless [k] occurs. That is the situation in the singular form of the noun : 'horn' and 'juice' are pronounced as [ruk̠] and [sok̠] respectively (Kenstowicz and Kisseberth 1979:72–3). Neutralisation is one of the key concepts in phonology. We shall come back to it in Chapter 8.

While Trubetzkoy was primarily concerned with phonological typology, Jakobson and his collaborators concentrated their investigations on phonological oppositions that occur UNIVERSALLY. Jakobson hypothesised that although languages show an almost infinite amount of phonetic variation, the range of phonemically contrasting features is severely restricted by universal principles. The initial proposal was that just a dozen acoustically defined pertinent contrasts (other than prosodic ones, involving such things as tone and stress which are usually associated with an entire syllable or word) would be found in all languages.

Jakobson and his co-workers further hypothesised that the presence of certain oppositions in a language precludes the existence of other oppositions. For instance, they suggested that no language phonemically contrasts labialised consonants (i.e. consonants produced with rounded lips) with pharyngealised consonants (i.e. consonants made with a constriction in the pharynx). Although labialization and pharyngealisation are distinct as far as articulation is concerned, they are phonologically merely implementations of the same acoustic distinctive feature FLAT.[1]

Another aspect of the Jakobsonian feature system was its BINARISM. Jakobson *et al.* (1952) insisted on a binary interpretation of all features. This was done by pushing the phonemicist's principle of distinctiveness to its logical conclusion: in order to distinguish between the meanings of words, they argued, what counts is either the presence or absence of a given feature (respectively indicated by a '+' or '−' before the feature in question). For example, to discriminate between the words in [3.4] what is crucial is the presence or absence of voicing in the first segment:

[3. 4]

[+ voice]	[− voice]
bet	pet
den	ten
ghoul	cool
zinc	sink

Admittedly, binarism works well where there exists a two-way opposition, but it does not yield entirely satisfactory results where multilateral contrast is involved. Take the case of a language which distinguishes four degrees of vowel height and has the vowels [i e ɛ a] or a language that distinguishes four places of articulation and has the bilabial, alveolar, palatal and velar nasal consonants [m n ɲ ŋ]. In neither case can a binary characterisation of opposition be employed without some degree of arbitrariness, or at the very least, without obscuring the fact that what is involved is a cline rather than a dichotomy.

Binarism has remained controversial and there has developed a powerful lobby (Ladefoged 1971, 1975; Vennemann 1972) for multivalued features where GRADUAL OPPOSITIONS (like those found in vowel contrasts) or MULTIVALUED OPPOSITIONS (involving say, places of articulation) are concerned. Nevertheless, the dominant view among phonologists, and the the view adopted in this book, is that although the case for multivalued features is not without merit, from a phonological point of view, distinctiveness is the paramount consideration and its interests are best served by binary distinctive phonological features; for on every occasion, the hearer has to make a decision as to whether the speaker has said either this word or that word. True, the phonetic features which specify the phonetic realisation of a given feature, say voicing of stops in English, could be put on a multivalued scale like:

[3.5] [d]:   [3 voice] as in *ladder* where [d] is surrounded by voiced segments
[d]:   [2 voice] as in *date* where [d] occurs at the beginning of a word
[d]:   [1 voice] as in *laid* where [d], which is word final, is almost completely devoiced

Phonetically, English voiced stops are fully voiced between vowels; less fully voiced word-initially and minimally voiced word-finally. In principle we could indicate the amount of voicing by using an infinite number of points on the voicing scale. Phonologically, however, this kind of low level detail is overlooked. Thus, for instance, although acoustically the final sound in a word like *late* may be virtually identical to the final consonant of *laid*, the two sounds are phonologically different: the former belongs to the /t/ phoneme and the latter to the /d/ phoneme. Phonetic features may be multivalued but phonological features need not be. A binary distinctive feature system is adequate because, what is relevant linguistically, is simply whether or not the sound uttered by a speaker is a realisation of phoneme /t/ or /d/. As a rule, it is a dichotomous choice.

3.3 The SPE system of distinctive features

Various shortcomings of the Jakobsonian features came to light in the 1950s and 1960s. It was discovered that the model was too parsimonious. The dozen or so features which it allowed were insufficient to account for all phonological contrasts found in the languages of the world. Furthermore, it was criticised for using the same phonological feature to characterise phonological oppositions which in some cases were manifested by different phonetic properties. For instance, if a sound was described as GRAVE (which means that most of the acoustic energy used in its production is concentrated in the lower part of the spectrum) you would not be able to tell whether it was a labial like [p], or a velar like [g], since the acoustically defined phonological property GRAVE could be correlated with either labial or velar articulation.

Because of these and other inadequacies, Chomsky and Halle (1968) in their book *The Sound Pattern of English* (henceforth SPE) proposed a major revision of the theory of distinctive features. They replaced acoustically-defined phonological features with a set of features that have, in most cases, articulatory correlates. Furthermore, the number of features was also substantially increased. But, like their original Jakobsonian precursors SPE features remain binary. They have only two coefficients or values, plus (+) indicating the presence of a feature and minus (−) its absence, so that, for example, among other things, a sound like [p] is said to be [−voice] and [−nasal] while [m] is [+voice] and [+nasal].

The list of distinctive features given below is based on SPE in the main, but it incorporates some of the modifications that have been proposed since 1968.

It is not important to 'master' all the details of distinctive feature theory at this stage. They are described mainly in order to show how the system works. But you should come back to this chapter to refresh your mind as the need to use features arises in later chapters.

3.3.1 Major class features

The major class features define the major classes of sounds

that are relevant in phonological analysis. The major classes include CONSONANTS and NONCONSONANTS, SYLLABICS and NONSYLLABICS, SONORANTS and NONSONORANTS (OBSTRUENTS).

1. CONSONANTAL – NONCONSONANTAL
   [± cons]
   Consonantal sounds are produced with a drastic stricture along the centre-line of the vocal tract; nonconsonantal sounds are made without such obstruction.
   Obstruents, nasals and liquids are consonantal; vowels and glides[2] are nonconsonantal.

2. SYLLABIC – NONSYLLABIC [± syllabic]
   Syllabic sounds are sounds which function as syllable nuclei; nonsyllabic sounds occur at syllable margins. Normally, syllabic sounds are auditorily more salient than adjacent nonsyllabic sounds. Vowels are syllabic and so are syllabic consonants such as [l̩] in *bottle* and *candle* or the nasal [n̩] in *cotton* and [m̩] in *bottom*.

3. SONORANT – NONSONORANT
   (OBSTRUENT) [± sonorant]
   Sonorants are produced with a vocal cavity disposition which makes spontaneous voicing easy while nonsonorants (obstruents) have a vocal cavity disposition which inhibits spontaneous voicing.
   In other words,the unmarked (normally expected and natural) state for sonorants is to be voiced, while for obstruents the unmarked state of affairs is to be voiceless.
   Vowels, nasals and liquids are sonorant; stops, fricatives and affricates are obstruents.

3.3.2 Cavity features

These features refer to place of articulation. They specify where in the vocal tract modifications of the airstream take place in the production of particular sounds.

4. CORONAL – NONCORONAL [± coronal]
   To produce a coronal sound, the blade of the
   tongue is raised towards the front teeth, the
   alveolar ridge or the hard palate; for noncoronal
   consonants the blade of the tongue remains in a
   neutral position.
   Dental, alveolar, alveo-palatal, retroflex and
   palatal sounds are coronal; labial, velar, uvular
   and pharyngeal consonants are noncoronal.

5. ANTERIOR – NONANTERIOR [± anterior]
   In the production of anterior sounds, the main
   obstruction of the airstream is at a point no
   farther back in the mouth than the alveolar ridge;
   for nonanterior sounds the main obstruction is
   at a place farther back than the alveolar ridge.
   Labials, dentals and alveolars are anterior
   while all other sounds are not.

6. LABIAL – NONLABIAL [± labial]
   A sound is labial if it has a stricture (narrowing)
   made with the lips; if there is no such stricture,
   the sound is nonlabial.
   In the literature the alternative feature
   ROUND is often used to refer to many of the
   sounds which can also be described as labial.
   Rounded sounds are produced with a pursing
   or narrowing of the lip orifice. There is a
   considerable degree of overlap between the
   groups of sounds covered by the features
   [+round] and [+labial]. Rounded sounds like
   [o] [u] and [w] are a subset of labial sounds;
   consonants like [p b m] are labial but not
   round. Labial sounds include bilabial and
   labiodental consonants as well as rounded
   vowels. All other sounds are nonlabial.

7. DISTRIBUTED – NONDISTRIBUTED [±
   distributed]
   Distributed sounds are made with an obstruction
   extending over a considerable area along the
   middle-line of the oral tract; there is a large area
   of contact between the articulators. In nondistri-

buted sounds, there is a smaller area of contact. This feature is primarily used to distinguish APICAL sounds from LAMINAL sounds. In apical sounds the tip of the tongue makes contact with the front teeth or the alveolar or alveo-palatal regions of the roof of the mouth while in laminal sounds it is the blade of the tongue that makes contact with those same areas. This feature also distinguishes labial from labiodental sounds.

The following sound types are distributed: bilabial fricatives like [ɸ ß] (lamino-)alveolar fricatives like [s z] (lamino-)alveo-palatal fricatives like [ʃ ʒ].

The following sound types are nondistributed: labiodental fricatives like [f v] (apico-)dental fricatives like [θ ð] retroflex fricatives like [ʂ ʐ].

3.3.3 Tongue body features

In SPE the neutral position of the body of the tongue is said to be the position which it assumes in the production of a mid front vowel. Other tongue configurations are regarded as departures from that norm.

8. HIGH – NONHIGH [± high]

High sounds are made with the tongue raised from neutral position while nonhigh sounds are made without such raising of the body of the tongue.

High sounds include vowels like [i u], the glides [w j], alveo-palatal, palatalized, palatal and velar consonants. All other sounds are nonhigh.

9. LOW – NONLOW [± low]

Low sounds are produced with the tongue depressed and lying at a level below that which it occupies when at rest in neutral position; nonlow sounds are produced without depressing the level of the tongue in this manner.

Open vowels like [a ɑ ɒ] are low and so are the pharyngeal consonants [ħ] and [ʕ]. All other sounds are nonlow. (MID vowels are both NONHIGH and NONLOW.)

10. BACK – NONBACK [± back]

Sounds produced with the body of the tongue retracted from neutral position are back. Sounds produced with the body of the tongue either in neutral position or pushed forward are nonback.

This feature distinguishes between back vowels like [u o ɔ] and front vowels like [i e ɛ]. (Note that because in SPE the position of the tongue in the production of a mid front vowel is taken as the neutral position, it is not only back vowels that are [+ back], but also central ones like [+ ə ʉ]. (Because the feature system is binary, there is no way of showing that certain vowels are neither front nor back; central vowels are grouped together with back vowels. This does not appear to be entirely satisfactory on purely phonetic grounds.)

Of the consonants, velars, uvulars and pharyngeals are back while labials, dentals, palatals as well as glottals are nonback.[3]

11. VELAR SUCTION – NONVELAR SUCTION [± velar suction]

This feature is used to characterise CLICK SOUNDS like the *Tut tut*! used in English to show disapproval.

While in English clicks are not fully-fledged speech sounds which can combine with other sounds to form words, in some languages (which happen to be almost exclusively found in Southern Africa) clicks are used as regular speech sounds.

The production of a click involves two crucial phases. First there must be a stricture made using the back of the tongue and the velum; this is called VELIC CLOSURE. Secondly there must be some constriction in the labial, dental, alveolar or alveo-palatal area. The feature [+velar suction] itself describes the pulling back of the body of the tongue which creates a partial vacuum between the velic closure at the back and the forward closure, say at the alveolar ridge. The resulting sound is a click.

Clicks are produced with an INGRESSIVE VELARIC AIRSTREAM MECHANISM (which is different from the more common pulmonic egressive airstream mechanism described in Chapter 1 which is used in English). The soft palate and the back of the tongue are the initiators of the movement of air and the direction of the airflow is inward.

Clicks are velar suction sounds; other sounds are not. Zulu has a dental click [ʇ], an alveolar lateral click [ʖ] and an alveo-palatal click [ʗ].

3.3.4 Tongue root features

The vocal tract is a long tube with holes at both the lip end and the throat end. The shape of this tube can be modified by rounding the lips and making them protrude – and thus elongating the tube. Alternatively, the tongue root position can be adjusted by pushing it forward or retracting it so that the vocal tract is either lengthened or shortened. Either of these actions has the effect of modifying the shape of the resonating chamber in the vocal tract in much the same way as differences in size and shape of wind instruments affect the notes which they produce.

12. ADVANCED TONGUE ROOT – NONAD-VANCED TONGUE ROOT [± ATR]
The tongue root is pushed forward in the production of advanced tongue root sounds, thus expanding the resonating chamber of the pharynx and possibly pushing the tongue body upward; if the tongue root is not advanced, it remains in a neutral position.

Vowels like [i e o] in many West African languages are made with the tongue root pushed forward while [ɪ ɛ ɔ] are made with the tongue root in neutral position.

13. TENSE – LAX [± tense]
The validity of the feature TENSE has always been controversial. I quote Halle and Clements (1983:7) who give this cautious definition: 'Tense vowels are produced with a tongue body or tongue root configuration involving a greater degree of constriction than that found in their lax counterparts; this greater degree of constriction is usually accompanied by greater length. (Tense vowels vs. lax vowels.) We note that this feature and the last [ATR] are not known to co-occur distinctively in any language and may be variant implementations of a single feature category.'
The English 'long' vowels and diphthongs [i, ɑ, ɔ, u, eɪ, aɪ, ɔɪ, əʊ, ju] are tense while the 'short' vowels [ɪ, e, æ, ʊ, ʌ, ɒ] are lax.

3.3.5 Laryngeal features

14. SPREAD GLOTTIS – NONSPREAD GLOTTIS [± spread]
Pushing the vocal cords wide apart augments the airflow through the glottis and inhibits voicing. This gesture, which is associated with voicelessness and aspiration, is absent in nonspread sounds.
Spread sounds include aspirated stops; murmured and breathy voice sounds, voiceless vowels and voiceless glides. All other sounds are nonspread.

15. CONSTRICTED GLOTTIS – NONCONSTRICTED GLOTTIS [± constr]
Constricted sounds are GLOTTALISED. They are produced with a severe obstruction of the glottis which is made using the vocal cords. This inhibits or prevents the free vibration of the vocal cords. No such gesture occurs in the production of nonconstricted sounds.
Constricted sounds include implosives, ejectives, glottalised and laryngealised consonants

as well as creaky voice and glottalised vowels and glides. All other sounds are nonconstricted. In the opening chapter of this book we observed that English only uses speech sounds made with the pulmonic airstream mechanism, but there are languages which employ additional mechanisms. Earlier in this chapter (see section 3.3.3) you will recall that I remarked on the use of clicks in many Southern African languages when another airstream mechanism, namely the velaric airstream mechanism was introduced. Here I shall briefly describe the remaining airstream mechanism found in languages. It is called the GLOTTALIC AIRSTREAM MECHANISM.

To understand how it works, I suggest that you begin by making a big constriction in your throat – pretend that you are just about to cough. Get your vocal cords firmly together and shut off the glottis. At this stage, an upward movement of the larynx will push out the air above the larynx while a downward movement of the larynx will suck in air and loosen the constriction; the vocal cords will vibrate vigorously as the air flows in.

Stops made with the GLOTTALIC AIRSTREAM MECHANISM, with the air above the larynx being expelled, are called EJECTIVES. Ejectives are voiceless. An example of an ejective is the [t'] in Tlingit, a language of Alaska, in the word [t'ij] 'elbow'.

Stops made with the GLOTTALIC INGRESSIVE AIRSTREAM MECHANISM are called IMPLOSIVES. The air drawn into the larynx as it is pulled downward normally causes heavy voicing. An example of this is the bilabial stop, in the word [ɓaɓa] 'father' in Shona (Zimbabwe).

16. VOICED – VOICELESS [± voice]

Voiced sounds are produced with the vocal cords vibrating at regular intervals; voiceless sounds are produced without such periodic vibration.

3.3.6 Manner features

These characterise the way in which the airstream is obstructed in the production of a consonant.

17. CONTINUANT – NONCONTINUANT [±cont]
Continuants are produced by impeding, but not completely blocking, the flow of air through the glottis, or the pharynx or through the centre of the oral tract; noncontinuants are made by completely blocking the flow of air through the centre of the vocal tract.
   Affricates, laterals, nasals and oral stops are noncontinuant. All other sounds are continuant.

18. LATERAL – NONLATERAL [± lateral]
A lateral sound is produced if the airflow through the centre of mouth is blocked and air only escapes over one or both sides of the tongue. In nonlateral sounds air flows out through the centre of the mouth. The English [l] is an example of a lateral LIQUID. (The term 'liquid' is conventionally used to refer to 'l' and 'r'-like sounds.)
   Languages may have lateral sonorants, fricatives and affricates made at various places of articulation.

19. NASAL – NONNASAL (ORAL) [± nasal]
In the production of a nasal sound the velum is lowered to allow air to escape through the nasal cavity. Oral sounds are produced with the velum raised so as to block access to the nasal cavity and to allow air to go out only through the mouth.
   Nasal sounds include nasal stops like [m n ɳ ɲ ŋ] (which are made with complete blockage of air at the place where the articulators meet) as well as nasalised consonants, glides and vowels. All other sounds are oral.

20. STRIDENT – NONSTRIDENT [± strident]
Only fricatives and affricates can be strident. Acoustically, strident sounds are characterised by

more random noise than their nonstrident counterparts.

In the SPE system, where features are generally defined in articulatory terms, the feature [strident], which is acoustically-defined is different from the rest – it is a relic retained from the original Jakobsonian system.

Fricatives which have high pitched strident noise are referred to as SIBILANTS. The feature strident distinguishes fricatives as follows:

	[+strident]		[-strident]	
	Voiceless	voiced	Voiceless	voiced
Sibilant	s	z	ɸ	ß
			θ	ð
	ts	dz	ç	j
	tʃ	dʒ		
nonsibilant	f	v		
	pf	bv		
	X	ʁ		

21. DELAYED RELEASE – INSTANTANEOUS RELEASE [± del rel]

This feature is only applicable to sounds produced in the mouth cavity and distinguishes stops from affricates. In stops, the closure is released abruptly while in affricates it is released gradually: the initial **hold phase** of an affricate is similar to that of a stop but in the later **release phase** an affricate is like a fricative.

Only affricates can have the property [+del rel]; all other sounds are [-del rel].

3.3.7 Prosodic features

Prosodic features such as tone and stress, which are usually associated with an entire syllable or word, are difficult to describe. Although their phonological relevance is clear, their phonetic properties are not easy to specify satisfactorily.

The account of prosodic features given in this chapter

is provisional. It is based on the SPE position which was dominant for a long time, and is reflected in much of the literature that appeared during the 1970s, but has been superseded by recent theories which will be outlined in the last four chapters of this book.

22. LONG – SHORT [± long]

This feature refers to the duration of a sound. Clearly, in purely physical terms this feature cannot be binary since length is always relative. In the SPE system, and in its Jakobsonian predecessor, length is not regarded as a basic phonetic property but rather as an incidental attribute of the feature [tense], which is binary. Thus in English, for example, the contrast between [i] and [ɪ] (as in /sik/ 'seek' and /sɪk/ 'sick') is regarded as being essentially a tense versus lax opposition; the fact that /i/ is longer than /ɪ/ is viewed as secondary.

But even if this were the correct analysis, using the feature [tense] to subsume length would be questionable where differences in duration involve consonants since the feature [tense] is meant to specify vowels only.

If we use the feature [±long], however, these difficulties are avoided because it is equally applicable to vowels and consonants. No problems arise when we encounter a language like Luganda (Uganda) which distinguishes long consonants from short ones in words like /ta/ [ta] 'release! (imperative)' and /tta/ [t:a] 'kill! (imperative)' as well as long and short vowels as in /kula/ [kula] 'grow up! (imperative)' and /kuula/ [ku:la] 'uproot! (imperative)'.

In principle, the feature [long] is multi-valued. A language could contrast more than two degrees of length. Kikamba (Kenya) contrasts three degrees of vowel length.[4] In practice most languages which have distinctive vowel length only distinguish between long and short vowels. A binary approach, while not ideal is not altogether inappropriate.

23. STRESS [± stress]

Stress is an elusive concept. All stressed (or accented) syllables in a word are more salient than their unstressed counterparts but the phonetic manifestation of stress varies. The prominence of stressed syllables is due to an admixture of raised pitch, greater length and increased intensity of the signal, which is perceived as loudness. In addition, in some languages, e.g. English, stressed vowels retain their full vowel quality while unstressed vowels are reduced to some muffled vowel sound like schwa [ə].

It is generally agreed in principle that stress need not be binary. In SPE, for instance, three degrees of stress are recognized for English. In practice, however, phonologists often treat stress as binary for convenience.

24. TONE

It is important to distinguish between tone and pitch. The pitch of an utterance depends on the rate of vibration of the vocal cords, the higher the rate of vibration, the higher the resulting pitch becomes. Any time a voiced sound is produced, the vocal cords must vibrate at a certain rate: all languages have sounds which show pitch differences. In a TONE language those pitch differences are used phonemically either to differentiate between word meanings or to convey grammatical distinctions.

Commonly used tone features (which are normally indicated by writing the appropriate diacritic above the appropriate tone-bearing element) are:

[±] High: (marked by ('))
[±] Mid: (marked by (−))
[±] Low: (marked by (`))
[±] Rising: (marked by (ᷓ))
[±] Falling: (marked by (^))
[±] Fall-rise: (marked by (ˇ))

The use of tone to distinguish lexical meanings can be illustrated with this example from Igala, a Nigerian language (Welmers 1973):

[3.6] áwó 'guinea fowl'   àwó 'a slap'
     áwō 'an increase'   àwō 'a comb'
     áwò 'hole (in a tree)' àwò 'star'

The use of tone to signal grammatical distinctions is illustrated with this example from Engenni (Nigeria), appearing in Bendor-Samuel (1974), where the distinction between declarative and negative sentences is marked using tone:

[3.7]

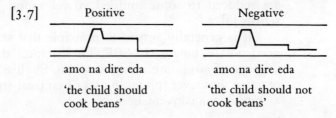

Positive	Negative
amo na dire eda	amo na dire eda
'the child should cook beans'	'the child should not cook beans'

I shall sum up the discussion so far by showing charts of distinctive feature matrices which contain arrays of features necessary for the representation of various sounds.

[3.8] Distinctive feature matrix for vowels

	i	ɪ	y	u	ʊ	e	ɛ	з	ə	ɨ	ʉ	ʌ	ø	œ	o	ɔ	æ	a	ɑ	ɒ	ɯ	ɣ
high	+	+	+	+	+	−	−	−	−	+	+	−	−	−	−	−	−	−	−	−	+	−
low	−	−	−	−	−	−	−	−	−	−	−	−	−	−	−	−	−	+	+	+	+	−	−
back	−	−	−	+	+	−	−	−	−	+	+	+	−	−	+	+	−	+	−	+	+	+	+
tense	+	−	+	+	−	+	−	+	−	−	+	−	+	−	+	−	−	−	+	−	+	+
round	−	−	+	+	+	−	−	−	−	−	+	−	+	+	+	+	−	−	−	+	−	−

[3.9] Distinctive feature matrix for sonorants

	m	n	ɳ	ɲ	ŋ	N	l	ɭ	ʎ	r	ɾ	j	w
cons.	+	+	+	+	+	+	+	+	+	+	+	−	−
cont.	−	−	−	−	−	−	+	+	+	+	+	+	+
nas.	+	+	+	+	+	+	−	−	−	−	−	−	−
lat.	−	−	−	−	−	−	+	+	+	−	−	−	−
lab.	+	−	−	−	−	−	−	−	−	−	−	−	+
ant.	+	+	−	−	−	−	+	−	−	+	−	−	−
cor.	−	+	+	+	−	−	+	+	+	+	+	+	−
high	−	−	−	+	+	−	−	−	+	−	−	+	+
back	−	−	−	−	+	+	−	−	−	−	−	−	+

[3.10] Distinctive feature matrix for obstruents

	b p	ɓ p'	d̪ t̪	d' t'	d t	ɟ c	g k	g' k'	G q	ʔ	β φ	v f	ð θ	z s	z̧ ṣ	ʒ ʃ	ʝ ç	ɣ x	ʁ χ	ʕ ħ	ɦ h	bv pf	dz ts	dʒ tʃ
+voice	+	+	+	+	+	+	+	+	+	−	+	+	+	+	+	+	+	+	+	+	+	+	+	+
−voice	+	+	+	+	+	+	+	+	+	+	+	+	+	+	+	+	+	+	+	+	+	+	+	+
cont.	−	−	−	−	−	−	−	−	−	−	+	+	+	+	+	+	+	+	+	+	+	−	−	−
strid.	−	−	−	−	−	−	−	−	−	−	−	+	−	+	+	+	−	−	+	−	−	+	+	+
distr.	+	+	+	+	−	+	−	−	−	−	+	−	+	−	−	+	+	−	−	−	−	−	−	+
ant.	+	+	+	+	+	−	−	−	−	−	+	+	+	+	−	−	−	−	−	−	−	+	+	−
lab.	+	+	−	−	−	−	−	−	−	−	+	+	−	−	−	−	−	−	−	−	−	+	−	−
cor.	−	−	+	+	+	+	−	−	−	−	−	−	+	+	+	+	+	−	−	−	−	−	+	+
high	−	−	−	−	−	+	+	+	−	−	−	−	−	−	−	+	+	+	−	−	−	−	−	+
low	−	−	−	−	−	−	−	−	−	−	−	−	−	−	−	−	−	−	−	+	−	−	−	−
back	−	−	−	−	−	−	+	+	+	−	−	−	−	−	−	−	−	+	+	+	−	−	−	−
constr.	−	+	−	+	−	−	−	+	−	+	−	−	−	−	−	−	−	−	−	−	−	−	−	−
spread	−	−	−	−	−	−	−	−	−	−	−	−	−	−	−	−	−	−	−	−	+	−	−	−

3.4 Segment structure redundancy

One striking thing about the distinctive feature matrices presented in the previous section is the amount of REDUNDANCY which they reveal: not every single phonetic property of every segment of a MORPHEME (i.e. minimal distributional or meaningful part of a word, such as *un-*, *kind*, and *-ly* in *unkindly*) is distinctive. Many properties are REDUNDANT. This means that they are predictable by general principles.

On the one hand, there are feature combinations that are predictable by universal SEGMENT STRUCTURE CONSTRAINTS. These feature combinations (e.g. [+nasal, +sonorant, + voice]) go together hand in glove: they are UNMARKED, they are the norm. On the other hand, there are feature combinations that are normally incompatible (e.g. [+high, +low] or [− sonorant, +syllabic]). It is unusual for a language to have segments with combinations of features other than those predicted by universal segment structure constraints. Though not absolute, (e.g. a language can have syllabic obstruents or voiceless vowels or voiceless nasals) such restrictions on the combination of features play a key role in delimiting the inventory of possible speech sounds. Odd sounds like voiceless vowels, voiceless nasals or syllabic obstruents are extraordinary. They are MARKED.

In addition to conforming to universal segment structure constraints languages may have their own idiosyncratic rules regulating feature combinations in their segments. An English example will clarify the point. In English (and indeed in most other languages), the feature [−back] cannot be combined with the feature [+round]. Rounded front vowels like [y] are not permitted in English (but they are allowed in French, occurring in words like [ty] *tu* [vy] *vu*). To take another example, [l] is the only lateral allowed in English. If you know that a segment is lateral, then you know that it is also consonantal, sonorant, alveolar and voiced. However, although voiceless [l] is disallowed in English and most other languages, it does occur in a few languages. For instance, the sound spelled with 'll' in Welsh words like *Llandudno* is a voiceless lateral fricative [ɬ].

Besides segment structure redundancy, there also exists SEQUENTIAL REDUNDANCY. As we shall see in the coming chapters correct inferences can often be made about a segment if the context in which it occurs is known. Thus, in spoken English, whenever there is a cluster of three consonants occurring syllable initially, the first consonant in the sequence is the fricative [s]. No other consonant can occur in that position: *splash* and *scream* are English words but *ftlash* and *zgream* are not – and could not be. We shall explore this problem more fully in Chapter 9.

Clearly, not all the phonetic properties of a sound are crucial in every case in distinguishing word meaning. Some properties are REDUNDANT, i.e. predictable and nondistinctive. When writing phonological rules, the convention of omitting redundant properties is normally observed. Thus [p] [b] and (ejective) [p'] may be represented simply as in [3.11]:

[3.11]	p	b	p'
son.			
voice	−	+	−
cont.	−	−	−
lab.	+	+	+
constr.	−	−	+
high			
back			
nasal			

Write down the values of redundant features which have been omitted in [3.11]. Check with table [3.10]

Exercises

1. Circle the segments which are:
   example (i) [+syll] w p ⓘ ⓔ m h ⓤ g v ⓐ
   (ii) [+ant] d z ʔ p b̃ n N ß ð f
   (iii) [−cons] a f v l r h ø j x u
   (iv) [+cor] v t r n j ʃ ŋ x d k
   (v) [+round] w t i u ɔ y o e l æ
   (vi) [−voice] o w s p l t g m i q

2. For each segment alter the value of the feature indicated, keeping all the other features unchanged. Write down the phonetic symbol for the resulting segment.

Original segment		Feature value changed	New segment
example	(i) i	[+syll]	j [−syll]
	(ii) u	[+back]	
	(iii) b	[−nasal]	
	(iv) e	[−round]	
	(v) d	[+voice]	
	(vi) g	[−nasal]	

3.(a) Write down the phonetic symbol for the initial segment of each one of the words below:

> that   cat   band   wet   write
> philosophy   shy   June   knee   tea

(b) Fill in the feature values of the initial segment of each of the words above for features listed below. Follow the example which is given.

> e.g. [ð]   *th*at
> cons   +
> son   −
> syll   −
> voice   +
> cont   +
> nas   −
> ant   +
> cor   +
> lab   −
> back   −
> high   −

Notes

1. FLAT consonants are contrasted with PLAIN ones. A flat consonant is produced by rounding the lips or by pharyngeal contraction. The resulting modification of the oral tract produces the acoustic effect of **flattening**, i.e. downward shift in the formants in the spectrum (Jakobson *et al.* 1952).

2. In SPE the class of glides includes the semi-vowels [j] and [w] as well as the glottal stop [ʔ] and the glottal fricative [h]. However, the case for formally recognising a class of glides which includes [w j h ʔ] is not altogether overwhelming. Some writers like Fromkin (1970) and Lass (1984) only recognise [w] and [j] as glides and argue for treating the glottal fricative [h] and the glottal stop [ʔ] as obstruents on articulatory grounds.

3. Although they are not made in the front of the mouth, glottals are not back because, by the definition given in SPE, only sounds produced with the tongue pulled back from neutral position are back. In the production of glottals the tongue is in neutral position, and does nothing. The vocal cords are the articulators.

4. Ladefoged (1971), citing Whiteley and Muli (1962), reports that Kikamba phonemically contrasts *four* degrees of vowel length: short, half-long, long and extra-long /V V. V: V::/ as in:

kwelela 'measuring'	kuʃa	'start'
kwele.la 'moving backward	_____	
and forward'		
kʊele:la 'aiming at'	kuʃa:	'giving birth'
_____	kuʃa::	'giving birth frequently'

CHAPTER 4
Phonological representations

4.1 Phonetics and phonology

PHONOLOGY is the branch of linguistics which investigates the ways in which speech sounds are used systematically to form words and utterances. By now it will be obvious that in order to understand phonology one must have a grasp of the basic concepts of phonetics, which as we saw in the first chapter, is the study of the production of speech sounds by speakers, their perception by hearers and their acoustic properties. Most speakers of a language like English, with a long tradition of writing, who have not made a study of phonetics and phonology tend to think of the sounds of speech through the medium of the ordinary alphabet. Becoming literate involves, among other things, mastering one particular rough-and-ready scheme of analysis for the phonetics of a given language.

In the particular case of the English language, it happens that the analysis implied by the ordinary spelling is very 'rough' and inaccurate indeed. Probably most people who are literate in English are aware of this fact although few of them could state explicitly and systematically what these shortcomings are. Someone who has not studied phonetics has scarcely any vocabulary for describing spoken English other than the names of the letters of the alphabet (and possibly terms like 'consonant', 'vowel' and 'syllable'; but these are often interpreted as graphological, i.e. pertaining to the study of the written language). So, the most that can be done by the average speaker towards pointing out the shortcomings of English spelling is to cite particular instances of 'illogicality', such as the various pronunciations which correspond to the spelling -oo- in *foot*,

fool, and *blood* or the various spellings that correspond to
[eɪ] in *maid* and *made, break* and *brake, weigh* and *way.*
Although people are aware of many individual cases of this
kind, their general understanding of what speech is like is
moulded almost wholly by the nature of the writing system
that we use to record speech. Much of the point of a study
of phonetics lies in acquiring the ability to penetrate behind
the rough-and-ready analysis of speech which is implied by
the standard orthography and to grasp what is really going
on, especially in cases where the standard orthography is
misleading. Moreover, as we shall see in the final section
of this chapter, the ability to analyse and record speech in
a more sophisticated way than that provided by the standard
alphabet is not only of theoretical interest, it also has many
practical applications.

Answer this question before you read on: if traditional
English orthography inculcates, in everyone who masters
it, a crude theory about the nature of speech sounds, what
would that theory be like, if it were stated explicitly?

Most obviously, the English alphabet tells us that
spoken utterances consist of linear sequences of elements:
UNITARY SOUNDS occurring one after another. It is a
fundamental characteristic of alphabetic writing to be one-
dimensional; letters follow one another across the page, it
never happens that two letters occupy the same position in
the left-to-right sequence as in [4.1].

[4.1] h̃ or m̃ or f́

And, although in handwriting individual letters blend each
into the next without sharp boundaries between them, this
is just regarded as a hasty, convenient way of transcribing
what are intended as a row of separate marks and appear
as such in print.

Secondly, the writing system tells us that these unitary
elements differ from each other discretely, like beads on a
string or chemical elements, rather than continuously, like
shades of colour. If you ask me what colour a dress is, it
makes perfectly good sense for me to say it is between green
and yellow – perhaps more towards yellow than green; but

if you asked a geologist what metal a sample of moon rock consisted of, it would make no sense at all if the reply you got was that it was a metal somewhere between aluminium and molybdenum, a bit more molybdenum-y than aluminium-y. (Of course, it might be a mixture or alloy, containing both aluminium and molybdenum atoms; but each individual atom would be either aluminium or molybdenum: atoms do not shade into each other as colours do.)

Do letters of the alphabet shade into each other as colours do or do they differ discretely like chemical elements?

The answer, as we have already seen, is that letters of the alphabet resemble chemical elements rather than colours in this respect: a given word, say *key* either begins with the letter *k* or it does not, and there would be no sense whatsoever if, for instance, when playing a game of 'I spy with my little eye' one child said to another that she spied something beginning with a letter halfway between *k* and *t*.

In brief, alphabetic writing teaches us:

(i) that speech consists of linear sequences of unitary, discretely-different sounds;

(ii) that there are only a small number of types of sound in a language;

(iii) that a sound occurring at a given place in one word can be identified with certain sounds occurring at different places in other words.

When children learn to read in the early years at school, the above statements (i)–(iii) about the nature of speech sounds are not, of course, taught to them in so many words – indeed they are rather abstract statements which small children could hardly understand if they did hear them stated explicitly. But the fact that these propositions about how speech works are left implicit does not make them any less influential in moulding adults' perception of the nature of their language. Rather, the reverse: precisely because these propositions are not explicitly articulated, it does not, on the whole, occur to people to question them. As you work your way through this book, you will realise that each of these assumptions is, if not down-right false, at best a very partial and crude approximation to the truth.

Of the points (i)–(iii) that I have listed, the one that *is* often called into question by adult English speakers without special knowledge of phonetics is (ii). People are well aware that the inventory of English sounds is not to be identified with the twenty-six letters of the English alphabet. They may recognise that, for instance, the two letters *sh* in words like *shop* and *push* stand for one rather than two sounds while the single letter *x* stands for two sounds in words like *tax* and *box;* and they may also be aware that the sound spelled *c* in *rice* is not the same as the sound spelled *c* in *coal*, but that the latter sound is the 'same' as the sound spelled by the different letter *k* in *koala* or by the letters *ck* in *back*. This does not mean that people generally question the existence of a limited inventory of English sounds – on the contrary, the general principle that speech is appropriately represented by means of an alphabet of a few dozen letters is usually taken for granted; but people think of English as a language whose alphabet regrettably fails to represent the spoken language accurately, partly because it needs a few more letters than it has got.

The student of phonetics, however, knows that even the fundamental assumption of the linearity of sound segments in (i) is misleading as a model of what happens when we speak. A speaker does not articulate just **one** holistic speech sound at a time. Speech sounds are the result of many **separate** articulatory gestures which are made simultaneously. As we saw in the last chapter the speaker changes the position of the vocal cords as the utterance progresses; at the same time the soft palate is raised and lowered; the shape and position of the tongue and of the lips is also modified while all that is going on. A writing system faithful to this aspect of the nature of speech would record speech not as a linear sequence of letters, but more after the fashion of an orchestral score which includes separate staves, one above the other, for the activities of the various instruments (in the phonetic case, the various vocal organs). The 'score' for the articulation of the word *mat*, for instance might look like this:

[4.2]

LIPS	close . . open.		
TONGUE	neutral . . lower front	raise blade make closure with alveolar ridge	return blade to neutral position
VOCAL CORDS	together and vibrating	stop vibrating	
VELUM	down . . . . up		
[	m . æ	t	]

As we saw in the last chapter, sounds can be thought of as bundles of distinctive features; they are the result of more or less simultaneous articulatory activities of various organs which imperceptibly merge with each other. Sounds are not neatly separated from one another in the way suggested by the self-contained, separate letters in a line of print. True, some of the articulatory events in a stretch of speech are fairly abrupt; during the production of [m], for instance, the lips stop the escape of air from the mouth until the bilabial closure is abruptly released. But even in cases like this where events on one stave of the orchestral score occur at precise moments, it is the exception rather than the rule for events on all the various staves to be synchronised. You can see in [4.2] that all the gestures involved in the production of a given sound do not necessarily start and stop at exactly the same time. Moreover, many of the events happening on the different staves will, by their nature, be gradual and not abrupt. For example, the raising of the velum takes time, and consequently, the first section of the vowel in *mat* will be somewhat nasalised during the transition from [m] to [æ]; movements of the body of the tongue are gradual and even a bilabial stop closure is not released as suddenly as all that. To take another example, conventionally, the English word *hour* is phonetically transcribed as a TRIPHTHONG (i.e. a vowel with three vowel qualities) [aʊə] but it would be a travesty to suggest that an utterance of this word consists of an initial period during which the tongue-body is depressed and the lips spread; a middle period in which the tongue is humped up in the back of the mouth and the lips pursed; and a final period in which the tongue has an intermediate shape and the lips are spread again. We humans do not have tongues and lips which are controlled by ratchets which click instantaneously from one configuration to another in that fashion; rather, throughout the utterance of *hour* the configurations of the tongue and lips are constantly changing, in complex ways, without stable intervals.

Furthermore, the fact that the vocal organs are controlled by muscles rather than clicking mechanical ratchets, means that speech sounds (or, to be precise, the separate articulatory gestures of which speech sounds are composed) are much more similar to colours which shade into each other gradually than to chemical elements which are sharply, discretely different. In terms of English orthography it makes no sense to talk of a letter halfway between a *k* and a *t*; phonetically, however, it is perfectly reasonable to talk of a sound somewhere in between [k] and [t]. For instance, a palatal stop [c] could be so described. But even the three phonetic symbols [k c t] do no more than crudely indicate three broad areas at which the tongue may make contact with the roof of the mouth.

This is the reason: between the ends of the upper teeth and the *uvula* (the fleshy bit of your anatomy hanging down from the middle of the soft palate at the very back of the roof of your mouth beyond the velum (see [1.2])) there is an infinity of slightly different areas against which the tongue can make a total closure and, at the same time, the areas of the tongue involved in contact vary continuously rather than discretely.

The implication of the continuously, rather than discretely varying nature of articulatory parameters is that, even if stretches of speech could be chopped up into separate 'sounds', there would not be a limited inventory of possible sounds. Rather, the range of pronounceable sounds is as infinitely variable as the range of possible shades of colour, and the number of different objects one chooses to label with distinct colour-names – or phonetic symbols – depends purely on how finely one wishes or is able to discriminate.

Let us ignore for one moment the problems of segmenting an utterance into a sequence of sounds. Admittedly, although the range of physically possible sounds is infinite, within any one language only a small, finite set of sounds is used. For instance, in English there are no speech-sounds, such as clicks, implosives or ejectives, which are made otherwise than with the pulmonic egressive airstream mechanism; there are no front rounded vowels like the [y] in French words such as *lu*, and so on. But equally clearly, within the range of sounds that do occur in a given language, all the same arguments about variation will apply – so that the range of slightly different sounds produced by English speakers will be enormous, even though that range is only a small part of the more extensive range of sounds which are produced by speakers of all the languages of the world.

Finally, we come to point (iii). The English version of the Roman alphabet has just twenty-six letters; but, of course, speakers of English produce a lot more than twenty-six physically distinct sounds. Often, sounds that are different are represented using the same letter. In learning to spell, we learn to think of the first sound of say, *car* as the 'same' as the first sound of *keys* although they are not phonetically identical (see section 2.1.1). This is misleading.

4.2 The domain of phonology

In terms of the physical properties of speech, then, sounds are endlessly diverse, and the appearance of a few discrete units suggested by the Roman alphabet is seriously misleading. To study phonetics is, partly, to learn to penetrate beyond that fiction to the chaotic wealth of slightly different sounds that we actually use. However, if we turn from considering the physical properties of speech-sounds to thinking about how they FUNCTION in a language as a communicative system, the picture suggested by the traditional orthography becomes rather more appropriate. It is this alternative approach to speech-sounds, examining them from the point of view of how they are actually USED in different languages, which is adopted by the student of PHONOLOGY.

What I mean by saying that the alphabet-based analysis of speech-sounds is reasonably adequate from a functional point of view is that, if we think of phonetic variation in connection with the work it does in language, then it ceases to be true that variation is continuous and not discrete. The phonetic symbols [t c k], we noted earlier, impose a three-way classification on what is physically an infinitely graded series of slightly different areas of the palate where the tongue can make contact. But the English language, as a tool of communication, imposes an even cruder classification on that series, treating it as if it had only two members *t* and *k*, with no in-between sound.

That does not mean that the initial sound in every utterance of a word such as *tea, time, tell*, etc., involves exactly the same area of contact between the tongue and the roof of the mouth; it does not mean that the tongue makes contact with exactly the same part of the roof of the mouth in the articulation of the *k* sound at the beginning of *key, coal* etc. Speakers could no more achieve that sort of consistency in their speech than darts players could manage to place the dart at exactly the same point on the dartboard as the dart before it.

To discover in a practical way what this means, find a dozen different words beginning with a *t* and a *k* sound respectively. Identify the exact points of contact between the tongue and the roof of the mouth when you say each one of the words which you have chosen.

You will notice that the sounds tend to cluster into two groups, rather in the same way that the holes made in the dartboard would cluster into two groups if the players were attempting to aim for one or other of two points selected as targets. Furthermore, speakers of English have learned as hearers to listen for the phonetic 'targets' and not the precise phonetic properties of each sound, so that if a speaker uttered in the middle of an utterance a 'word' which is transcribable as [cul], with an initial sound intermediate between [k] and [t], and if it were perceived as such by the hearer, it would be dismissed as a mistake. What is more likely is that the 'word' would be perceived as a rather unsuccessful or inelegant way of saying [tul] *tool* or [kul] *cool*, whichever seemed appropriate in the context.

The view that the phoneme is a TARGET SOUND in the minds of speakers and hearers was originally proposed by the Polish linguist Baudouin de Courtenay in 1894. He suggested that much of the precise phonetic detail that is physically present in speech (from an articulatory or acoustic point of view) is irrelevant from a FUNCTIONAL point of view.

In the intellectual climate of the first half of this century, especially in America, de Courtenay's mentalist definition of the phoneme was rejected by most linguists. Because they considered themselves empirical scientists, they saw no value in speculating about the workings of the invisible mind (Twaddell 1935:57).

While objections to the mentalist approach to the phoneme cannot be ignored, it does nonetheless seem to offer some useful insights. If you say *tea* and *key*, for example, there will inevitably be some very slight difference in the way you produce the first consonant on various occasions but all that matters is that each time these words begin with an articulation whose target is either /t/ or /k/. Another language may well have three targets on this particular dimension (indeed, many languages have).

Variation in the physical execution of a given phonetic target need not be random. For instance, of the two English clusters of tongue/palate contact-areas just discussed, the area I am calling the /k/ cluster, if it could be plotted, would turn out to involve a scatter not round a single point but round a line. This is because, typically, velar consonants preceding front vowels tend to be made with contact farther forward on the soft palate than velar consonants preceding relatively back vowels (section 2.1.1).

You can verify this by pronouncing the following words very carefully and observing the movement of your tongue:

[4.3]   car key   King Cole
         keep cool   Ken Carr

I hope you observed that the *k*'s in *car, cool, Cole* and *Carr* are made farther back than those in *key, keep, King* and *Ken*.

Although this variation in the *k* sound is systematic

rather than random, it is not functionally significant. The distinction between a fronted *k* and a more back *k* cannot be used to contrast word meaning in English. It is not phonemic. Fronted [ḳ] (see [4.7] below) and nonfronted [k] are allophones of the same phoneme. Phonology focuses on functional differences. Phonology is sometimes referred to as FUNCTIONAL PHONETICS.

4.3 Recapitulation: levels of representation

To sum up the discussion so far, we recognise at least two distinct levels of representation of speech: the PHONETIC LEVEL and the PHONEMIC LEVEL. At the PHONETIC LEVEL, our task is to provide an accurate description of the characteristics of the sounds that occur in speech; at the PHONEMIC LEVEL the emphasis is on those properties of sounds that are functionally significant in the formation of words and utterances.

4.4 Phonetic and phonemic transcription

We have seen in the preceding sections the ways in which the standard orthography fails to provide an adequate representation of speech. In this section we are going to see how the use of PHONETIC and PHONEMIC TRAN-SCRIPTION might improve matters. In addition to introducing you to transcription, this section is intended to familiarise you with aspects of the consonant system of English. The section should also serve as a practical demonstration of the use of phoneme theory which was introduced in Chapter 2.

Phonemic transcription (also called BROAD TRAN-SCRIPTION) only shows functional differences, i.e. differences between sounds which are used to distinguish word meaning. It only uses enough symbols to represent each phoneme of the language in question with a symbol of its own. Phonetic transcription (also called NARROW TRAN-SCRIPTION) on the other hand, is much more detailed and attempts to provide a more faithful representation of speech. It normally represents the allophones of a phoneme that occur in various contexts, but can be made to show even finer detail, if necessary. To do this it uses a much larger number of symbols together with diacritic marks to distinguish subtle nuances of pronunciation. In [4.4] and [4.5] I exemplify broad and narrow transcription respectively:

[4.4] Broad transcription
    attend /ətend/   two   /tu/
    eighth /eɪtθ/   seat /sit/
    nutmeg /nʌtmeg/

[4.5] Narrow transcription
[ətʰend] the raised (h) shows ASPIRATION i.e. there is a slight delay between the release of the stop [t] and the onset of voicing in the vowel [e]. An aspirated stop is released with greater force than a unaspirated one.

[tʷu] the raised (w) shows lip-rounding (the speaker starts rounding the lips before the production of [t] is completed in anticipation of the vowel [u] which is made with rounded lips.

[eɪt̪θ] the subscript (̪) marks dental sounds; here, in anticipation of the dental fricative [θ], the tongue makes contact with the upper front teeth rather than the alveolar ridge.

[siʔt] the symbol (ʔ) marks pre-glottalisation. There is glottal reinforcement – with a glottal stop coinciding with or slightly anticipating the allophone of /t/ that occurs in word final position. The airstream is simultaneously obstructed at two points like a river dammed at two points. In some accents the word ends in a glottal stop, with no [t] element at all.

[nʌʔtmeg][1] the symbol (ʔ) again marks pre-glottalisation; that is glottal reinforcement when [t] is followed by another consonant.

The various *t* sounds are in complementary distribution; each one has got its special contexts in which it occurs. They are allophones of the phoneme /t/. Below I have written informal rules stating the distribution of these allophones:

[4.6] /t/ is realised as:

[tʰ],   an aspirated voiceless alveolar stop when it occurs at the beginning of a stressed syllable as in [ətʰend];

[tʷ],   a labialised (rounded) voiceless alveolar stop before rounded vowels; The word *two* also has a voiceless aspirated alveolar stop and we could have written it phonetically as [tʷʰ]. But, as you can see, diacritics can crowd each other out. For the sake of clarity we may use only those diacritics that are necessary to clarify the point we wish to focus on;

[t̪],   a voiceless dental stop before dentals;

[ʔt],   a glottalised alveolar stop in word final position or before another consonant.

In order to describe the allophones of a phoneme or to make a narrow phonetic transcription you will need to know various DIACRITICS devised by phoneticians for this purpose. An annotated list of common diacritics is provided in [4.7].

[4.7]   ° VOICELESS: examples (voiceless) [g̊ ḁ] This indicates that a segment type that is normally fully voiced is fully or partially devoiced (e.g. in English, word-final voiced stops like /g/ are realised as [g̊] as in *bag* [bæg̊].

   ʰ ASPIRATED: examples (aspirated) [pʰ tʰ kʰ] This indicates that a segment is aspirated (e.g. voiceless stops in English are aspirated when they occur at the beginning of a stressed syllable in words like [ətʰend] *attend*, [pʰet] *pet* and [kʰæt] *cat*).

   ʷ LABIALISED: examples (labialised) [pʷ tʷ kʷ] It indicates labialisation (lip-rounding) (e.g. non-labial consonants followed by round vowels are labialised in English words like [tʷu] *two* and [kʷul] *cool*).

   ' SYLLABIC: examples (syllabic) [l̩] and [n̩]

It indicates that a consonant functions as a syllable nucleus (e.g. in English the nasals and [l] are syllabic when they occur at the end of a word if they are preceded by another consonant as in [ketl̩] *kettle* and [kɒtn̩] *cotton*).

˞ RHOTACISED (i.e. r-coloured)
It indicates that a vowel has 'r-colouring' (e.g. the pronunciation of words such as [kɑ˞] *car* and [kɑ˞t] *cart* in American and English west country accents).

+ shows that a segment is FRONTED (e.g. velar is made with the back of the tongue moved forward close to the hard palate when it is followed by a front vowel as in [ki̟] *key*).

~ NASALISED
It indicates that air escapes through the nose as in American [pæ̃n] *pan* or French [bɔ̃] *bon*.

: LONG
It shows that a segment is long (e.g. the vowel in the word *see* [si] can alternatively be transcribed as [i:]²).

The list in [4.7] is not exhaustive but it contains most of the diacritics you are likely to need frequently. For a more comprehensive list refer to the IPA chart in [1.13] in the first chapter.

4.5 A guide to phonetic transcription

This section contains a few practical hints about transcription.

(i) Start by reading the word or passage aloud several times in a manner which is as close as possible to natural conversation. If possible, make a recording of your reading so that when doing the transcription you work from the recording. This is because it is virtually imposisble to repeat an utterance consistently from one time to the next.

When working with informants, do not start transcribing until you can mimic their pronunciation to their satisfaction.

(ii) Write on alternate lines.

(iii) Avoid using letters of the alphabet (such as the capital letter A) which are not part of the phonetic alphabet. Avoid using capital letters (at the beginning of sentences or in proper names) because they may have a different phonetic value from that of lower case letters, e.g. [n] is an alveolar nasal but [N] is a uvular nasal.

(iv) Do not confuse the spelling of a word with its pronunciation.

(v) Mark off intonation group boundaries using vertical lines like these | |
e.g. | *The aim of this exercise* | *is to identify some of the phonemes in your speech* |

(vi) Avoid confusion. Do not use any of the standard punctuation marks like question marks, because many of them have a different value in the phonetic alphabet e.g. the colon [:] represents length; the symbol for a glottal stop [ʔ] is like a question mark [?] without the dot, etc.

(vii) If you are transcribing English, remember that unstressed vowels are in most cases realised as [ə] (or [ɪ] or [ʊ]). E.g. [bənænə], not *[bænænæ], for *banana*.

(viii) You may mark off those syllables which carry stress by a raised, small vertical line before the syllable carrying the main stress of a word, e.g. ['entə] *enter*. Where in addition to a main stress there is a secondary stress, you can mark it with a lowered vertical line, e.g. [ˌdʌbl̩'edʒd] *double-edged*.

4.6 Why study phonology?

In this chapter we have seen that it is necessary to recognise at least two levels of speech representation: the phonetic and the phonemic. We have further seen that corresponding to each level there is a system of transcription, namely phonemic (broad) and (phonetic) narrow transcription. But you might still wonder why anyone should be interested in working out ways of representing speech, other than the standard orthography which, in spite of its limitations, has served us so well. In the closing remarks of this chapter, I briefly address this question.

First there is the theoretical motivation: theoretical linguists are interested in exploring the ways in which language uses the medium of sound, which is in itself meaningless (a sound like [t] or [e] in itself means nothing) to build words which convey an infinite range of meanings. They are interested in the restrictions on the ways in which sounds can combine to form words; they are interested in the ways in which phonology relates to grammar and meaning. They are interested in both the language-specific and universal dimensions of these questions.

The answers to these questions are relevant to other areas of linguistics.

(a) Psycholinguists investigate the acquisition of phonological knowledge by infants and the disintegration of that knowledge in aphasia (the loss of linguistic ability through brain damage) – these are windows through which the nature of human cognition in general can be glimpsed.

(b) Historical linguists investigate the evolution of sound systems because it provides the surest evidence of languages sharing common descent. (For example, /p/ in Latin words like *pater* and *piscis* corresponds to /f/ in the English words *father* and *fish* which have the same meaning). There tends to be a significant degree of sound-meaning correspondence between languages descended from a common ancestor.

(c) Sociolinguists investigate the correlation between geographical dialect, social sub-groupings and pronunciation. (For example, in England, middle-class speakers of English are very much less likely than their working-class counterparts to drop their aitches initially in nouns, adjectives and verbs and pronounce the words *heat*, and *hat*, for instance, as [it] and [æt] respectively, rather than [hit] and [hæt]. Both sociolinguists and historical linguists, for instance, attempt to explain why *look* and *luck* rhyme in the North of England, both being pronounced [lʊk], but not elsewhere, and why [həʊm] home and [stəʊn] stone are pronounced as [he:m] and [ste:n] in Scotland.

For all these groups of linguists it is essential to be able to understand the workings of the spoken language. At the very least, they all need to be able to make adequate broad and narrow transcriptions of spoken language data so that they have a proper representation of the subject matter which they examine.

Phonetics and phonology are not esoteric academic disciplines with no relevance to the real world. Beyond the confines of linguistics, there are many kinds of specialists working with language who need to be able to analyse and represent speech in a more sophisticated way than that provided by the standard orthography. They include literacy experts, especially those devising orthographies for unwritten languages (a famous book on phonemics by Kenneth Pike has the sub-title '*a technique for reducing languages to writing*'). An orthography ensuring that there is just one symbol for every contrastive sound in a language is ideal for writing down a language and introducing literacy to a speech community. Even for a written language like English, literacy workers wishing to understand the problems of their pupils or clients need to have the grasp of spoken English and its relationship with the standard orthography which is derived from a study of phonology. Not least because often spelling mistakes – such as misspelling *feel* as *feeyal* – can be understood and remedied if the instructor realises that phonetically that word is frequently pronounced as [fiʲəl]. The incorrect spelling is, in fact, phonetically well motivated.

For teachers of foreign languages, too, a good under-standing of phonetics and phonology is desirable, for it facilitates the diagnosis of learners' errors and provides the concepts and notation needed to represent accurately both the learner's speech and the target pronunciation.

Actors need to be convincing mimics of a wide range of accents. An understanding of the phonological charac-teristics of social and geographical dialects hinted at above is invaluable in that profession. Phonetics (in some form) is usually one of the subjects studied at drama school.

Speech therapists treat patients with speech defects which sometimes are due to inability to produce certain sounds, or a failure to produce certain allophones of phonemes, or again a failure to master some principles that govern phonological patterning. Not only do they need to be able to transcribe their raw data phonetically and analyse aspects of their patients' pathological speech case histories, but they need also to have a thorough knowledge of normal phonological behaviour which their patients are expected to approximate. For the same reasons, specialists in speech hearing science and teachers of the deaf need to have a good understanding of phonetics and phonology in order to enable their speech-impaired clients to communicate using the spoken language.

Neurologists and neurolinguists often have to treat aphasics (brain-damaged patients) who have lost the ability to produce or process the spoken language but who may, in some cases, have retained the ability to communicate through the written word. They need to know how speech is produced and heard, they need to know about the neurological wiring responsible for speech, and they need to know how sounds are organised in speech, in order to help restore speech in their patients.

Speech is a very important personality trait: in everyday life we all make judgements about people on the basis of how they talk. We can judge whether they are lugubrious, excitable or depressed on the basis of their voice quality, volume, tempo, and so on. In a professional context, psychiatrists can diagnose certain mental abnormalities by focusing their attention on these and other aspects of speech.

The police, too, in recent years have increasingly used 'forensic phonetics' in order to track down suspects on the basis of their geographical dialect, occupation and social class as well as physical characteristics such as sex, age and size which can be established on the basis of their speech. But although the popular press speaks of 'voice prints' which are supposedly as individual as finger prints, phoneticians are much more cautious. The contribution of phonetics in this area is still modest.

It is probably in the development of modern communications that phonetics has had the greatest impact. Alexander Graham Bell, the inventor of the telephone, was a Scottish phonetician, like his father and grandfather before him. Initially, like his father and grandfather, he was interested in clinical applications of phonetics, but later he realised that phonetics had other uses. He emigrated to

America and there his invention, the telephone, was developed and marketed by the Bell Telephone Company. To this day, the Bell Telephone Laboratories in America remain at the forefront of acoustic phonetics research.

Communications engineers are interested in increasing the efficiency of telephone systems. To a great extent this means cutting out redundant, non-distinctive aspects of speech so that more messages can be carried on their networks without reducing the level of clarity and intelligibility. To do this effectively, a good model of the physics of speech has to be complemented by an equally sophisticated understanding of phonological systems.

More recently, there has been a surge of interest in speech processing by computer. Acoustic phonetics and phonology are both central disciplines in the production of synthesised speech and the decoding of spoken language using computers. Both have great future promise. Once computers are capable of inputting and transcribing spoken language and producing good quality synthesised speech, they will possibly become as easy to use and as ubiquitous as the telephone. The commercial possibilities of talking computers which give verbal responses to questions, in naturalistic plain speech, without the user needing to spend hours tied to the keyboard, have attracted massive investment in phonetics research in the last few years.

But even if the study of the spoken language had absolutely no practical applications it would still be an important discipline because it is central to understanding who we are. More than anything, the ability to speak, the ability to use language is what sets us apart from the rest of the animal kingdom.

Exercises

1. Read aloud the following words which are written in phonetic script:

(i)	[den]	(vi)	[lɪŋgwɪstɪks]
(ii)	[pæn]	(vii)	[haʊsbreɪkəz]
(iii)	[saɪəns]	(viii)	[ɪndɪvɪdjʊəl]
(iv)	[sɪkstin]	(ix)	[naɪthʊd]
(v)	[æŋgl̩]	(x)	[prəfjuʒn̩]

2.   Make a *broad transcription* of the following words:
(a)   full   fool   foot   coot   cut   but   boot   tuck   took
(b)   glass   path   mast   plastic   bath   last   laugh
(c)   stair   stare   fare   rare   fair   fur   where   wear   were
(d)   philosophy   finish   enough   fish   caution
(e)   ringing   wringing   bringing   longer   long

3.   Using the symbols for allophones introduced earlier in
      this chapter, and where appropriate using diacritics,
      make a **narrow phonetic transcription** of your
      relaxed pronunciation of the following words:
(a)   apart   attention   atmosphere
(b)   button   cotton   bottom   bacon   baking
(c)   kettle   little   medal   metal
(d)   drain   train   strain   play   splay   sweep   scream

Notes

1.   Speakers of Northern English may have the vowel
      [ʊ] in [nʊʔtmeg].

2.   There is some controversy surrounding English
      vowels. Some regard the basic distinction as that
      between long and short vowels and hence transcribe
      them as /iː uː ɑː ɔː/, the set of long vowels, which is
      opposed to /ɪ ʊ æ ɒ/, the set of short vowels. Others
      regard the quality difference as more basic and think
      the features tense/lax bring this out more appropri-
      ately. They would prefer to use the symbols /i u ɑ
      ɔ/ for the tense vowels and /ɪ ʊ æ ɒ/ for the lax vowels.
      It is the latter position which is adopted in this book.

CHAPTER 5

Phonological processes

5.1 Introduction

The phonological systems of different languages are obviously different. No two languages have exactly the same inventory of phonemes which are realised by the same set of allophones; no two languages have exactly the same phonological rules regulating the deployment of their sounds. However, while all that is true, it would be wrong to ignore the similarites between languages because they are no less impressive than the differences. In the discussion of phonological symmetry in Chapter 2, we noted that languages tend to exploit the same phonetic parameters in building their phonological systems and that there are certain patterns that recur frequently.

In Chapter 3 we observed that it is feasible to use a relatively small number of DISTINCTIVE FEATURES like [± back], [± high], [± low], [± round], [± voice] etc. to characterise the phonological contrasts found in all the world's languages. One possible explanation for this is the fact that human anatomy and physiology impose limits on the range of sounds which people can produce as speakers and discriminate as hearers. Thus, for instance, since no human is endowed with a tongue which is so long that the tip can curl all the way back to the throat, it is safe to predict that no language has apico-uvular consonants made with the tip of the tongue and the uvula as the articulators (the uvula is the fleshy bit that hangs down from the centre of the soft palate at the very back of the mouth). On the other hand, given the ease with which the tip and the blade of the tongue can be raised towards the upper front teeth and the teeth ridge, it is not surprising to discover that all languages have either dental or alveolar sounds, if not both. Distinctive feature theory claims that there is a universal inventory of phonological construction materials from which various languages choose different elements which they use in building their phonological systems. Alternatively, distinctive features can be likened to cooking ingredients on a supermarket shelf. The selection of ingredients that a particular language puts in its shopping basket depends on the recipe which it wishes to concoct. (Of course, I do not mean this in a literal sense. Languages cannot be credited with intentional behaviour!)

It is significant, but not unexpected, that the phonological recipes which are available fall within the range permitted by human biology. What is intriguing is the fact that not everything that is biologically possible is equally likely to occur. Within the range of possible sounds, certain articulatory parameters are exploited by languages much more commonly than others.

Furthermore, besides exhibiting similarities in the features they use in structuring their sounds, languages also show other phonological similarities. For example, although the phonological systems of different languages are governed by different rules, the variation which occurs does, for the most part, fall within certain parameters. Similar phonological processes turn up, in language after language.

5.2 Assimilation

In Chapter 2 we saw that often in language a phoneme has several allophones, with the allophone selected in a particular position being dependent on the other sounds that are adjacent to it. The commonest phonological process responsible for this is ASSIMILATION. Assimilation, as you will recall from the discussion in Chapter 3, is the modification of a sound in order to make it more similar to some other sound in its neighbourhood. The advantage of having assimilation is that it results in smoother, more effortless, more economical transitions from one sound to another. It facilitates the task of speaking. The speaker usually tries to conserve energy by using no more effort than is necessary to produce an utterance. (Guardians of linguistic good taste in a speech community might view many instances of assimilation as nothing less than culpable sloppiness. But their admonitions 'to uphold standards' tend to go largely unheeded.)

Usually, the alternation in the phonological realisations of a MORPHEME (i.e. minimal meaningful or distributional unit in a language, which may be a simple word like *dog*, or a suffix like the -*s* plural marker in *dog-s*, or the negative prefix *un-* in *un-do*) can be accounted for in terms of assimilation.

Consider the regular plural ending in English. It is written as *s*, but it may, in fact, be pronounced as [-s] as in [pet-s] *pets*, or as [-z] as in [bel-z] *bells* or even as [-ɪz] as in [rəʊz-ɪz] *roses*. The choice is not random. The principle that determines the shape of the suffix is VOICE ASSIMILATION: this suffix must always agree in voicing with the preceding sound. Turning voicing on and keeping it on throughout, or alternatively, not turning voicing on at all is much easier than the alternative of turning it on or off part-way through a sequence of sounds.

More data is provided in [5.1] to illustrate the pattern of alternation of the plural ending. Study the data and answer the questions which follow:

[5.1] English Plural Formation

A		B		C	
Singular	Plural	Singular	Plural	Singular	Plural
dog	dogs	dock	docks	witch	witches
bid	bids	bit	bits	nose	noses
rib	ribs	tip	tips	marsh	marshes
love	loves	giraffe	giraffes	badge	badges
sea	seas	moth	moths	bus	buses

(a) Add five more examples of your own to each column.

(b) Suggest a rule to predict the shape of the ALLO-MORPH (i.e. alternative realisation of the morpheme) that occurs with the nouns in each column.

If you have answered [5.1] correctly, you have established that the English plural suffix has the following allomorphs:

[5.2] (i)   [-z]   occurring with the words in column A

(ii) [-s]   occurring with the words in column B

(iii) [-ɪz]   occurring with the words in column C

Typically, as these examples show, the alternation in the shape of a morpheme is not arbitrary. Rather, it is PHONOLOGICALLY CONDITIONED. This means that the allomorph of a morpheme that occurs in a given context is partly or wholly determined by the sounds found in the allomorphs of adjacent morphemes. It is not merely coincidence that is responsible for the allomorphs of the plural morpheme and the third person singular being [-z -s -ɪz]. The suffix AGREES IN VOICING with the preceding sound. We shall provisionally state the rule thus:

the plural suffix is realised by a voiced or voiceless alveolar fricative depending on whether the noun ends in a voiced or voiceless segment. (The rule will be embellished presently to take into account the forms in column C.)

Note that this voice assimilation is not an idiosyncratic property of the plural morpheme. It is a rule that applies more generally to English suffixes consisting of plosives or fricatives (i.e. obstruents). For instance, the /-z/ suffix, whether it is the noun plural marker as in [5.1], or the third person singular present tense suffix, shows the same pattern of alternation. You can verify this by examining [5.3]:

[5.3] English third person singular present tense suffix

	A		B		C
see	sees	paint	paints	teach	teaches
love	loves	hate	hates	wish	wishes
rub	rubs	talk	talks	judge	judges
mend	mends	make	makes	kiss	kisses
come	comes	laugh	laughs	rise	rises
call	calls	wipe	wipes	lose	loses
know	knows	keep	keeps	catch	catches

Instead of listing separately the three allomorphs of the plural morpheme and those of the third person singular present tense morpheme (and for that matter, of any other regular, phonologically conditioned morpheme in any language), we can posit a single UNDERLYING REPRESENTATION (or BASE FORM) which is entered in the 'DICTIONARY'. The various allomorphs can be derived by rule from that underlying representation.

In this case, if we assume that the base form of the noun plural suffix is /-z/, and if we further assume that the base form of the third person singular present tense morpheme is also /-z/, we can derive the various allomorphs of each morpheme using the informal VOICE ASSIMILATION rules in [5.4]:

[5.4] English voice assimilation
  (i)   The underlying, dictionary representation of the plural and of the third person singular present tense markers is /-z/.
  (ii) Insert [ɪ] (or [ə]) after any root ending in a sibilant (i.e. a sound such as [s z ʃ tʃ dʒ] which has high pitched fricative noise). See words like *witch* in column C in (5.1).
  (iii) Make sure that the suffix agrees in voicing with the segment preceding it. After a voiceless segment, like the final [k] of *dock*, the underlying /-z/ is changed to [s] so that the root and the suffix become more similar: /dɒk-z/ → [dɒk-s]. See words in column B in (5.1).
  (iv) After a root that ends in a voiced segment like a vowel or like the voiced stop /g/ in *dog* the suffix is realised as [z], which is also voiced, i.e. the underlying /-z/ in that case surfaces unmodified:
        /dɒg-z/ → [dɒgz]
        See the words in column A in (5.1).
  (v)   Likewise, after the vowel [ɪ] has been inserted after roots ending in a sibilant, the underlying /-z/ is realised as [z] so that it agrees in voicing with [ɪ]:
        /wɒtʃ/ → [wɒtʃ-ɪ/ → [wɒtʃ-ɪz/.
        See words in column C in (5.1).

In the next section we shall explore some general issues regarding assimilation before returning to voice assimilation in 5.3.3 below.

5.2.1 Direction of assimilation

When discussing assimilation, it is useful to look at processes in terms of DIRECTIONALITY, i.e. we can say whether a sound becomes more like either the sound that **precedes** it or the sound that **follows** it. If a sound becomes more like the sound that precedes it, the process is called PROGRESSIVE assimilation; if, on the other hand, a sound is modified so that it becomes more like the sound that follows it, the process is called REGRESSIVE assimilation.

In all the English examples above, the suffix consonant is made to agree in voicing with the root segment that precedes it. Hence, the rule of suffix voice agreement is an instance of progressive assimilation.

Now consider the following examples from Luganda (Uganda) and determine the direction of assimilation.

[5. 5] m–bala   I count   n–tema   I cut
       m–pa   I give   ɲ–ɟagala   I like
       m–mala   I finish   ɲ–ɲumya   I converse
       n–daga   I show   ɲ–coppa   I become destitute
       n–sika   I pull   ŋ–kola   I work
       n–neɲa   I blame   ŋ–gula   I buy

You will have observed how, in these data, the nasal always shares the place of articulation of the consonant that follows it. Anticipating the place of articulation of the following consonant, the speaker adjusts the place of articulation of the nasal. The direction of assimilation in [5.5] is REGRESSIVE (also called ANTICIPATORY):

[5.6] The nasal is realised as
      (i) [m] before bilabial consonants (e.g. when one of [p b m] follows)

(ii)   [n] before alveolar consonants (e.g. when
       one of [t d n s] follows)
(iii) [ɲ] before palatal consonants (e.g. when one
       of [c ɟ ɲ] follows)
(iv)   [ŋ] before velar consonants (e.g. when [k or
       g] follows)

Stop reading and write down at least two fresh examples from English (or any other language you know) which
exemplify progressive and regressive assimilation.

Examine the data [5.7], again taken from Luganda, and
determine whether the direction of assimilation is
progressive or regressive.

[5.7] A   B
       βakula grab! (imp.)   m-bakula   I grab
       βala count! (imp.)   m-bala   I count
       ka-βuzi small goat   m-buzi   goat
       ka-βogo small buffalo   m-bogo   buffalo

The process whereby the nasal is altered to agree in
place of articulation with the **following** consonant must be
viewed as anticipatory (i.e. regressive) assimilation. However, if you examine the data closely, you will observe that
there is another process going on at the same time. The
bilabial fricative [β] alternates with a plosive: the fricative
occurs word initially (see column A) while the plosive [b],
which shares the same place of articulation, occurs after a
nasal (see column B). The fricative, which is a continuant,
assimilates the property of being noncontinuant (i.e. being
a stop) from the nasal immediately preceding it.

What [5.7] shows is BIDIRECTIONAL assimilation.
The nasal prefix assimilation rule which ensures that all
nasals have the same place of articulation as the **following**
consonant exemplifies regressive assimilation; but the
STRENGTHENING of continuants so that they are realised as stops when they are **preceded** by a nasal stop is an
example of progressive assimilation.

5.3 Assimilation processes

Another way in which assimilation processes can be seen is in terms of whether a vowel or consonant acquires vowel or consonant features, respectively, of a neighbouring segment. Various patterns are examined in turn below. The coverage is not intended to be exhaustive. It is only meant to show some of the commonest assimilation processes found in the languages of the world.

5.3.1 Palatalisation

Say the following words and describe the position of your tongue during the production of the first consonant in each one of them:

[5.8] key [ḳi] car [kɑ]   then say: [kɑ ḳiz]
     keep [ḳip] calm [kɑm]   [kip ḳɑm]
     get   [get] garlic [gɑlɪk]   [get gɑlɪk]
     give [ḡɪv] guns [gʌnz]   [ḡɪv gʌnz]

Observe that, in each case when a velar consonant is followed by a front vowel, there occurs some slight anticipatory fronting of the part of the tongue that makes contact with the roof of the mouth. This fronting is indicated by a subscript (+) under the consonant. The effect of the fronting is that the velar consonant is made partly in the palatal region. This process is called PALATALISATION. Velar consonants often have slightly palatalised allophones which occur before front vowels because the tongue is raised towards the hard plate in the production of front vowels and speakers anticipate that gesture and start making it before they have completed the articulation of [k] or [g].

Palatalisation is not limited to velar consonants. It is equally possible to palatalise anterior consonants. In fast, casual spoken English, for instance, alveolar consonants are usually palatalised when they occur at the end of a word and are followed by another word which begins with an alveopalatal consonant:

[5.9] his shoes   [hɪz ʃuz]   → [hɪʒ ʃuz]
     nice shirt   [naɪs ʃɜt] → [naɪʃ ʃɜt]
     miss Ure   [mɪs juə] → [mɪʃ juə]
     John's shorts [dʒɒnz ʃɔts] → [dʒɒnʒ ʃɔts]

Now use the notion of palatalisation to help account for the alternative pronunciations of the words in [5.10].

[5.10]	A	B	C
issue	[ɪsju]	~ [ɪʃju]	~ [ɪʃu]
consume	[kənsjum]	~ [kənʃjum]	~ [kənʃum]

Add at least two more examples of your own.

If the forms in A are taken as the CITATION FORMS that would be listed in a dictionary, B can be explained as a case of palatalisation. The speaker, anticipating the palatal approximant which follows, places the tongue in the alveo-palatal region instead of the alveolar region. In C the speaker once again anticipates the palatal approximant and has the tongue making contact with the alveo-palatal region and drops the [j] sound which triggered off the palatalisation in the first place.

5.3.2 Labialisation

Palatalisation is not the only vowel feature which can be acquired by consonants. Say the words in [5.11] and then get another person to say them. Watch your partner's lips very carefully. Describe the lip position adjustment process which you observe as the initial consonant of each pair of words in A and B is said.

[5.11]	A		B
peel	[pil]	pool	[pʷul]
tea	[ti]	two	[tʷu]
she	[ʃi]	shoe	[ʃʷu]
leek	[lik]	Luke	[lʷuk]
get	[get]	got	[gʷɒt]

In each case, the word in B is said with some degree of secondary lip rounding. Anticipating the next segment, which is a rounded vowel, the speaker starts rounding the lips before the articulation of the consonant is completed. This assimilation process is called LABIALISATION (or ROUNDING). It can be indicated in a phonetic transcription by using the raised ʷ after a consonant [Cʷ].

Find two examples of labialisation in any language you know and write them down using a narrow phonetic transcription.

5.3.3 Voice assimilation

You will remember that in section 5.2 of this chapter we saw that in English suffixes agree in voicing with the last segment of the stem to which they are attached. That is a classic example of VOICE ASSIMILATION: whatever happens to be the specification for the feature [voice] of the preceding segment of the root is automatically carried over into the suffix. The relevant examples are not repeated here. If you want to refresh your memory, please read section 5.2 again.

The phonetic cause of voice assimilation is well–understood. Given the fact that speech is a continuum, the process of putting the vocal cords close together to produce voicing or keeping them wide apart to produce voicelessness is not always perfectly synchronised with other articulatory gestures. This may mean voicing spilling over into an adjacent segment. This frequently happens where a voiceless consonant occurs between two (voiced) vowels. In many languages, in that position, 'voiceless' consonants acquire a certain amount of voicing. This happened historically as Spanish developed from Latin. One of the changes that occurred was the voicing of voiceless stops between vowels. For instance, Latin *fāta* 'fate' became *fada* in Spanish. The converse situation is also attested. In some languages a vowel is devoiced when it occurs between voiceless consonants. That is the case in Japanese in a word like [k̥ita] 'came'.

Cast your mind back to the French problem in Chapter 2. The data is reproduced below for convenience. Recall that in French, at the end of a word the LIQUIDS (i.e. /l/ and /r/) as well as the nasals agree in voicing with the preceding consonant: they are voiced after voiced consonants (as in [5.12]), and voiceless after voiceless ones (as in [5.13]):

[5.12] French voice assimilation: word final nasals and liquids are voiced after a voiced segment.

matinal 'morning' (adj.)
li:r 'to read'
film 'film'
tabl 'table'

[5.13] French voice assimilation: word final nasals and liquids are voiceless after a voiceless segment.

metr̥ 'to put'
tãpl̥ 'temple'
ʃifr̥ 'figure'
rymatism̥ 'rheumatism'

Examine the data in [5.14] and describe the rule responsible for the voice assimilation in Kalenjin (Kenya) (Toweett 1975).

[5.14]	kep	to notch	kebe:t	is notching
	nap	to sew	nabe:t	is sewing
	luk	to fight	luge:t	is fighting
	ku:t	to blow	ku:te:t	is blowing

There is a twist in the data. While labial [p] and velar [k] acquire voicing in intervocalic position, alveolar [t] does not. It remains voiceless between vowels.

5.3.4 Place of articulation assimilation

We saw in [5.6] that in Luganda the place of articulation of a nasal is predictable from the place of articulation of the consonant that comes after it.

Now apply the same kind of analysis to the Malay data in [5.15] and state the distribution of the allomorphs of the agentive nominalising prefix /pəŋ/. This prefix can be attached to most verbs to form a noun with a meaning similar to that of a noun derived from a verb in English using the -er suffix.

[5.15] Malay (Dodds 1977)

baca	read	pəmbaca
bəli	buy	pəmbeli
bərənan	swim	pəmbərənan
dənar	hear	pəndənar
dakwa	prosecute	pəndakwa
cakap	speak	pəɲcakap
curi	steal	pəɲcuri
gosok	polish	pəŋgosok
gali	dig	pəŋgali

In [5.15], the nasal is HOMORGANIC with the consonant that goes after it, i.e. the nasal shares the place of articulation of the following consonant. Hence the use of the label HOMORGANIC NASAL ASSIMILATION to refer to this assimilation process. The homorganic nasal assimilation rules which were suggested for Luganda in [5.6] would also cover Malay. In both languages the assimilation is automatic. It applies wherever a nasal is followed by another consonant in the same word.

Homorganic nasal assimilation also applies in English, albeit somewhat sporadically. Compare the two columns in [5.16] which show the negative prefixes *in-* and *un-* respectively:

[5.16]   A   B
  [ɪn] in-appropriate   [ʌn] un-exciting
  [ɪm] im-plausible   [ʌn] un-pretentious
  [ɪn] in-decent   [ʌn] un-deserving
  [ɪŋ] in-gratitute   [ʌn] un-grateful

Add three fresh examples to each column, choosing a different consonant after the prefix, but avoiding the prefixes *ir-* and *il-* (see next section). Say carefully each word that you add to the list, noting the changes in the place of articulation of the nasal in column A in anticipation of the place of articulation of the consonant that follows. Assume that the underlying representation of the prefix in A is *in-* since that is the form that appears before vowels, a position where there is no phonetic motivation for modifying the place of articulation (given the fact that vowels have no place of articulation).

Homorganic nasal assimilation is not an automatic and obligatory rule of English phonology. It applies selectively to certain forms and is not triggered by phonological information alone. There are words which contain nonhomorganic nasals. The homorganic assimilation rule normally applies to *in-* but not to *un-*, except in casual speech where, for example, *unkempt* and *unpleasant* may be pronounced [ʌŋkempt] and [ʌmplezənt] respectively.

It is interesting that across word boundaries, in fast speech, consonants (especially alveolar ones), can be optionally homorganic with the following consonant. There, no grammatical restrictions seem to apply:

[5.17] bad man   [bæd mæn] → [bæb° mæn]
      ten men   [ten men] → [tem men]
      what car   [wɒt kɑ] → [wɒk° kɑ]
      top ten   [tɒp ten] → [tɒt° ten]
      (C° = unreleased stop: normally there is no audible release of a stop followed by another stop.)

Find two more examples of assimilation similar to those in [5. 17].

5.3.5 Manner of articulation assimilation

In the last section we established that the underlying representation of the negative prefix which occurs with adjectives in [5.16] must be *in-*. If that assumption is correct, how can we explain the historical development shown in [5.18]?

[5.18] in-legal   → illegal
      in-licit   → illicit
      in-rational   → irrational
      in-revocable   → irrevocable

The answer seems to be that before roots whose first consonant is a LIQUID (/l/ or /r/) the nasal of the negative prefix assimilates the manner of articulation features of the liquid so that /n/ becomes [l] before /l/-commencing roots or [r] before /r/-commencing roots. However, this alternation is not purely phonetically conditioned since [n] can be followed by [l] or [r] in words such as *unloved* or *unreasonable*. In fact, this is a historical assimilation which took place in Latin, and is simply reflected in modern English through Latin borrowing.

An example of a manner of articulation assimilation rule which is still active in a contemporary language is given in the Cairo Arabic data in [5.19]. The underlying representation of the definite article is /il-/. However, it is not realised as [il-] in all contexts. Whether it is realised as [il-] or as something else depends on the first consonant of the root to which it is prefixed.

Study [5.19] and suggest a rule to account for the realisation of the definite article.

Here is a clue: the definite article is realised as [il-] unless the noun to which it is attached shares some place of articulation features with /l/.

[5.19]   Cairo Arabic (Harms 1968)

kursi	'chair'	ilkursi	'the chair'
dars	'lesson'	iddars	'the lesson'
innimra	'the grade'	ilmudarris	'the teacher'
issatr	'the line'	ilwa:gib	'the assignment'
ilba:b	'the door'	ilqism	'the section'
issanta	'the bag'	ilge:b	'the pocket'

We could state the rule this way informally:

the [l] of the definite article takes on the manner of articulation features of the initial root consonant and becomes indistinguishable from it, where like [l], that consonant is anterior and coronal (i.e. made at the alveolar place of articulation).

The motivation for this kind of change is not difficult to see. Ensuring that segments made at the same place also agree in manner of articulation is a way of minimising articulatory effort. Instead of making two articulatory gestures the speaker only makes one and holds it for a longer period.

5.3.6 Nasalisation

NASALISATION is a process whereby an oral segment acquires nasality from a neighbouring segment. Again, the articulatory motivation for this is self-evident. In order to produce a nasal segment, it is necessary to lower the velum (soft palate) and allow air to escape through the nose (the lower the soft palate is, the higher will the degree of nasalisation be); to produce an oral sound, it is necessary to completely block off access to the nasal cavity by raising the velum as high as it can go. Any leakage of air past the velum will cause some nasalisation. To maintain an absolute distinction between oral and nasal consonants would require perfect synchronisation of velic closure with the other articulatory parameters of (a) PHONATION (i.e. production of voicing), (b) the PLACE OF ARTICULATION and (c) the MANNER OF ARTICULATION. This is not always possible. Typically some nasalisation seeps through and affects an oral segment which is adjacent to a nasal. In many languages the nasalisation is prominently audible. Examples of nasalised vowels (Ṽ) are the sound [ɛ̃] and [ã] in the French words [pɛ̃] *pain* 'bread' and [mãmã] *maman* 'mum'.

In Kikuyu (Kenya), vowels have nasal variants which occur in the neighbourhood of nasal consonants, as you can see in [5.20]:

[5.20] Kikuyu nasalisation (Leakey 1959)

mõndu	person	tato	three
mõãnake	young man	ihiɣa	stone
nyɔ̃ni	bird	iðə	father
ŋgõlo	heart	koɣolo	foot
kehẽmbe	drum	oholo	news

Historically it is almost certain that nasalisation is always a consonant feature which is assimilated by vowels. However, in a synchronic description of a language it is possible to find vowels which are always nasal and which must be presumed to be underlyingly nasal. That is the case in Yoruba (Nigeria) where nasal vowels occur in the absence of nasal consonants in words like [odũ] 'year'. At one time there would have been a nasal consonant conditioning the vowel nasalisation but it has disappeared.

5.4 Dissimilation

We have seen in the preceding section of this chapter that assimilation processes typically have a transparent phonetic basis that can be stated in terms of ease of articulation. But not all phonological processes can be plausibly explained in terms of assimilation. If we recognise the fact that phonological systems have to meet the needs of language users both as speakers and as hearers, we can easily appreciate that while assimilation (by making sounds more similar to each other) facilitates speech production, it does also have the undesirable effect of making the hearer's task of discriminating between sounds somewhat more difficult.

Phonological processes which ensure that differences between sounds are enhanced so that sounds become more auditorily distinct make speech perception easier. DISSIMILATION is the term used to refer to processes of that kind. The effect of dissimilation is to make sounds more distinct from other sounds in their environment. After a dissimilation rule has applied, phonological elements are less like each other than they were before the rule applied.

Let us begin by examining a very limited set of data from English which illustrates dissimilation. In English, the adjective forming suffix -al has two phonetic manifestations. Sometimes it is -al, as in column A in [5.21] below and sometimes it -ar, as in column B. Bearing in mind the fact that dissimilation plays a role in this, study the data and describe the factor which determines the allomorph that occurs in any particular instance. Pay special attention to the last segment of the noun which is adjacent to the adjective ending. Say the words aloud and transcribe the final segment phonetically.

[5.21]

	A		B
noun	*adjective*	*noun*	*adjective*
electric	electrical	angle	angular
region	regional	circle	circular
orbit	orbital	table	tabular
baptism	baptismal	tubule	tubular
genitive	genitival	title	titular
culture	cultural	single	singular

The pattern is clear. The shape *-al* is the base form. It is the form which you add in column A where the last consonant of the noun is a sound other than [l]. Verify this by looking at the transcription which you have made. The shape *-ar* is the alternant which is normally added where the last consonant of the noun is [l]. The addition of *-al* after a root ending in [l], which would have resulted in two [l] sounds merely separated by a schwa, is thus avoided. But like many other rules, this rule has exceptions, e.g. *linear* not **lineal* although *line* does not end in *-l*. (Note also in passing that in column B, [jʊ] is inserted between the final [l] and the consonant preceding it.)

The English dissimilation process is another Latin relic. It survives in words borrowed from Latin but is not a productive rule. It is often difficult to know where to draw the line between a synchronically relevant phonological process and a historical relic which is no longer relevant. We shall return to this problem in Chapter 8.

For our next example we shall consider a productive synchronic dissimilation process. In many Bantu languages there is a rule which requires a consonant in a prefix to DISAGREE in voicing with the first consonant of the root to which it is attached:

a voiced stem initial segment requires a voiceless consonant in the prefix and a voiceless stem–initial segment requires a voiced consonant in the prefix.

Consider the Kirundi (Burundi) examples in [5.22]:

[5.22] (Kirundi dissimilation (Kenstowicz and Kisseberth 1977)

a. *Imperative*   *1st person singular present*
    rya   eat   tu-rya

	mwa	shave	tu-mwa
	va	come from	tu-va
	bona	see	tu-bona
b.	soma	read	du-soma
	te:ka	cook	du-te:ka
	seka	laugh	du-seka
	kubita	hit	du-kubita

This dissimilation rule in Bantu is called Dahl's law, after the scholar who first described it.

5.5 Conclusion

In this chapter a number of common phonological processes have been examined. It has been shown that there are often good phonetic reasons for phonological processes. For the most part, phonological alternation in the shape of a morpheme has a phonetic motivation and that motivation tends to be similar in different languages. This largely explains the considerable degree of similarity between the phonological patterns found in different languages.

Exercise

1. Before attempting this question read [5.2] again. Next do the following:
(a) Make a broad phonetic transcription of the English data in example [5.1] above.
(b) Propose a rule which predicts the shape of the genitive suffix which goes with each one of the nouns in [5.1].

2. Study the data below showing the realisation of the regular past tense ending in English:

present	past	present	past
walk	walked	paint	painted
look	looked	want	wanted
trap	trapped	part	parted
wish	wished	fit	fitted
laugh	laughed	court	courted
watch	watched	land	landed
launder	laundered	sound	sounded
arm	armed	fade	faded

warn	warned	pad	padded
sue	sued	row	rowed

(a) Make a broad phonetic transcription of the data above.
(b) Suggest a rule to account for the realisation of the regular past tense ending.
(c) Make a single statement to account for the realisation of both the plural suffix and the past tense suffix.

CHAPTER 6
Naturalness and strength

6.1 Introduction

It will have become clear in the last chapter that the alternation in the phonological realisation of morphemes is for the most part not arbitrary. The same segment types turn up in similar processes found in diverse languages. Phonologists have used the term NATURALNESS to refer to the fact that there is, for the most part, a phonetically well-motivated relationship not only between the allophones of a phoneme, but also between the various phonological manifestations of a morpheme. Naturalness can be approached in terms of MARKEDNESS. What is NATURAL can be said to be UNMARKED, and what is not natural can be said to be MARKED, i.e. in some sense unusual. The purpose of this chapter is to explore this phenomenon.

6.2 Natural segments, natural classes and natural processes

It is not only classes of sounds which are affected by the same phonological processes that tend to be made up of segments which are phonetically natural. Individual segments themselves also tend to contain phonetic features which are natural. Partly due to physiological constraints, not every conceivable combination of features results in permissible segments. At a very obvious and trivial level, the fact that nobody has lips long enough to make contact with the uvula precludes labio-uvular consonants. More significant, however, is the fact that not all physically possible feature combinations are equally probable. Certain feature combinations are more likely; they are the ones that recur again and again in various languages. They are the unmarked combinations.

For instance, voiceless sonorants such as the nasals [m̥ n̥ ɲ̥ ŋ̥] are much less common than their voiced counterparts [m n ɲ ŋ]. Likewise, voiceless approximants like [w̥ j̥ l̥ r̥] are less common than voiced ones. Sounds produced with the velaric airstream mechanism (i.e. clicks) and those produced with the glottalic airstream mechanism (i.e. implosives and ejectives) are less common than sounds produced with the pulmonic airstream mechanism. Front rounded vowels are rare (the main concentration of front rounded vowels is north-western Europe where they occur in languages such as French, German and Swedish) but front unrounded vowels are not. Nasalised vowels, though widespread, are still much less frequent than their oral counterparts both in the world's languages and in those languages where they occur. That certain combinations of features are more favoured, more natural than others is beyond dispute. We shall consider some possible reasons for this at the end of this chapter.

I invite you now to determine which of the segments in each pair below is marked (less natural). State your reasons.

[6.1] A   B
      u̥   u
      õ   o
      œ   ɛ

In each case the sound in column A is marked. Vowels are normally voiced like [u] and not voiceless like [u̥]; vowels are normally oral like [o] and not nasal like [õ]; front vowels are normally unrounded like [ɛ] and not rounded like [œ].

Languages typically have both natural segments and natural phoneme inventories. In Chapter 2 we noted that phoneme inventories tend to be SYMMETRICAL. That observation can be restated in terms of naturalness. As a rule, creating symmetrical phoneme inventories entails maximising the use of a few phonological parameters. Such an arrangement is economical and has the merit of reducing the burden on memory during language acquisition: a small number of features is learned and is reused many times. This is preferable to having phonemes which have little in common with each other and which entail mastering numerous distinctive features.

Contrast the inventories in [6.2] with those in [6.3]:

[6.2] (a) Swahili vowels

i		u
e		o
	a	

(b) Turkana (Kenya) consonants (Dimmendaal 1983)

p	t	c	k
b	d	ɟ	g
m	n	ɲ	ŋ
	s		
	l		
	r		
j		w	

[6.3] (a) i   (b) p   t   ʔ

     ɪ   d   g

     e   m   ɲ

     ɛ

     æ

A phoneme inventory like that in [6.3b], with its many holes in the pattern, is less likely to be attested in natural languages than the symmetrical Turkana inventory in [6.2b], which distinguishes voiced stops, voiceless stops and nasals at each one of the three places of articulation exploited. Likewise, the balanced Swahili system in [6.2a] where front vowels are paired with back ones is a more likely vowel inventory than the skewed one containing only front vowels which is shown in [6.3a].

While recognising the importance of symmetry, we need to constantly bear in mind the fact that it is not an absolute imperative. Inelegant, skewed phonological systems are not unheard of. The Kikuyu plosives system, for instance, contains no bilabial voiceless stop:

[6.4] Kikuyu (Kenya)

	t	k
b	d	g

We shall end this section by re-examining data first introduced in the last chapter, which are reproduced below as [6.5] for convenience. These data illustrate the role of NATURAL CLASSES in the phonology of Luganda:

[6.5]

m–bala	I count
m–pa	I give
n–daga	I show
n–sika	I pull
ɲ–ɟela	I sweep
ŋ–gula	I buy
ŋ–kuba	I hit

The segments [m n ɲ ŋ] which acquire the place of articulation of the following consonant are not a random collection of segments; rather, they are a coherent class of phonetically similar sounds. They form a natural class. The homorganic nasal assimilation rule affects only the natural class consisting of nasal consonants.

The other phonological processes discussed in Chapter 5 also affect natural classes. The segments which condition or undergo a phonological process do share in each instance some phonetic characteristic. Thus, typically, palatalisation of velar consonants occurs in the context of front vowels (especially high ones like [i]) which are themselves produced with the tongue approximating the hard palate. Labialisation occurs in the neighbourhood of labial vowels like [u] which are themselves produced with rounded lips. Nasalisation of vowels occurs when they are adjacent to nasal consonants. Voiceless consonants may acquire some voicing when juxtaposed with inherently voiced segments like vowels or sonorants (such as nasals), and so on.

Important though they are, naturalness and markedness are not absolute concepts. Rather, they are both relative. What is marked or unmarked will often depend on the circumstances. A nonlinguistic analogy should help to clarify this: wearing a bikini or a kilt and sporran are in a sense marked modes of dress. Most people most of the time do not go about their business so attired. However, a woman in a bikini on the beach on a hot, sunny day or a Scotsman in a kilt at a Burns Supper would respectively be very 'unmarked'. So it is in phonology. Nasal vowels, to take one example, are marked. Indeed, we would be extremely surprised if we found a language which had only nasal vowels and no oral ones. However, between two nasal consonants, or before a nasal plus consonant cluster like [nd], nasalised vowels would be unmarked. It would be somewhat unusual for vowels occurring in those contexts to have no nasalisation. Using an oral [æ] in [mæn] is marked but using a nasalised [æ̃] and saying [mæ̃n] is unmarked. The same would apply to palatalisation of velars before high front vowels or labialisation before rounded vowels. Markedness cannot be interpreted with total disregard for context.

For the next example look back at the discussion of voice assimilation in English in section 5.2 of the last chapter. The consonants in the suffixes -s, -z, -ɪz; -t, -d, -ɪd that figure in English voice assimilation are either fricatives or stops. This is not accidental. In many languages fricatives and stops (together with affricates) form a natural class to which the label OBSTRUENT (or NON-SONORANT) is given. These sounds share the phonetic characteristics of having very significant obstruction in the oral tract and of being typically voiceless. They also tend to display similar phonological behaviour.

[6.6]	A	B	C	D
	bat	tab	pat	tap
	goal	log	coal	lock
	vine	save	fine	safe
	zoo	as	sue	ass
	gin	edge	chin	etch

Say the words in [6.6] aloud again and again. Compare the voicing of the words on the same line carefully and see if there is some kind of pattern.

What you will discover is that in English obstruents are more heavily voiced at the beginning of a word than they are word-finally. Generally, word-final voicing is so attenuated that it is barely detectable. In fact, the distinction between 'voiced' and 'voiceless' obstruents word-finally is less important in discriminating between words than the lengthening of the vowel that precedes a 'voiced' consonant.

It is natural for obstruents to be voiceless. Many languages have more voiceless obstruents than voiced ones and some have no voiced obstruent phonemes at all. That is the situation in many Australian languages. And numerous languages, with voiced obstruents, have a rule which devoices them in syllable final position. Such an obstruent devoicing rule can be seen at work in Turkish:

[6.7] Turkish obstruent devoicing (Kenstowicz and Kisseberth 1977:50)

objective	*absolute*	*plural*	*gloss*
ip–i	ip	ip-ler	rope
dib–i	dip	dip-ler	bottom
at–i	at	at-lar	horse
ad–i	at	at-lar	name

The stops /b/ and /d/ are devoiced in syllable-final position, i.e. when they occur in preconsonantal or word final position.

6.2.1 Phonological strength hierarchies

In the last chapter we saw that assimilation and dissimilation are useful concepts for elucidating phonological alternation. Many natural phonological processes involve some kind of assimilation or less commonly, dissimilation. But assimilation and dissimilation are not the only concepts in terms of which naturalness can be discussed.

Many phonological processes can be fruitfully examined using the notions of STRENGTHENING (also called FORTITION) and WEAKENING (also called LENITION). These two concepts are not independent of each other. They are merely two poles of the same gradient. As in everyday life, strength and weakness are relative. In [6.8]

I have reproduced a commonly accepted phonological strength hierarchy (> indicates a step towards a 'weaker' pronunciation):

[6.8] (a) VOICELESS > VOICED
(b) STOP > AFFRICATE > FRICATIVE > APPROXIMANT > ZERO

Before you proceed, I suggest that you work out the phonetic parameter(s) on which this hierarchy is based. Is it place of articulation, manner of articulation, airstream mechanism, phonation or something else? Now use your answer to rank the following sounds on the hierarchy which you have established. In some cases you might need to have more than one sound occupying the same place:

[6.9] t   r   o   β   z   s   k   d
g   m   w   ð   θ   p   b   a

In [6.8a] SONORITY is the parameter in question. As a first approximation, sonority is related to voicing. The greater the propensity a sound has of spontaneous voicing, the more sonority it has:

[6.10] Sonority hierarchy
least sonority
1 | voiceless obstruents (e.g. *t s k*)
2 | voiced obstruents (e.g. *d g β z*)
3 | nasals (e.g. *m*)
4 | liquids (e.g. *r*)
5 | glides (e.g. *w*)
6 | vowels (e.g. *a o*)
greatest sonority

The sonority hierarchy is an inverse restatement of the strength hierarchy (see also [9.6] page 158 below). In view of this, some phonologists question the need to distinguish between the strength hierarchy and the sonority hierarchy. Under the heading of strength they would prefer to include not only stricture (i.e. obstruction of the airstream) but also sonority.

Grouping together stricture and sonority under the rubric of the strength hierarchy might strike you as odd.

On the face of it, the two phenomena appear unrelated. However closer examination reveals an interesting relationship, especially where language evolution is concerned. To understand this relationship we need to draw a distinction between SYNCHRONIC and DIACHRONIC approaches to the study of language. Synchronic linguistics studies the state of a language during one period in its history. A grammar of mid-twentieth century English is a synchronic description. Diachronic (or historical) linguistics on the other hand, studies the evolution of a language during successive periods.

Frequently, both synchronically and diachronically, voiceless consonants change into voiced ones in environments similar to those where the reduction in the strength of the obstruction in the production of consonants takes place. Indeed, one process may facilitate the other. It is significant that the sounds at the weak end of the strength hierarchy are typically voiced, while those at the strong end are normally voiceless. Voiced sounds are weaker than their voiceless counterparts – [d] is weaker than [t], [z] is weaker than [s] and so on. When a voiceless sound like [t] becomes voiced, we can speak of 'weakening'.

If you are in any doubt as to what the answer to [6.9] ought to be, turn back to the first chapter and work out the manner of articulation of each sound. The strength hierarchy in [6.8b] is based on manner of articulation i.e. the way and the extent to which the airstream is obstructed in the articulation of a particular sound. Stops involve the strongest obstruction and approximants the weakest, with the remaining types of sound falling in between. Of course, having no obstruction at all and dropping a sound altogether is the ultimate form of weakening.

Many phonological concepts like assimilation, strengthening, etc., refer to processes that can be understood from either a synchronic or diachronic point of view (see Chapter 8). Strengthening and weakening are exemplified below using some data from historical phonology. Compare the forms in [6.11] (Hooper 1976):

[6.11] (a) Latin Italian Spanish French
         vita   vita   vida   vie   'life'
       (b) Latin   Italian   Spanish French

voiceless ——►voiceless ——►voiced ——► zero
stop   stop   stop
t ——►   t ——►   d ——►   ø
(where ————► = becomes)

The changes exemplified involve movement down the
sonority hierarchy.

In some cases, before being deleted a voiced stop may
go through a fricative phase. The word meaning 'loyal' in
modern Spanish is derived from Latin *legale* whose [g]
weakened to the velar fricative [ɣ] in Medieval Spanish
when it was pronounced as *leɣale*. The velar fricative was
eventually lost, resulting in the modern Spanish form *leal*.
In this case the progression down the sonority hierarchy is
from a voiced stop to a voiced fricative before deletion takes
place.

The examples presented so far have been of weakening.
But sounds can also move up the strength hierarchy. In
Luganda [l], an approximant, becomes a stop [d] when it is
immediately preceded by a nasal stop:

[6.12]   [laga]   'show'   [ndaga]   'I show'
         [kaliga]   'lamb'   [ndiga]   'sheep'

Some linguists have added PLACE OF ARTICU-
LATION as a parameter of the universal strength hierarchy:

[6.13] LABIAL > ALVEOLAR > VELAR

This dimension of the hierarchy seems to be valid for the
languages of Western Europe, like Danish, where in intervocalic position, velar /g/ undergoes the most extreme
form of lenition (i.e. weakening), being deleted altogether;
alveolar /d/ is moderately weakened, being changed to the
fricative [ð] but labial /b/ remains unchanged.

However, the universal validity of a place of articulation hierarchy is doubtful. In many Bantu languages, for
instance, it is the labial place of articulation that is weakest.
Many languages in this family historically weakened and
completely dropped the labial stops /p/ or /b/ while
retaining the alveolar and velar ones. Thus in Kikamba
(Kenya) the reflex of the Proto-Bantu noun class prefix *ba-
is a-. The labial [b] was deleted except where it was
preceded by a nasal. After a nasal it survives as prenasalised

[ᵐb]. Proto-Bantu /p/ is equally prone to lenition *p→h in Sukuma (Tanzania), Rundi (Burundi), Pare (Tanzania) etc.; *p > φ in Pokomo (Kenya), and Rimi (Tanzania) etc. Typically velars and alveolars do not undergo lenition to the extent that labials do. Given this evidence, it would be unwise to insist on the universality of a strength hierarchy based on place of articulation.

It is arguable that the sonority and manner of articulation strength hierarchies in [6.8] should be replaced by the single hierarchy shown in [6.14]. This, for the reasons given above excludes the dimension of place of articulation.

[6.14] VOICELESS STOP > VOICED STOP > VOICELESS AFFRICATE > VOICED AFFRICATE > VOICELESS CONTINUANT > VOICED CONTINUANT > NASAL > APPROXIMANT

One type of consonant not included in [6.14] which there is strong evidence for is the GEMINATE consonant like [t:] or [d:], usually represented by doubling consonant letters ([tt] or [dd]). Gemination occurs when two identical consonants are adjacent to each other as in English *penknife* [pen:aɪf]; in other words, gemination occurs when a particular segmental articulation is prolonged to cover what would otherwise be two distinct segments. Geminate consonants occupy the highest rung of the hierarchy.

The strength hierarchy, re-stated now in [6.15], is manifested in synchronic phonological alternation and in historical sound change in numerous languages:

[6.15] GEMINATE VOICELESS STOP > GEMINATE VOICED STOP > VOICELESS STOP > VOICED STOP > VOICELESS AFFRICATE > VOICED AFFRICATE . . . .

The relative strength remains the same with other manners of articulation.

Synchronically, in many languages in positions of weakening, for instance between vowels, geminate segments like [t:] (spelled with *tt* in the examples which follow) alternate with plain segments like [t]. Thus in Luganda the singular of the word 'branch' is *ttabi* [t:aßi] but

the plural is *matabi* [mataßi]. An historical example of the
same kind is provided by the word for 'drop' in Romance
languages where the reflexes of Latin *gutta* are *gota* in
Spanish and *goutte* in French. The original geminate has
changed to [t] in both languages.

6.3 Explanations of naturalness

The assimilatory phonological processes of the kind which
we explored in the last chapter all have a firm basis in
articulatory phonetics. We can point to a good articulatory
reason for a process like palatalisation, labialisation or nasalisation. Where possible, adjacent sounds are made similar
to each other so that one avoids using any more effort than
is required to ensure that one is understood by the
addressee. But while assimilation makes the task of speech
production easier, it can make speech perception more
difficult. It is easier to discriminate between sounds if they
are very different from each other than it is to distinguish
them when they are very alike. To counterbalance assimilation, there are natural processes which have the effect of
enhancing differences between sounds. These facilitate the
task of the hearer. In Chapter 5, voice dissimilation in
Kirundi was introduced as an example of dissimilation.
When this rule applies, the prefix and the root end up not
having the same value for voicing, which makes them more
different from each other than they would otherwise be.

Vowel patterns also frequently obey the principle of
MAXIMUM PERCEPTUAL DIFFERENTIATION. The
set in [6.16] turns up in language after language with a three
vowel system (see section 3 of Chapter 2).

[6.16]

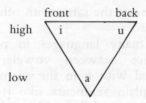

The choice of these vowels is not accidental. These three vowels occupy the most peripheral positions in vowel space: [i] is the highest front vowel, [u] is the highest back vowel and [a] is the lowest vowel. Perceptually they are maximally distinct. If a language has only three vowels, in order to avoid hearers getting them confused (and as a consequence getting the meanings of words in which they occur confused), it is almost invariably the three vowels [i a u] that are selected. Languages as diverse as Greenlandic Eskimo and Australian Pitta-Pitta have /i a u/ as their only vowel phonemes.

Languages with a five vowel phoneme system consisting of /i e a o u/, if they have rules which neutralise vowel distinctions in certain environments, tend to maintain the opposition between /i a u/ in the places of neutralisation. An example should clarify this. In many Bantu languages with the five vowel phonemes /i e a o u/, only the peripheral vowels /i a u/ occur in noun class prefixes which mark the class (or gender) of a noun, as you can see in the Luganda forms below:

[6.17] *mu*-sota   snake   *mi*-sota   snakes
       mu-ntu   person   *ßa*-ntu   people
       ki-ntu   thing   *ßi*-ntu   things
       ka-tale   market   *ßu*-tale   markets

6.3.1 Natural phonology

Pholonogists do not agree on the place of naturalness in phonological theory. Those who belong to a school called NATURAL PHONOLOGY which was pioneered by Stampe (1973) argue that the phonological component of language is not merely the result of CONVENTION, rather it is the way it is for very good reasons. It reflects, on the one hand, the auditory, articulatory and speech processing capacity of humans, and on the other hand the functions which language serves. They maintain that in all languages, phonemes and phonological processes are the residue of UNIVERSAL PHONOLOGICAL PROCESSES. Typically these are assimilation processes like homorganic nasal assimilation, palatalisation, nasalisation, voice assimilation, and so on. It is claimed that in acquiring the phonological system of its language, a child has to learn to SUPPRESS in different ways and to different language-specific degrees various innate universal phonological processes. A rump of those processes survives, tailored to fit whatever quirks a particular language may have acquired over the centuries. It is suggested that the striking similarity that exists between the phonological processes found in unrelated languages can be largely explained in terms of their having preserved the same or similar aspects of universal natural processes.

In this approach, a sharp distinction is drawn between rules and processes. The term RULE is used to refer to phonetically wholly or partially unmotivated alternations, like those exemplified in the next paragraph, which are governed by the conventions of a particular language. PROCESSES are alternations which are regulated by universal phonetic or functional factors. Unlike processes, rules are idiosyncratic properties of particular languages and do not form part of humankind's common phonological inheritance. Natural processes are more common than idiosyncratic rules. Donegan and Stampe (1979:127) claim that natural phonology 'follows naturally from the nature of things' because essentially phonological patterning is not merely a matter of convention.

Nonetheless, even the most ardent natural phonologist would admit that not everything in synchronic phonology is natural. The alternation in the shape of some morphemes either has a tenuous phonetic basis or is entirely arbitrary: there are numerous UNNATURAL alternations which are motivated by lexical or grammatical considerations rather than phonetic factors. For instance, in English the plural of a noun is normally formed by suffixing an alveolar fricative which agrees in voicing with the last segment of the noun root. But in a few irregular forms like *ox*, which becomes *oxen* instead of the expected **oxes* in the plural, or *sheep*, which remains *sheep* in the plural instead of the expected **sheeps*, the regular natural process of assimilation does not apply.

A case has been made in the literature for restricting phonology to processes with a genuine phonetic basis and reserving for the morphological component of the grammar any rules regulating alternations that are determined by nonphonetic factors: This dichotomy between processes and rules is justified on the grounds that natural processes are easier to master in language acquisition than rules, which are not natural. Furthermore, when the language faculty disintegrates in aphasia, control of idiosyncratic rules, vanishes before control of natural processes. The theory predicts, for example, that an English-speaking aphasiac is more likely to continue correctly forming regular plurals like *ships* and *boxes* which obey the natural process of voice assimilation than irregular plurals like *sheep* and *oxen* which obey an *ad hoc* rule.

But there are complications. There is not always a simple dichotomy between natural processes and unnatural rules. With the passage of time, natural processes may have severe constraints imposed on their application without their natural basis becoming entirely lost. Re-examine the treatment of place of articulation in the last chapter. In section 5.3.4 we considered the process of place of articulation assimilation in English and in various African languages. You will recall from section 5.2.1 that in a language like Luganda all nasals always take the place of articulation of the following consonant, this being the universal natural process. In English too, this principle does apply, albeit in a very restricted way, as we saw in the examples in [5.16]. It automatically affects the prefix *in-* but not the prefix *un-*. In Luganda the universal natural process of homorganic assimilation is preserved intact but in English it is inhibited, though not completely suppressed. It applies not across the board, but rather in restricted, morphologically defined environments. But this is still less arbitrary than the rule which says add nothing to form the plural of *sheep*.

Continue exploring the notion of 'degrees of naturalness' by examining some more data, this time taken from Swahili.

[6.18]

noun class 9/10		*noun class* 1		*noun class* 3	
mbuzi	goat	ŋtu	person	m̩vi	grey hair
nguruwe	pig	ŋke	wife	m̩fereʄe	gutter
ɲʄugu	peanut	ŋze	old person	mlaŋgo·	doorway

mbuni	ostrich	ṃbuni	inventor	ṃbuni	coffee plant
ndizi	banana	ṃpya	new person	ṃkono	arm
ŋgao	shield	ṃgaŋga	doctor	ṃʃale	arrow
ɳtʃi	country				
ɳtʃa	point				
ŋge	scorpion				

State the circumstances in which nasals are:

  (a) homorganic   (b) syllabic

Be warned! You will need to take into account some of the information provided about MORPHOLOGY. Information about noun class membership is important as different morphemes may behave in different ways in identical phonetic contexts.

I hope you have been able to see that in Swahili, a word-medial nasal or a nasal prefix marking classes 9/10 must be homorganic with the following consonant but that a nasal prefix marking class 1 or 3 need not be homorganic. While assimilation of a nasal to the place of articulation of the following consonant is itself a natural process, its implementation in Swahili is sensitive to nonphonetic factors – it depends on the noun class which the nasal represents. The homorganic nasal assimilation rule is MORPHOLOGISED. It is not automatically triggered by phonetic information. It requires morphological information.

Likewise, the distribution of syllabic nasals, is morphologised. Any class 1 or class 3 nasal prefix is syllabic but a class 9/10 prefix is syllabic only if the root to which it is attached is monosyllabic. The distinction between monosyllabic and longer roots is clearly phonological but information concerning noun class membership is morphological.

Rule morphologisation represents a cline rather than a dichotomy. Some rules may be more morphologised than others; the extent to which the natural basis of a phonological alternation is subverted by nonphonetic factors varies greatly.

Besides morphologisation, another common cause of

the loss of naturalness is TELESCOPING. Telescoping occurs when some intermediate stages in a series of natural historical changes get eclipsed or completely lost, leaving behind a phonetically bizarre set of synchronic alternations. Normally alternants of the same morpheme are related by phonological processes that are plausible. Occasionally, however, we find phonetically triggered, automatic alternations which are arbitrary from a synchronic point of view.

In Luganda, for instance, we find /p/ alternating sometimes with [j] and sometimes with [w], which is extraordinary. It is very odd for a bilabial voiceless stop to have palatal and labio-velar approximants as its allophones. Allophones of the same phoneme ought to be phonetically similar; these sounds have very little in common.

Study the data in [6.19] and state the distribution of the allophones of /p/.

[6.19]	kuwa	to give	kujita	to call	kuweta	to bend
	wa	give! (imp.)	tujita	we call	tuweta	we bend
	mpa	I give	mpita	I call	mpeta	I bend

The fact that [p j w] are in complementary distribution is strange. But we can easily write a rule stating their distribution:

/p/ becomes (i) [j] when followed by [i] and not preceded by a nasal;

           (ii) [w] when followed by any other vowel provided it is not preceded by a nasal;

          (iii) where it is preceded by a nasal, it is realised as [p] regardless of the vowel that follows it.

When Luganda is compared with another very closely related Ugandan language, Runyankole, the missing stages in Luganda can be reconstructed thus:

[6.20] $p > p^h > h > j$ or w (depending on the following vowel)

Evidence for [6.20] is contained in sound correspondences in forms like:

[6.21] *Runyankole* *Luganda*
kuha   to give   kuwa
kuhaisa   to cause to give kuweesa
kuheɟera   to pant   kuweɟeela
omuhiigi   hunter   omujizzi

Natural phonology opens new perspectives on the problems of phonological analysis. However, there remain some nagging doubts. The explanation of phonological alternation which it offers is essentially FUNCTIONAL, emphasising as it does natural assimilation processes, and implicitly ease of articulation. But a functional account in terms of ease of articulation which works well for speech production will not be as satisfactory when the focus shifts to speech perception, since what makes the articulation of sounds easier tends to make their discrimination more difficult. The two viewpoints are in conflict. In concrete terms, what this means is that we cannot always explain why in a given case assimilation rather than dissimilation is the preferred solution. The explanation proferred by a natural phonologist might appear to a sceptical observer to be a somewhat arbitrary, *post hoc* rationalisation whose explanatory value is doubtful.

Consider the claim, for instance, that the ideal syllable type is CV, i.e. the kind of syllable that ends in a vowel (see section 9.5, page 175). It is said that the function of many rules is to maximise preferred CV syllables. It is sometimes suggested that this explains why, in many languages, a word final consonant not followed by a vowel is deleted. For example, in French, the final [t] is dropped in words like *petit* [pəti] 'little' (masculine); in the feminine where it is followed by [ə] as in *petite* [pətitə] 'little' the consonant is kept. Similarly, the desire to maintain the preferred CV syllable type is said to explain the insertion of extra vowels in English loanwords like *hospital* when they are borrowed by languages that require consonants to be followed by vowels. Thus *hospital* is often rendered as *hosipitali* in Swahili and many African languages.

At present there is no way of determining which natural process takes precedence where alternative natural processes are available. Even if it turned out to be true that naturalness determines rule application, we would be none the wiser when it comes to providing an explanatory account of a specific phonological event. It is not yet possible to explain why, to create a CV sequence, in one instance a vowel is added and in another a consonant is deleted. Intuitively naturalness seems to be a valid concept. However, its predictive value and hence its place in a rigorous theory of phonology is still uncertain.

Exercises

1. All the segments; except one; in each set below form a natural class. Circle the odd one out and state the phonetic property that makes it different from the rest.

   (a)   r l m (k)   *example* [k] is an obstruent
                                      [r l m] are sonorants
   (b)   p t x g k s f
   (c)   l r n ɲ d w j t
   (d)   f ʃ t p g b θ
   (e)   s z f v x ʃ t
   (f)   pf d ts tʃ bv dʒ
   (g)   ã õ i ũ ỹ
   (h)   p m t s b d
   (i)   b ɗ g d
   (j)   e i ɛ ø

2. Tairora (Papua New Guinea) (SIL: 1980:39)

bu'rauka	I went	bi'lo	he goes
bi'ßa	he went	bi'reɾa	I will go
'tei'rima	I understand	bu'araßa	you went
'bulo	I'm going	bi'reße	will you go?
'iɾia	listen!	'binaßu	we went
aluke'loma	he killed it		

   'biɾi 'timilo He brought it down and gave it to me
   (Note: ' marks stress)

   (a) Are [l] and [ɾ] distinct phonemes? What is the evidence?
   (b) State the distribution of [b] and [ß]. They are in complementary distribution.
   (c) Explain the natural basis of the alternation of [b] with [ß].

3. Account for the realisation of the final consonant of the noun root in the data below.

singular	genitive	plural
wife	wife's	wives
knife	knife's	knives
hoof	hoof's	hooves
thief	thief's	thieves

CHAPTER 7

Interaction between rules

7.1 Introduction to rule formalisation and ordering

Previous chapters have shown the need for more than one level of phonological representation. If we assume that there are underlying representations from which surface (phonetic) representations are derived, we shall often need more than one rule to map underlying representations on to surface representations. The situation can be compared to rush hour city traffic at a road junction, with rules queueing up to be applied. Police officers or traffic lights are needed to regulate the flow of traffic. Likewise, in phonology a mechanism is needed to determine which one of several rules affecting a piece of data has precedence over other rules. Obviously, where rules do not interfere with each other, where they are like traffic on parallel one way streets, the question of regulation does not arise. I illustrate this with English examples in [7.1]:

[7.1] [pʰɪt]   pit   [pʷʰul]   pool
       [tʰɪk]   tick   [tʷʰʊk]   took
       [kʰïl]   keel   [kʷʰul]   cool
       [ətʰend]   attend   [əkʷʰʊstɪk] acoustic

The rules we needed to account for [7.1] are listed informally in [7.2]

[7.2] (a) voiceless stops are aspirated at the beginning of a stressed syllable;
       (b) consonants are labialised (rounded) before rounded vowels;
       (c) velar consonants are fronted (palatalised) before high front vowels.

Rules [7.2b] and [7.2c] do not affect each other. There is no interaction problem since they do not have the same *structural description*, i.e. the phonetic properties of their inputs are different. Rule [7.2b] requires the presence of a rounded vowel, and all such vowels are back in English while rule [7.2c] stipulates that there must be a high front vowel. The two rules are like traffic on different highways. There is no possibility of their interfering with each other.

Determine whether rule [7.2a] interferes with either of the other two rules.

The answer must be 'no' since the voiceless stop at the beginning of a stressed syllable is aspirated regardless of the vowel that follows. Here again no traffic control system is needed. It would make no difference whatsoever to the final output which order the rules were applied in. Regulation of rule interaction is required only if one rule affects in some way the potential input to another rule.

Before we examine more closely the problem of rule interaction, I shall introduce you to the basic formal conventions used by generative phonologists because normally rules are written using distinctive features and formal notation. The motivation for rule formalisation is that it increases the explicitness of linguistic descriptions and makes it easier to expose woolly or incoherent analyses. I shall introduce the basic formal conventions of GENERATIVE PHONOLOGY, by restating formally in [7.3] the rules outlined above in [7.2]:

[7.3] input   *becomes*   output   *in the environment*

(a) $\begin{bmatrix} -\text{cont} \\ -\text{voice} \end{bmatrix} \longrightarrow [+\text{spread}]/\_(C)\begin{bmatrix} -\text{cons} \\ +\text{stress} \end{bmatrix}$

e.g. /k/   becomes   [kʰ]   before a stressed vowel (as in *acoustic*)

(b) $[+\text{cons}] \longrightarrow [+\text{round}]/\_\begin{bmatrix} -\text{cons} \\ +\text{round} \end{bmatrix}$

e.g. /t/   becomes   [tʷ]   before a rounded vowel (as in *too*)

(c) $\begin{bmatrix} + \text{cons} \\ + \text{back} \\ + \text{high} \end{bmatrix}$ $\longrightarrow$ $[-\text{back}] /\underline{\hspace{1cm}}$ $\begin{bmatrix} + \text{high} \\ - \text{back} \end{bmatrix}$

e.g. /k/ becomes [$\overset{k}{+}$]   before a
                                                high front
                                                vowel (as
                                                in *key*)

A formal rule consists of the following:

  (a) the *input*, which states the sound or sounds affected by the rule;

  (b) the *arrow*, which means 're-write as' or 'is realised as' or 'becomes' (but no historical development is implied);

  (c) what occurs to the right of the arrow is the *output* of the rule;

  (d) following the output, there is a diagonal line '/' to the right of that line is the *environment*, the _____ line which forms part of the environment and shows precisely where the changed segment is located:

  (e) brackets round an element (like (C) in [7.3a]) indicate that a given element is optional – the rule applies regardless of the presence or absence of any optional element. In this instance it indicates that a voiceless plosive is still aspirated even where a consonant intervenes, as in *prayer*.

We shall turn to French for our next example of rule interaction and rule formalisation.

Usually in French, an underlying word final consonant is deleted unless it is followed by a vowel. This produces alternations like [triko] (*le*) *tricot* 'knitted wear' and [trikɔte] *tricoter* 'to knit'. A good place to look for examples of this is the alternation between the masculine and feminine forms of nouns and adjectives:

[7.4] FINAL CONSONANT DELETION

Masculine			Feminine			
/bɑs/	[bɑ]	bas	/bɑsə/	[bɑs]	basse	'low'
/ʃat/	[ʃa]	chat	/ʃatə/	[ʃat]	chatte	'cat'
/ʃod/	[ʃo]	chaud	/ʃodə/	[ʃod]	chaude	'hot'

In the underlying representation the feminine form ends in [ə]. Phonetically, however, that final vowel is normally deleted in contemporary French – it is the so-called 'silent e'. In fact, this vowel has not always been 'silent'. It was weakly pronounced as [ə] in Old French. Even today, when French poetry is recited, 'silent e' is scrupulously pronounced as [ə] in certain contexts. The rules regulating the pronunciation or omission of [ə] are complex. Their main function is to determine whether [ə] contributes to the syllable count. See Grammont (1961). The rule of final consonant deletion which applies to underlying representation can be formalised as [7.5]:

$$[7.5] \quad [+\text{cons}] \longrightarrow \varnothing / \underline{\hspace{1cm}} \left\{ \begin{array}{c} C \\ \# \end{array} \right\}$$

Remarks on the notation:
  (i) ø means *zero* i.e. the segment is rewritten as zero – in other words it is deleted.
 (ii) # = word boundary
(iii) the *curly brackets* { } indicate alternatives; here deletion of a consonant occurs **either** before a consonant **or** before a boundary at the end of a word.

Next consider VOWEL NASALISATION, another phonological process which occurs in French:

[7.6]

[fɛ̃]	fin	'end'
[dɑ̃]	dans	'in'
[rɔbɛ̃]	robin	'lawyer (pejorative)'
[fɛ̃]	faim	'hunger'
[sɑ̃]	sans	'without'
[ɔ̃]	on	idef. pron. 'one'
[ɑ̃]	en	'in'
[tɑ̃]	tant	'so much'
[mulɛ̃]	moulin	'mill'

The rule to account for [7.6] is given in [7.7].

$$[7.7] \quad V \longrightarrow [+\text{nasal}] / \underline{\hspace{1cm}} \overset{C}{[+\text{nasal}]} \left\{ \begin{array}{c} C \\ \# \end{array} \right\}$$

Strictly speaking distinctive features should always be used in the formal statement of rules. But in practice, for convenience, instead of using distinctive features, we often adopt the convention of using V to represent any vowel, C to represent any consonant, G to represent any glide and N to represent any nasal.

Rule [7.7] states that a vowel is nasalised if it is followed by a nasal consonant which in turn is followed by

either another consonant or a word boundary in the underlying representation.
If you turn now to [7.8], you will see that rule [7.7]
does not apply to the vowels in [7.8b] because in the
underlying representation, none of them is followed by
either a nasal consonant which is in turn followed by
another consonant or appears in word final position. But
nasalisation does apply to the vowels in [7.8a] because their
underlying representations satisfy the requirements of the
nasalisation rule. (We shall use the abbreviations UR and PR
to stand for Underlying Representation and Phonetic
Representation respectively):

[7.8a] *UR*   *PR*
     /bɔn/   [bɔ̃] bon (masc.) 'good'
     /amerikɛn/   [amerikɛ̃] américain (masc.)
                             'American'
     /dɑns /   [dɑ̃] dans 'in'
     /mɑrin /   [marɛ̃] marin 'marine' (masc.)[1]
     /tɑnt /   [tɑ̃] tant 'so much'
     /an/   [ɑ̃] an (masc.) 'year'
     /mulin/   [mulɛ̃] moulin (masc.) 'mill'
     /fɔnd]   [fɔ̃] fond (masc.) 'bottom'
     /fɔndamɑntal/ [fɔ̃damɑ̃tal] fondamental
                             'fundamental'
     /fin/   [fɛ̃] fin (fem.) 'end'

[7.8b] *UR*   *PR*
     /bɔnɔmi/   [bɔnɔmi] bonhomie (fem.)
                            'good nature'
     /amerikɛnə/   [amerikɛn] américaine (fem.)
                            'American'
     /dada/   [dada] dada (masc.) 'hobby-
                     horse'
     /marinə/   [marin] marine 'marine' (fem.)
     /ta/   [ta] ta 'your' (sing.)
     /a/   [a] à prep. 'to'
     /ane/   [ane] année (fem.) 'year'
     /mulina:ʒ/   [mulina:ʒ] moulinage 'milling
                             (noun)'
     /fwa/   [fwa] fois (fem.) 'time, occasion'
     /finalite/   [finalite] finalité (fem.)
                            'finality'

Before moving on, list separately words in [7.8a] which have nasalised vowels:
(a) due to being followed by a nasal in word final position:
(b) due to being immediately followed by a nasal which is in turn followed by another consonant.

The words *bon* and *fin* are obvious examples of the effects of rule (a) and *fondamental* of rule (b).

7.2 Linear rule ordering

The French data in [7.8] pose a rule ordering problem. A word like *an* [ã] is subject both to the rule that deletes final consonants which are not immediately followed by a vowel and also to the nasalisation rule. To determine the order in which the two rules should be applied, we can try out the two derivations in [7.9] and [7.10] and see which one yields the correct output.

[7.9] Underlying representation /an/
First apply
Rule [7.5]: Final consonant deletion

$$[+\text{cons}] \longrightarrow \emptyset / \_ \left\{ \begin{matrix} C \\ \# \end{matrix} \right\}$$

(This deletes the /n/ of *an* as it is word-final.)
Then apply
Rule [7.7]: Vowel nasalisation

$$[-\text{cons}] \longrightarrow [+\text{nasal}] / \_ [+\text{nasal}] \left\{ \begin{matrix} C \\ \# \end{matrix} \right\}$$

The nasalisation rule fails to apply because the nasal which triggers off the nasalisation process is absent, having been deleted by [7.5]. Consequently the final output is *[a]. This is obviously incorrect.

Let us now try applying the two rules in reverse order, assuming again that the underlying representation is /an/.

[7.10] First apply
Rule [7.7]: Vowel nasalisation

$$[-\text{cons}] \longrightarrow [+\text{nasal}] / \_ [+\text{nasal}] \left\{ \begin{matrix} C \\ \# \end{matrix} \right\}$$

This yields [ãn] (and a lowering rule affecting nasalised vowels subsequently turns it into /ãn/).
Then apply
Rule [7.5]: Consonant deletion

$$[+\text{cons}] \longrightarrow \emptyset \;/ \; \underline{\quad} \left\{ \begin{matrix} C \\ \# \end{matrix} \right\}$$

By this rule /ãn/ loses its final /n/ and becomes [ã], which is the correct phonetic form.

This example shows that there are situations where the order in which rules apply makes a difference. That being the case, principles regulating the order in which rules apply are needed.

In SPE Chomsky and Halle proposed that rules should be LINEARLY ORDERED. To illustrate this, suppose in the phonological component of the grammar of a given language there are thirty rules. By this principle, the rules would be arranged in a list and it would be stipulated that each rule applies after all the rules that precede it and before all the rules that follow it on the list. It would not be possible, for instance, to apply rule two after rule ten, where both rules are applicable. Once a particular order has been established, it is strictly observed in every derivation in a language. Furthermore, a rule can only apply once in a derivation. This means that a rule cannot re-apply in the same derivation either to its own output or to the output of another rule ordered after it which satisfies its structural description.

If the application of one rule has absolutely no effect on the potential input to another rule, the question of the sequence of application of those rules simply need not be raised. This was established at the beginning of the first section of this chapter. However, the question of linear ordering arises in a very interesting way where one rule can affect another, as in the French data above. We shall explore this again by examining some data from Luganda.

[7.11] Luganda glide formation

Column A		Column B	
UR	PR	UR	PR
/mu+ana/	[mwa:na] 'child'	/mu+ti/	[muti] 'tree'

/mu+ojo/ [mwo:jo] 'soul' /mu+kazi/ [mukazi] 'woman'
/li+anda/ [lja:nda] 'coal' /li+no/ [lino] 'this'
/mi+aka/ [mja:ka] 'years' /mi+ti/ [miti] 'trees'
(+ is a sign for a morpheme boundary.)

Contrast the realisation of the underlying high vowels /i/ and /u/ in columns A and B. Write in your own words the rule which captures the relevant generalisation.

In [7.12] I have written the rule out formally (ignoring for the moment the fact that the vowel that follows the glide is lengthened).

[7.12] V
[+high] ⟶ [−syllabic]/ __ V

[7.12] states that a high vowel becomes a nonsyllabic glide when it is followed by another vowel.

Luganda has another rule which is of interest in this context. It is an optional rule which deletes a root-initial /j/ which is preceded by certain CV prefixes. The effect of that rule is shown in [7.13].

[7.13] UR   PR
/tu+jagala/ [twa:gala] or [tujagala]
                       'we like, want'
/ku+jaka/   [kwa:ka] or [kujaka]
                       'to blaze'
/mu+jola/   [mwo:la] or [mujola]
                       'you (pl.) carve'
/tu+jela/   [twe:la] or [tujela]
                       'we sweep'
/mu+jiko/   [mujiko] or [mwi:ko] 'trowel'

Where a prefix is represented by a lone V, root-initial /j/ is not deleted:

[7.14] UR   PR
/a+jagala/ [ajagala] 'he/she likes, wants'
/e+jaka/   [ejaka] 'it blazes'
/a+jola/   [ajola] 'he/ she carves'
/a+jela/   [ajela] 'he/ she sweeps'

The / j/ deletion rule, can be written as [7.15]:

[7.15] $/j/ \longrightarrow \text{ø} / CV_{[+Pref.]} + \underline{\quad} V$

These Luganda examples show that in order to derive the correct output in [7.13] for words like [twe:la] 'we sweep', it is necessary to apply the /j/ deletion rule in [7.15] **before** the glide formation rule in [7.12].

Work out the reason for this before you read on.

If we assume that rules apply linearly, until [7.15] has been applied to a form like /tu+jela/, the vowels /u/ and /e/ are separated by /j/ and the input to glide formation is not available and so glide formation cannot be applied. For glide formation to apply, a high vowel must be adjacent to another vowel. The deletion of /j/ creates the input to glide formation. The implications for rule ordering are obvious: /j/ deletion must precede glide formation if both rules are to apply. Technically, this kind of rule relationship where one rule opens the door to the application of another rule is called FEEDING ORDER.

The reverse is also possible. One rule may prevent or pre-empt the application of another. In that case the rules are said to be arranged in a BLEEDING ORDER. We shall explore this type of rule interaction using data from Swahili.

Swahili has a rule of homorganic nasal assimilation. Here it is illustrated applying to forms in noun class 9. This class contains many nouns referring to non-humans:

[7.16]
UR	PR	
/ N+boga/	[mboga]	'vegetable'
/ N+bu/	[m̩bu]^2	'mosquito'
/ N+dizi/	[ndizi]	'banana'
/ N+dama/	[ndama]	'calf'
/ N+jugu/	[ɲɟugu]	'peanut'
/ N+guruwe/	[ŋguruwe]	'pig'
/ N+goma/	[ŋgoma]	'drum'

The nasal prefix /N/ undergoes homorganic nasal assimilation. If a noun root begins with a voiced consonant, the nasal class prefix adjusts to its place of articulation so that it is labial, or alveolar or velar depending on whether the first consonant of the noun root is labial, alveolar or velar (see section 5.3.4).

To write this rule formally we need to use Greek letter variables like α (alpha), β (beta) and γ (gamma) which range over both plus and minus values of a given feature. Thus,

$$\begin{matrix} N & C \\ [\alpha ant] & [\alpha ant] \end{matrix}$$

means that the nasal and the consonant after

it are either both [+ant] or both [−ant];

$$\begin{matrix} N & C \\ [\beta\ back] & [\beta\ back] \end{matrix}$$

means that the nasal and the consonant after it are either both [+back] or both [−back] etc. Building on that, we can account for [7.16] using this formal homorganic nasal assimilation rule:

[7.17]
$$\begin{matrix} N \\ [+nas] \end{matrix} \longrightarrow \begin{bmatrix} \alpha\ ant \\ \beta\ cor \\ \gamma\ back \end{bmatrix} / \_\_ \begin{bmatrix} \alpha\ ant \\ \beta\ cor \\ \gamma\ back \end{bmatrix}$$

Where, however, the noun root begins with a voiceless stop, the assimilation rule in [7.17] is blocked. In that case, the stop following the nasal is aspirated and the nasal itself is dropped, as you can see:

[7.18] / N+pange/   [pʰaŋge]   'gadfly'
       / N+taa/   [tʰaa]   'lamp'
       / N+kubwa/   [kʰubwa]   'big (adj.)'

The rules at work here are shown in [7.19] and [7.20].

[7.19] Voiceless stop aspiration ([+spread] means 'aspirated')

$$\begin{bmatrix} -cont. \\ -voice \end{bmatrix} \longrightarrow [+spread] / N+ \_\_$$

(Voiceless stops are aspirated after the class 9 nasal prefix.)

[7. 20] Nasal deletion

$$N \longrightarrow \emptyset / \_\_ + \begin{bmatrix} -cont. \\ -voice \\ +spread \end{bmatrix}$$

(The nasal prefix is deleted before aspirated voiceless stops.)

The nasal deletion rule, it turns out, applies not only where a nasal is followed by a voiceless stop, but also where any other obstruent (that is, a fricative or affricate or stop) follows a nasal:

[7.21]   /N+fimbo/ [fimbo] 'stick' (not *[mfimbo])
/N+siku/   [siku]   'day'   (not *[nsiku])
/N+tʃumvi/[tʃʰumvi] 'salt' (not *[ntʃumvi])

If we turn our attention to rule interaction, we observe
that the nasal deletion rule BLEEDS the homorganic nasal
assimilation rule. Having been deleted by [7.20], the nasal
is no longer available to the assimilation rule in [7.17].

Now work out how nasal deletion [7.20] interacts with
aspiration [7.19].

Since it is the presence of a class 9 nasal prefix which
triggers off aspiration, the aspiration rule in [7.19] must
precede nasal deletion [7.20], if we assume that these rules
apply in a linear order. Having conditioned the aspiration,
the nasal can be subsequently deleted. If the order were
reversed, and [7.20] applied first, deleting the nasal, the
input to [7.19] would be destroyed and the correct surface
form would not be derived. The upshot is that given two
obligatory rules, one of which can POTENTIALLY
BLEED the other, they must be ordered in a manner that
ensures that bleeding is avoided.

Now return to the French consonant deletion and
vowel nasalisation examples above and see how these rules
affect each other. You will recall that in order to get the
right output, it is important that vowel nasalisation precedes
consonant deletion; if the order is reversed, vowel nasalisation is blocked because the deletion of the consonant robs
nasalisation of its input.

When two rules interact in such a way that one of them
would be blocked if their order were reversed, those rules
are said to be in a COUNTER-BLEEDING relationship.
The French rules [7.5] and [7.7] are in a counter-bleeding
relationship: unless vowel nasalisation precedes consonant
deletion the derivation aborts because nasal deletion would
destroy the input to vowel nasalisation. There are a number
of other rule relationships which we need not go into in an
introductory book of this kind.

7.3 Abandoning extrinsic ordering

The linear ordering hypothesis is presented above without considering any possible alternatives. It is assumed that phonological rules must be ordered so as to ensure that their interaction is correctly handled. For instance, where one rule would destroy the input to another (i.e. where rules are in a BLEEDING RELATIONSHIP) or where the prior application of one rule opens up the possibility of applying another (i.e. where rules are in a FEEDING RELATION-SHIP) it is claimed that the linguist needs to order the rules in the appropriate linear sequence. In fact, this linear ordering position is controversial.

Before we see why the above ordering hypothesis is controversial we need to clarify two important concepts. We shall do that by distinguishing between two kinds of ordering relationships: INTRINSIC and EXTRINSIC linear ordering. Rules are said to be **extrinsically ordered** if their interaction is governed by tailor-made ordering statements designed for that specific set of rules in a particular language. But rules are **intrinsically ordered** if the order in which they apply follows automatically from the way in which they are formulated. For instance, as we saw above, if two obligatory rules are in a feeding relationship, for both of them to apply the feeding rule must necessarily apply before the rule that is fed. In such a case an *ad hoc* decision needs to be made as to which rule applies first: when rules are intrinsically ordered, the order in which they apply follows automatically from universal principles. We shall consider some of these principles presently.

The approach presented in the last section allows both extrinsic and intrinsic linear ordering. Some linguists (like Koutsoudas *et al.* 1974, Ringen 1972, Hooper 1976, Pullum 1978) have argued strongly against extrinsic linear ordering, proposing instead that intrinsic ordering is the only kind of rule interaction that should be allowed. Essentially, the case against extrinsic linear ordering is that it gives the linguist more latitude than is warranted. However, if extrinsic ordering is disallowed, the range of legitimate rule inter-actions is reduced. This has the merit of making it difficult to set up underlying representations which differ greatly from phonetic representations. This seems to be desirable. The greater the distance between surface and underlying representations, the greater the likelihood of having a very involved set of rules interacting in a complex or idiosyncratic way with each other in the mapping of underlying onto surface representations. A ban on linear rule ordering effectively means that only those underlying representations which require rules interacting in a straightforward way can be successfully mapped on phonetic representations. Derivations requiring complex rule interaction would abort.

Let us now see how the phonological rule system might operate without extrinsic linear ordering. One proposal that has been made involves SIMULTANEOUS RULE APPLICATION. It is assumed that the question whether or not a given rule applies can be answered by inspecting the underlying representation: rule application is solely dependent on whether the underlying representation satisfies the structural description of a given rule.

We shall return to the Swahili example in [7.18] which is reproduced here as [7.22] to illustrate this point:

[7.22]   UR   PR
    / N+pange/   [pʰaŋge]   'gadfly'
    / N+taa/   [tʰaa]   'lamp'
    / N+kubwa/   [kʰubwa]   'big (adj.)'

The underlying representations of these data satisfy the structural descriptions of both the nasal deletion rule in [7.20] and the obstruent aspiration rule in [7.19]. So, both these rules apply directly and simultaneously to the underlying representations:

[7.23] UR / N+taa/
       / N+ tʰaa/ (by [7.19]) and / tʰaa/ (by [7.20])
       PR [tʰaa]

Extrinsic linear ordering is unnecessary, in cases of this kind.

Another situation in which simultaneous rule application could also be used is where rules are MUTUALLY NON-AFFECTING. In such a situation any ordering would be arbitrary. You can verify this by looking back at the English examples and rules in [7.1] to [7.3]. The rules aspirating voiceless stops, labialising consonants before rounded vowels and fronting velars before front vowels do not affect each other's input. Any ordering of these rules would make no difference to the final output. They can directly apply at the same time to the underlying representation whenever their structural description is satisfied.

Our next example of rule interaction will also be taken from English. The relevant rules are [7.24] and [7.25]

[7.24] *Shortening:*

$$[+\text{segment}] \longrightarrow [-\text{long}] / \underline{\quad} \begin{matrix} C \\ [-\text{voice}] \end{matrix}$$

(Vowels and consonant segments are shortened when followed by voiceless segments.)

The existence of this rule means that the vowel in *sat* is somewhat shorter than that in *sad*; it also means that the [l] in *colt* is shorter than that in *cold*.

[7.25] *Obstruent devoicing*

$$[-\text{sonorant}] \longrightarrow [-\text{voice}] / \underline{\quad} \#$$

(Nonsonorants (obstruents) i.e. stops, affricates and fricatives are (partially) devoiced in word final position.)

The effect of [7.25] is to make the last segment of each of the following words less fully voiced than the first one: *bib, did* and *gag*.

Proponents of extrinsic linear ordering would suggest that the fact that the vowel segment preceding the devoiced /g/ segment in a word like *gag* does not become shorter even when, after the application of [7.25], the word ends in a voiceless or partially voiceless velar, is evidence that [7.24] applies before [7.25] so that by the time [7.25] applies, the opportunity of shortening has already been missed. In other words, rule [7.25] on the face of it, could POTENTIALLY FEED [7.24] if the ordering of these two rules was reversed. But the reality is that it does not. Thus, ordering [7.24] before [7.25] ensures that a potentially feeding rule interaction is avoided.

In fact, where rules are in a potentially feeding (also called **counter-feeding** relationship), an approach which forbids extrinsic linear ordering would also yield the right result if it stipulated that rules apply directly to underlying representations which satisfy their structural descriptions. Thus, it is possible to show that [7.24] applies since its structural description is met by the underlying representation while [7.25] fails to feed [7.24] because the voiceless obstruents produced by this rule miss the application of [7.24] since both rules are assumed to apply directly to underlying representations. No further ordering statements are needed.

Another proposal that has been made by critics of extrinsic ordering is RANDOM SEQUENTIAL RULE APPLICATION. This principle states that rules apply one at a time, rather than simultaneously. But they are not strictly regimented in a fixed order. They apply, whenever a string that satisfies their structural description arises in a derivation. In cases of potential ambiguity, rules are arranged in that order which ensures that all obligatory rules are applied.

This principle is needed because the claim made above that rules only apply directly to underlying representations is not always correct. Earlier in this chapter we established that there are rules which cannot apply directly to underlying representations and which only become applicable after their input has been created by another rule during the course of a derivation. That is the case when rules are in a feeding relationship (see [7.11] – [7.15] above). The feeding rule must precede the fed rule. But this ordering need not be done on an *ad hoc* basis. The random sequential application principle, by ensuring that rules apply at any stage in a derivation when their structural description is met provides a simple mechanism for arriving at the correct order: the structural description of the feeding rule must, by definition, be met before the conditions for the application of the fed rule are created. So, feeding rules must always precede the rules that are fed.

A further universal principle which renders extrinsic ordering unnecessary is the ELSEWHERE CONDITION (Kiparsky 1973). The elsewhere condition states that where the input to two rules partially overlaps, the more specific rule applies before the more general rule. Discussion of this principle will wait until section 12.2.3.

7.4 Conclusion: why ordering matters

It would be wrong to think that in this chapter too much fuss has been made over an abstruse theoretical point. This is not the case. Rule interaction is not a fringe, esoteric issue. The importance of rule ordering lies in the fact that it offers us a way of constraining the power of the model. A phonological theory, which incorporates powerful rules which can insert, move and delete elements enables the linguist to perform a very wide range of operations, some of which may not be possible in human language.

It is therefore necessary to find ways of reducing the power of the model so that only those operations that are possible in human language are catered for. Restrictions on rule interaction have the effect of reducing the range of possible outputs of phonological rules. Furthermore, restrictions on rule interaction also indirectly curtail the distance between underlying and surface representations. Very complex extrinsic rule ordering is required where a large number of rules are needed to translate abstract underlying representations into phonetic representations.

The theme of constraining the remoteness of underlying representations from phonetic representations is developed further, from a different angle, in the next chapter.

Exercises

1. In fast, casual speech the words in the left-hand column may be realised as indicated in the right-hand column.
   Column A   *Column B*
   handball   [hæmbɔl]
   handbag   [hæmbæg]
   hand-made   [hæmmeɪd]
   (a) Formulate the rules needed to state the processes involved.
   (b) Should these rules be extrinsically ordered?

2. Study the data below and answer the questions which follow. Assume that the morphemes of the two dialects have identical underlying representations. The differences in the phonetic shape of morphemes are due to

differences in their phonological rules. Lumasaaba
(Uganda) (based on Brown (1972))

Dialect A		Dialect B
im-piso	needle	i:-piso
im-pale	trousers	i:-pale
im-fula	rain	i:fula
in-temu	snake	i:-temu
iɲ-cese	sheep	i:-cese
iŋ-kafu	cow	i:-kafu
in-sami	fly	i:-sami
im-beba	rat	im-beba
in-dali	beer	in-dali
in-zu	house	in-zu
iŋ-gwe	leopard	iŋ-gwe
im-bululuka	I fly	im-bululuka
in-dima	I run	in-dima
iɲ-cina	I dance	i:-cina
iɲ-ɟo:la	I grow	iɲ-ɟo:la
iŋ-kuba	I hit	i:-kuba

(a) Determine the underlying representation of each prefix.
(b) State formally the rules that account for the alternation
    in the shape of the prefixes in the two dialects.
(c) Describe the differences in rule interaction which you
    have observed in the two dialects.

Notes

1. Note, incidentally, that vowel nasalisation tends to
   induce lowering. Oral [i] corresponds to nasalised [ɛ],
   oral [o] to nasalised [ɔ], and so on. We do not have the
   space to explore this phenomenon in depth here.

2. This nasal prefix is both homorganic and syllabic
   before monosyllabic roots like /N+bu/[m̩bu] 'mosquito'.

CHAPTER 8

The abstractness of underlying representations

8.1 Abstractness

So far it has been assumed without much discussion that normally the alternation in the realisation of a morpheme is most appropriately stated by positing a single underlying form from which its various alternants are derived by rule. Thus, for instance, the forms *sign* [saɪn], *signal* [sɪgnəl], *signature* [sɪgnətʃə] and *signify* [sɪgnɪfaɪ] share the underlying representation /sɪgn/. It can be argued that in *sign* the word final /-gn/ consonant sequence makes underlying /ɪ/ change to [aɪ], and then /g/ disappears. But in the rest of the examples, where various affixes are present, the underlying representation /sɪgn/ remains unchanged because in those cases the string /-gn/ is not word final.

Note that the underlying representation /sɪgn/ is ABSTRACT, i.e. it is distant from the phonetic form [saɪn] which is actually uttered by speakers. Support for the abstract underlying form is drawn not only from the phonological and semantic relatedness of *sign, signal, signature* and *signify*, but also from the fact that several other sets of forms such as *malign* [məlaɪn] ~ *malignant* [məlɪgnənt] and *benign* [bɪnaɪn] ~ *benignant* [bɪnɪgnənt] show the same alternation. This suggests that the alternation is rule governed. It is not a unique characteristic of the form /sɪgn/. To capture the relevant generalisation rules changing word final underlying /-ɪgn/ into surface [-aɪn] are required.

The position which I have just outlined appears reasonable, but it is not entirely uncontroversial. The controversy centres round the extent to which phonetic realisations can differ from underlying representations. Is there a principled way of determining when underlying representations are too far removed from surface manifestations of a morpheme to be credible? Is there a principled way of determining when semantic relatedness is too dilute and phonological similarity too tenuous to justify deriving different forms from the same base form? Is there a principled way of determining when relatedness between different forms is only of diachronic interest and has ceased to be synchronically valid?

These questions are too important to be left to the linguist's common sense. Phonological theory would become empty if any sound was allowed to change arbitrarily into any other sound at the whim of the analyst. Principles are needed which would outlaw a maverick phonological gambit in which, for instance *hundred* and *centenary*, or *foot* and *pedal*, were derived from the same abstract synchronic base. Notwithstanding their semantic similarity and faint phonological resemblance, these forms are not closely enough related synchronically to be derived from the same base form. This begs the question of the degree of relatedness that is sufficient to allow the derivation of phonetic representations from the same base form. Can effective mechanical procedures that determine which forms are derivable from the same synchronic source ever be devised? Unfortunately, the answer is 'no'.

In the last chapter we saw one perspective from which the problem can be dealt with: restrictions can be placed on rule systems, making it impossible to derive phonetic representations from distant underlying representations where extrinsic linear rule ordering is required. But even if it were desirable, banning linear ordering in itself would not be enough. A two-pronged attack is what is needed: one prong being the incorporation in the model of as restrictive a theory of rule interaction as the facts of language allow and the other prong being the development of restrictive principles for the setting up of synchronic underlying representations.

8.2 Concrete phonology?

A knee-jerk reaction might be to simply resort to draconian measures like banning all abstract underlying representations (i.e. underlying representations that are remote from surface (phonetic) representations). The dichotomy between underlying and surface representations would be abandoned and we would have 'CONCRETE PHONOLOGY' with only one level of representation, namely the phonetic. But, for a number of reasons, this would not be a satisfactory solution.

Abandoning underlying representations would be unsatisfactory because, as we saw in section 3.4 there is redundancy in language. Many phonetic properties of a segment are predictable because certain feature combinations either presuppose or preclude each other (e.g. in English any nasal consonant is also noncontinuant, nonstrident and voiced). Other properties of a sound may be predictable, given the context in which it occurs (e.g. in English if we know that a syllable begins with a consonant cluster whose second segment is a stop, we can always correctly predict that the first consonant of that cluster is [s]). Having two levels of representation allows us the possibility of extracting all the predictable phonetic features of a morpheme so that we only include the idiosyncratic properties as part of the underlying representation. All predictable features are filled in later by redundancy rules. There would be no adequate way of dealing with this redundancy in a model of phonology which did not have more than one level of representation.

The second objection is that 'concrete phonology', in a literal sense is a chimera (and nobody has ever proposed it as a viable alternative) since even so-called 'concrete' phonetic representations do not exist. The phonetician, like all other scientists never deals with 'brute facts'. Raw data is always seen through the lenses provided by the analyst's theory. The measurements which laboratory instruments are calibrated to make depend on what sort of data the analyst considers relevant to testing certain theoretical claims. As for the phonetic transcriptions on which phonological descriptions are based, they can never be totally faithful to the brute facts. Phonetic transcription is a subtle art which involves a degree of interpretation. In view of this, a one-level phonological representation identical to a phonetic representation could never be concrete, except in a metaphorical sense.

The third objection to an approach which only recognises phonetic representations is that it fails to capture significant generalisations concerning relationships between allomorphs of a morpheme. You will recall that in Chapter 5 we saw that usually the relationship between allomorphs of a morpheme is not arbitrary. The realisation of allomorphs tends to be PHONOLOGICALLY CONDITIONED. For example, listing all the allomorphs of the past tense would fail to show the difference between the realisation of the regular endings [-t -d -ɪd] as in *walked, loved* and *wanted*, which are governed by voice assimilation, and the totally arbitrary past tense formation of *went* from *go*. If, on the other hand, underlying representations are set up we can show the non-arbitrary relationship between the various allomorphs by deriving them from a single base form as we did in [5.2].

However, the search for underlying representations cannot be allowed to proceed without any constraints. It is always essential to ensure that putative underlying representations are synchronically valid. This is by no means an easy matter because for better or for worse, languages have to live with undigested bits of their history. Often there is no clear division between synchrony and diachrony. Phonological processes which might have been regular, natural and motivated at an earlier period in the life of a language may only survive as sporadic alternations in a few isolated forms. That is true, for example, of the vowel alternation in English nouns like:

[8.1] | Singular | | Plural | |
|---|---|---|---|
| goose | [gus] | geese | [gis] |
| foot | [fʊt] | feet | [fit] |
| tooth | [tuθ] | teeth | [tiθ] |

During the Middle Ages, many Germanic languages underwent changes known as UMLAUT (or *i-mutation*). This is partial assimilation involving the fronting of a stressed back vowel in anticipation of a high front vowel or glide [i or j] in the next syllable.

In Old English (which was spoken circa 449–1100 and from which modern English is descended) umlaut probably began during the sixth century. Originally the nominative singular and the nominative/accusative plural of the noun *foot* were *fōt* [fo:t] and *fōtiz* [fo:tiz] respectively, but from about the sixth century, the plural form changed to *fētiz* [fe:tiz]. Later the ending was dropped and [fe:tiz] became *fēt* [fe:t]. (Later still, around the fifteenth century long /e:/ changed to long /i:/; but that change was never reflected in the orthography). After the loss of /i/ in the plural suffix /-iz/, the alternations survived as ways of marking plural in *feet* and a few other words. But there was no longer a phonetic reason for the umlaut alternation and it became fossilised.

If a new product was launched on the market, and it was called a *voot* [vʊt], there is no likelihood whatsoever that two of those objects would be called *veet* [vit]: this internal vowel change in the root is no longer a productive process, i.e. it cannot be extended to new forms. Yet, at the same time, as [8.1] shows, the alternation between [ʊ] and [i] still exists in English and it cannot be disregarded. Arguably, to show the relationship between the different shapes of the words in [8.1], we could set up a single underlying representation for each pair from which the surface representations are derived. However, in view of the lack of productivity of the alternation between [i] and [ʊ], there is a strong case for not setting up a single synchronic underlying form for each one of these pairs of words and instead showing the relationship between them directly using a rule which is part of the lexicon.

This is one way in which the search for underlying representations could be restricted: a single underlying representation is only warranted where a given phonological alternation can be shown to be alive and well in a language. This can be done by showing that it is productively extended to new forms entering the language. The fronting of [ʊ] (or [u]) to [i] as in [8.1] is unproductive while the addition of -*s* to *voot* to form *voots* [vʊts] is productive. Addition of -*s* rather than fronting of a back vowel (*umlaut*) is the rule which must be included in a grammar which aims to model speakers' knowledge of their language.

Unfortunately, our troubles do not necessarily end if we take that stance. The difficulty of determining what the native speaker knows still remains. If the grammar is a model of linguistic knowledge, we must be wary of assuming rashly that on every occasion when an ingenious linguist can spot a regularity in the alternation in the phonetic shape of a morpheme, for which a base form can be posited and a rule written, the native speaker too will necessarily have such a rule. This was the subject of a heated debate in the early seventies. The debate centred on data like these from English showing alternative shapes of a root, depending on whether a suffix is present:

[8.2] *tense vowel* [eɪ]	*lax vowel* [æ]
v*ai*n	v*a*nity
s*a*ne	s*a*nity
op*a*que	op*a*city
prof*a*ne	prof*a*nity
in*a*ne	in*a*nity
gr*a*ve	gr*a*vity

Write down in words the rule which determines the quality of the italicised vowel.

Note that no vowel change occurs in words like *fame* [feɪm] ~ *famous* [feɪməs], *base* [beɪs] ~ *basic* [beɪsɪk], *fate*, [feɪt] ~ *fatal* [feɪtl], *safe* [seɪf] ~ *safety* [seɪftɪ], etc.

From your solution can you see why this rule is called TRISYLLABIC LAXING? It is a rule which changes a tense vowel into a lax vowel when a short word is lengthened by adding a suffix so that it ends up having at least three syllables. Trisyllabic laxing applies in [8.2] but fails to apply to *famous, basic*, etc. because these contain only two syllables after the addition of a suffix.

This rule is not only responsible for the [eɪ] ~ [æ] alternation, but also for the [i] ~ [e] alternation in words like *serene* ~ *serenity*; the [au] ~ [ʌ] alternation in words like *pronounce* ~ *pronunciation*, the [aɪ] ~ [ɪ] alternation in words like *divine* ~ *divinity*, etc.

Find two other words exemplifying each of these patterns.

These alternations are a synchronic relic of the momentous upheaval in the English vowel system that took place during the late Middle English period, around the fifteenth century, to which the name the English GREAT VOWEL SHIFT is given. Trisyllabic laxing is part of the undigested history of the language.

Not having some kind of rule to show the regularity of these MORPHOPHONEMIC ALTERNATIONS (i.e. alternative phonological realisations of a morpheme) which we have observed would result in a failure to capture obvious generalisations. It would mean failure to show that the pairs of words in [8.2] are related. But, on the other hand, it would be somewhat misleading to claim that the rule that relates, say, *profane* to *profanity* is every bit as synchronically relevant and phonologically well-motivated as the allophonic rule aspirating a voiceless stop occurring initially in a stressed syllable that relates the aspirated [kʰ] of *cake* [kʰeɪk] to the unaspirated first [k] of [tʰikeɪk] *tea-cake*. The issue is that not all regularities that can be identified by the linguist have the same status for speakers of a language.

In view of this, phonologists belonging to the Natural Generative Phonology school (e.g. Hooper 1976; Vennemann 1974a) have argued that the phonological component need only deal with transparent, phonetically motivated, regular, productive processes like the aspiration of voiceless stops occurring initially in stressed syllables in English. All other regularities should be handled by the morphological component. Where psychologically valid synchronic relationship is doubtful, though some semantic and phonological link exists, LEXICAL VIA RULES located in the lexicon should be used to indicate the link.[1]

Hooper (1976:9), examines the Spanish forms in [8.3] which Harris (1969), who favoured a more abstract approach, had claimed to be synchronically related:

[8.3]	A			B	
leche	[letʃe]	'milk'	lactar	[laktar]	'to lactate'
ocho	[otʃo]	'eight'	octavo	[oktaβo]	'eighth'
noche	[notʃe]	'night'	nocturno	[nokturno]	'nocturnal'

Harris used phonological rules, closely reflecting the historical development of Spanish from Latin, to derive the words in each pair from a single underlying representation in contemporary Spanish. His underlying representations were respectively /lakte/, /okto/ and /nokte/. His proposed rules are illustrated with a derivation of *noche*:

[8.4] UR /nokte/

noyte (a) $k \rightarrow y/ \underline{\hspace{1cm}} \left\{ \begin{matrix} t \\ s \end{matrix} \right\}$

noytʃe (b) $t \rightarrow tʃ/y\underline{\hspace{1cm}}$

notʃe (c) $y \rightarrow \emptyset/\underline{\hspace{1cm}}tʃ$

PR [notʃe]

Though historically valid, the underlying representation /nokte/ and the two intermediate forms [noyte] and [notʃe] do not occur in modern Spanish. Harris is rebuked by Hooper for being too abstract.

In Natural Generative Phonology where the premium is on avoiding abstract solutions, the relationship between the pairs of words in [8.3] is shown by Hooper using a via rule in the lexicon. This is a statement to the effect that in certain forms *x* corresponds to *y*:

[8.5] $kt \rightarrow tʃ$

A via rule is not productive. Those few items linked by a via rule have to be individually marked. Furthermore, a particular via rule is not assumed to be part of every native speaker's linguistic competence.

You can see why this should be so by considering relationships between some English words, e.g. *stink* and *stench*, *drink* and *drench*, *break* and *breach*. The words in each pair are semantically and phonologically related. But probably most speakers of English are unaware of this fact. Those who are aware of the connection may have a via rule linking each pair.

The treatment of sounds in language acquisition, language change and dialectal variation would provide windows through which speakers' phonological knowledge could be glimpsed. For instance, the fact that the productive rule of plural formation in modern English is the addition of /-z, -ɪz, -s/ can be seen in the way children sometimes overgeneralise /-z/ and form *mans* (instead of *men*) as the plural of man. They do not analogise in the other direction making the plural of e.g. *pan* and *van* *pen* and *ven* (instead of the correct *pans* and *vans*). A fundamental contention of these scholars is that linguists should posit as underlying representations only those forms that can be plausibly *learned* by induction on the basis of the phonetic evidence which a child is exposed to. The sceptic might retort that the effect of these proposals is not to solve the problem but rather to shunt it into a morphological or lexical siding. Proponents of Natural Generative Grammar are aware of this possible criticism. They provide a battery of principles to be used in deciding whether or not a transparent phonological relationship exists between forms which the linguist wishes to relate using synchronic phonological rules so that problem cases are not dispatched too hastily to the lexical via rules.

We could simply insist that the underlying representation must be IDENTICAL to one of the phonetic representations of a given morpheme, i.e. one of the allomorphs should be selected as the underlying representation. Let us return to the data in [8.2] to illustrate this. If we choose /veɪn/ as the underlying representation of *vanity* [vænɪtɪ], there is no problem since all the segments of the root morpheme do surface in a single shape of the word *vain* [veɪn].

Unfortunately the principle stated above fails in somewhat more complex situations like that described below in Russian where the underlying form would need to be cobbled together from more than one surface form. Consider the data in [8.6] and [8.7] (based on Kenstowicz and Kisseberth:1979).

[8.6] vowel neutralisation

ļés	'forest'	ļisá	'forests'
górat	'town'	garadá	'towns'

[8.7] Final obstruent devoicing

górat	'town'	garadá	'towns'
sapók	'boot'	sapagá	'boots'
rás	'time'	razí	'times'
ruká	'hand'	rukʲí	'of the hand'

There is a rule which has the effect of neutralising vowels in [8.6]: in stressed positions Russian has the vowels / i a e o u/ but in unstressed position the contrast between underlying /i/ and /e/ is suspended and both are realised as /i/. Likewise, when unstressed, /o/ and /a/ do not contrast: they are both realised as [a]. Only /u/ appears in both stressed and unstressed syllables. (As a result of vowel neutralisation only the maximally perceptually distinct peripheral vowels /i a u/ occur in unstressed position.) The vowel neutralisation rule is presented in [8.8]:

[8.8] Vowel neutralisation

(a) $\begin{bmatrix} -\text{high} \\ -\text{back} \end{bmatrix} \rightarrow$ [+high] / [−stress] (i.e. /e/

        e   i   occurs

                                        unstressed)

(b) $\begin{bmatrix} -\text{high} \\ -\text{back} \\ +\text{round} \end{bmatrix} \rightarrow \begin{bmatrix} +\text{low} \\ -\text{round} \end{bmatrix}$ / [−stress] (i.e. /o/

        o   a   occurs

                                        unstressed)

To account for the devoicing of obstruents (d → t, z → s, etc.) seen in [8.7] the following rule is required:

[8.9] Final obstruent devoicing
    [−son] → [−voice] / __#

Explain why, given the existence of rules [8.8] and [8.9], establishing the underlying form of words like górat/garadá 'towns' is problematic if you assume that one of the allomorphs of a morpheme is the base form from which other alternants are derived.

The problem is that no single phonetic representation contains all the segments which must form part of the base form. Given [8.8] the unsuffixed forms in the left-hand column provide the correct representation of the underlying vowel which reveals itself under stress; but given [8.9], the forms in the right-hand column contain the underlying voiced obstruent which is devoiced in word final position.

This problem is solved by a weaker proposal which merely requires that SEGMENTS POSITED AS UNDERLYING APPEAR IN AT LEAST ONE ALLOMORPH of a morpheme. But not all the properties of the underlying representation need occur together in one of the allomorphs. The phonologist is allowed to posit as underlying a composite form containing segments which surface in distinct allomorphs of the morpheme. The underlying representations of the Russian forms are *ljés, górad, sapóg* and *rúk*, which are not necessarily attested as such in the superficial phonetic representations (Kenstowicz and Kisseberth 1979).

These Russian data also illustrate another important principle which has to be observed in setting up underlying representations. It is the principle of PREDICTABILITY. If two analyses appear to describe the data adequately, that analysis which has greater generality, i.e. greater predictive power, is preferred.

In order to account for the data in [8.6] and [8.7], we could have regarded the roots as either ending in voiced or voiceless obstruents in the underlying representation. We could have posited /lés/, /górat/, /sapók/, /ráz/ and /rúk/ as the underlying representations. A rule would have been needed to voice obstruents when they occur between vowels.

Write up that hypothetical obstruent voicing rule formally.

The obstruent voicing rule could be stated as:

$$[8.9a] \begin{bmatrix} \text{-son} \\ \text{-voice} \end{bmatrix} \longrightarrow [\text{+voice}] \quad / \text{ V} \underline{\hspace{1cm}} \text{V}$$

Rule [8.9a] would correctly predict [garadá], [sapagá] and [razi] but it would wrongly predict the voicing of the obstruent in *[lʲizá] and *[rugʲi]. By *ad hoc* measures, like using a diacritic to distinguish those obtruents which undergo voicing rule [8.9a] from those which defy it, embarrassing exceptions might be swept under the carpet. But there is nothing to commend such a solution.

There is a better alternative. If we posit underlying voiced obstruents as the last root consonants in /górad/, /sapóg/, and /ráz/, we can apply the devoicing rule [8.9] to all forms which satisfy its structural description. Base forms like /lʲés/ and /rúk/ which end in voiceless consonants are unaffected by the rule. There would be no need to resort to *ad hoc* measures to explain away exceptions.

8.3 Absolute neutralisation

In the SPE version of generative phonology a high degree of abstractness was tolerated if it enabled the linguist to capture generalisations – so long as it was not too 'costly'. Very abstract solutions and complex derivations though not encouraged, were not prohibited. It was considered legitimate to posit underlying abstract 'ghost segments' which never occur in the phonetic realisation of any morpheme of a language but which nonetheless can be inferred on the basis of regular phonological alternation.

I shall use some facts about French which have received considerable attention in the literature to explore the problem of abstractness and particularly the issue of ghost segments:

[8.10] (a) le pic   [lə pik] 'the pickaxe'
    l'abbé   [labe] 'the abbot'
  (b) le hasard [lə aza:r] 'the accident'
    la hirondelle [la irɔ̃dɛl] 'the swallow'

As [8.10a] shows, French has a rule of vowel deletion

[8.11] V → Ø / _____ + V

which, in this case, deletes the vowel of the definite article when the article is followed by a noun beginning with a vowel. This rule applies to yield [labe] from /lə abe/, but does not apply to /lə pik/ where the noun begins with a consonant.

In [8.10b], the nouns are spelled with consonant *h* as their first letter, but that *h* is not pronounced. Phonetically, the first sound of both [lə aza:r] and [la irɔ̃dɛl] is a vowel. Therefore one would expect the vowel deletion rule to apply to the article. In fact, as you can see, vowel deletion fails to apply in these and many other words beginning with the *h* in the orthography although that *h* is 'mute' e.g. *le hale* [lə al] 'tow-line', *la harengère* [la arɑ̃ʒɛ:r] 'fish-wife' *le hall* [lə ɔl] '(hotel) lounge', *le harem* [lə arɛm] 'harem', *le hideur* [lə idœ:r] 'hideousness', *le hongre* [lə ɔ̃:gr] 'gelding', *la houe* [la u] 'hoe' and even *le hold-up* [lə ɔldœp] 'hold-up' and *le home* [lə o:m] 'home (as in "children's home")'.

It has been proposed in the literature that although such

stems phonetically begin with a vowel, they should be deemed to begin with an abstract /h/ segment in the underlying phonological representation which is peculiar in that it always fails to surface phonetically (Schane 1968).

But others have suggested that it is unnecessary to insist that the sound that blocks the vowel deletion rule is indeed /h/. It is sufficient to assume that there is a very UNDERSPECIFIED consonant which is only represented by the residual feature [+consonant]. That is enough to block the vowel deletion rule since that rule is only applicable where the noun begins with a vowel. Furthermore, only being specified for the feature [+consonant] means that the abstract segment cannot surface phonetically (i.e. be uttered). Much fuller phonetic specification is required before pronunciation is possible (Clements and Keyser 1983). This line of argument is persuasive. We shall return to it in [9.6] below.

While with regard to French positing an abstract segment is plausible, there are situations where the arguments for abstract non-surfacing segments are less persuasive. That is the case with respect to Luganda vowels.

In this language the five vowels /i e a o u/ are the only ones which appear on the surface; vowel length can be distinctive:

[8.12] *Short vowel*   *Long vowel*
    [sima] 'dig a hole!'   [si:ma] 'be grateful!'
    [tema] 'cut!'   [te:ßa] 'guess!'
    [mala] 'finish!'   [ma:la] 'smear!'
    [wola] 'lend'   [wo:la] 'scoop!'
    [tuma] 'send'   [tu:ma] 'heap!'

Although phonetically there are two high vowels, namely [i] and [u] (which can be long or short), they condition different phonological processes. Sometimes a stop followed by [i] or [u] undergoes SPIRANTISATION (i.e. becomes a fricative) and sometimes it does not. Since sounds normally display consistent phonological behaviour, we would expect the same sound to behave in the same way when it occurs in identical phonetic contexts. Consider the data in [8.13] where no spirantisation occurs before high vowels:

[8.13] *No spirantisation before* [i] *and* [u]

[pima]	'measure!'	[kupuluka]	'to escape'
[mitima]	'hearts'	[kutu]	'ear'
[kiki]²	'what?'	[mukutu]	'canal'
[kiguli]	'cage'	[mudumu]	'pipe'
[kuginga]	'to notch'	[mugugu]	'burden'

In contrast with the [i] and [u] vowels in [8.13], those in [8.14] and [8.15] trigger off the spirantisation of a preceding nonlabial consonant. (Note that labials are exempt from spirantisation.)

After examining the data below, suggest a rule to account for spirantisation.

[8.14] *Spirantisation before* [i]

[le:ta]	'bring!'	[mule:si]	'bringer'
[ßu:ka]	'jump!'	[mußu:si]	'jumper'
[lo:nda]	'choose'	[mulo:nzi]	'elector'
[jiga]	'learn!'	[mujizi]	'student'
[kola]	'work!'	[mukozi]	'worker'

[8.15] *Spirantisation before* [u]

[kukwa:ta]	[makwa:fu]
'to turn (of milk)'	'turned (of milk)'
[kugo:nda]	[ßugonvu]
'to be soft'	'softness'
[laßuka]	[ßulaßufu]
'be alert!'	'alertness'
[jiga]	[ßujivu]
'learn!'	'learning'

In [8.16] I have stated the spirantisation rule informally:²

[8.16] (a) $\begin{bmatrix} t \\ k \end{bmatrix} \rightarrow s \ / \underline{\hspace{2em}} i$

(b) $\begin{bmatrix} l \\ d \\ g \end{bmatrix} \rightarrow z \ / \underline{\hspace{2em}} i$

(c) $\begin{bmatrix} t \\ k \end{bmatrix} \rightarrow f/\underline{\quad} u$

(d) $\begin{bmatrix} l \\ d \\ g \end{bmatrix} \rightarrow v /\underline{\quad} u$

The account of spirantisation so far is somewhat inexplicit. The word 'certain' is too vague to characterise the vowels which condition spirantisation. To make it more explicit one possible move that could be adopted is to use a DIACRITIC FEATURE. An advocate of this less abstract solution could argue that since the vowels triggering spirantisation are phonetically indistinguishable from those which do not, the best solution is to use an arbitrary diacritic, which is totally devoid of phonetic content, to identify the relevant vowels. In the dictionary morphemes which cause spirantisation would be marked with a 'flag' saying '[+spirantisation] rule'.[3] That would be done to morphemes like the agentive nominalising suffix /-i/ (similar in meaning to /-er/ in English words like *maker*) or the stative noun and adjective suffix /-u/.

On the other hand, a proponent of a more abstract approach might interpret the evidence differently. For instance, Herbert (1974) suggests that the fact that some high vowels cause spirantisation while others do not can be attributed to an underlying PHONOLOGICAL difference between the vowels. The vowels which cause spirantisation could be represented as /i/ and /u/ respectively. They have different distinctive feature matrices from those of /i�/ and /ų/ which do not cause spirantisation.

The phonological feature that distinguishes the vowels which cause spirantisation from those which do not might be [+tense] (or [+extra high]). Essentially, this position amounts to a claim that although only five vowels surface phonetically, there are seven vowels in the underlying phonological representation. The surface, phonetic vowels are [i e a o u] (which can be long or short) but the underlying vowels are /i̝ i e a o u ų/. The vowels /i̝/ and /ų/ are ABSOLUTELY NEUTRALISED i.e. they only occur in underlying representations. The contrast between vowels /i̝/

and /ụ/ vs. /i/ and /u/ respectively is **suspended** or **neutra-lized in all contexts** in the phonetic representation. In other words, the extra-high sounds are ABSTRACT SEGMENTS which never occur phonetically but they are said to be none-theless phonologically real. Their existence is inferred, as we have seen, from the phonological alternations in the language.

Such an abstract analysis is problematic. First, sanc-tioning absolute neutralisation means countenancing claims about neutralisation which are not normally regarded as legitimate. The orthodox view is that when a phonological opposition is neutralised, the opposition between sounds which contrast elsewhere in the phonetic representation is suspended in a specific context (Kiparsky 1968).

For instance, as you will recall from Chapter 2, in English voiced and voiceless stops are distinct phonemes. There are words like *pull* and *bull* which show that they contrast word meaning. In fact, they can contrast in any position – except after /s/. There is no possibility of [p] and [b] contrasting after /s/ in putative words like [spul] and *[sbul]. The latter is not a possible English word. In the Luganda example the opposition between /ị/ and /i/ (or between /ụ/ and /u/) is suspended not just in one specific context, but everywhere in the phonetic representation. The essence of the criticism is that absolute neutralisation over-extends the concept of neutralisation.

A further objection to positing abstract segments which are absolutely neutralised concerns LEARNABILITY. As our phonological theory attempts to model speakers' knowledge of the sound systems of their languages, we should not assume underlying segments which infants acquiring a language would not be able to infer from the phonetic input to which they are exposed. So, although the solution which allows two extra-high vowels which never surface phonetically is historically sound, it will not be warmly embraced here. True, Proto-Bantu, Luganda's ancestor, had the seven vowels /ị i e a o u ụ/; but at some point in the evolution of Luganda the vowel mergers shown in [8.17] took place:

[8.17] Proto-Bantu   ị   i   e   a   o   u   ụ

       Luganda   i   u

The abstract solution, while recognising the mergers at the phonetic level, denies their existence at the underlying level in present-day Luganda. This implies that phonological contrasts can be maintained long after they have ceased being realised phonetically. But how could Luganda-speaking children ever acquire the two extra-high vowels /i̥/ and /u̥/ which they never hear?

We can restrict the degree of abstractness of underlying representations by insisting that only those segments that could be plausibly learned by infants on the basis of the phonetic input should be considered possible underlying segments. Thus, abstract segments which never occur phonetically would be excluded. That would mean that the linguist might on occasion have to concede that some of the regularities in the phonetic realisation of morphemes are not phonologically relevant in a synchronic grammar.

8.4 Conclusion

Underlying representations need to be posited in order to show relationships between morphemes. But, in setting them up, care must be taken to avoid positing base forms which are at worst arbitrary or at best historically valid but synchronically unmotivated. For the working phonologist, the difficulty is that abstractness is a scale rather than a dichotomy. It is not possible to establish the absolute cut off point beyond which the degree of abstractness becomes intolerable: while it might be relatively uncontroversial to proscribe ghost underlying extra-high vowel segments in Luganda, it would not be as easy to proscribe some form of ghost segment in cases like that of the French *h- aspiré*. But we should not complain. That is what makes phonology so fascinating.

Exercises

1. Luo (Kenya) (Okoth 1979)
    Study the following data and answer the questions that follow:

	Singular		'vegetable'	Plural
(a)	alɔt	·	'vegetable'	alɔde
	luθ		'stick'	luðɛ
	gɔt		'hill'	gɔdɛ
	kɔθ		'rain'	kɔðɛ
	guok		'dog'	guogi
(b)	lɛp		'tongue'	lɛpɛ
	lak		'tooth'	leke
	adit		'basket'	adite

(The data is simplified. Many of the complications have been left out.)

(a) List the allomorphs of the plural morpheme. Do not attempt to predict their distribution.

(b) Determine the underlying representation of each noun root. Focus on the consonants. You should always select a base form which allows you to make the most general and consistent predictions about the behaviour of sounds.

(c) Write up formally the rule needed to account for the alternations in the final root consonant.

(d) Use these data to illustrate what is meant by **neutralisation** in phonology.

2. Luyia (Kenya)
Study the following data and answer the questions below.

Noun class 9		Noun class 12 (diminutive)
[mbako]	'hoe'	[xaßako]
[mbwa]	'dog'	[xaßwa]
[nduju]	'rabbit'	[xatuju]
[ndika]	'bicyle'	[xatika]
[ndimu]	'lemon'	[xatimu]
[ndemu]	'snake'	[xaremu]
[nɟusi]	'jackel'	[xajusi]
[nɟu]	'house'	[xaju]
[ɲama]	'meat'	[xaɲama]
[ɲumba]	'house'	[xajumba]

(a) List the allomorphs of the class 9 and class 12 prefixes.

(b) What is the class 9 form of the following words: [xaßusi] 'small goat' and [xateße] 'small chair'.

(c) State verbally the rule governing the alternation in the shape of the class 9 prefix and give it a suitable name. Why is the rule preferable to the list in (a) above?

(d) Write up formally the rule you have stated.

(e) State verbally the rules which account for the alternation in the shape of the first consonant of the noun root. Give each rule a suitable name.

(f) Re-write your rules in (e) formally.

(g) Must any of the rules you have formulated be extrinsically ordered? Justify your answer.

3. Hyman (1970) reports that in Nupe (Nigeria) consonants are **palatalised** before front vowels (see (a) below) and **labialised** before round vowels (see (b) below). Where the vowel following a consonant is neither front or round, as in (c), it has no effect on the preceding consonant.

    (a) [eg^{j}i]   child   (b) [eg^{w}u] mud
       [eg^{j}e]   bear   [eg^{w}o] grass
    (c) [ega]   stranger
       [ta]   to tell

However, palatalisation and labialisation also occur as in (d) and (e) where there are no front or round vowels following the consonant. Suggest a possible explanation for this.

    (d) [eg^{j}a] blood   (e) [eg^{w}a] hand
       [t^{j}a]   to be mild   [t^{w}a]   to trim

Notes

1. The interaction between phonology, morphology and the lexicon is one of the main issues in linguistic theory today. In Chapter 12 another approach, which to me appears more promising, is presented.

2. The vowel [i] causes palatalisation of a preceeding velar so that /k+i/ → [k^j] and /g+i/ → [g^j] (but this will be ignored as it is not central to the problem which we are focusing on).

3. These spirantisation processes affect several other morphemes. For instance the perfective and the causative suffixes have the same effects as the agentive nominalising suffix shown here.

CHAPTER 9
The syllable

9.1 The syllable

The syllable is at the heart of phonological representations. It is the unit in terms of which phonological systems are organised. It is a purely phonological entity. It cannot be identified with a grammatical or semantic unit. There are syllables like [ʌn] as in *unusual* which are co-extensive with the morpheme; there are syllables like [kæt] *cat* which are co-extensive with the word; there are syllables like [kæts] *cats* which represent more than one morpheme (the noun root *cat* and the plural marker -*s*) and there are syllables like [mʌn] and [kɪ] in [mʌŋkɪ] *monkey* which represent only part of a morpheme.

9.2 The representation of syllable structure

The syllable has received a very considerable amount of attention from phonologists, especially in recent years, and a number of alternative models of the syllable have been offered. A serious attempt to compare them is beyond the scope of an introductory textbook of this kind. All that can be presented here is a very brief outline of some of the main trends before focusing on the one that we shall be using.

Many phonologists envisage a BRANCHING, HIER-ARCHICAL syllable structure. For a traditional structuralist statement of this position see Pike (1967) and Pulgram (1970). More recently, writers like like Kiparsky (1979), Halle and Vergnaud (1980), Steriade (1982) and Harris (1983) have presented a revamped version of the hierarchical branching theory in the framework of a MULTI-TIERED

PHONOLOGICAL THEORY. (This is an approach where phonological representations are viewed as consisting of a number of independent levels that are linked to each other. See Chapter 10). On this view, syllable structure can be represented as in [9.1]:

[9.1] (a)

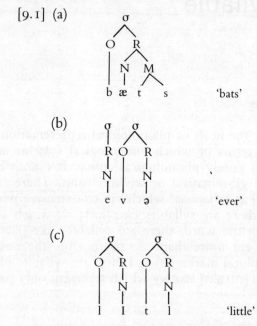

Note: σ = syllable, O = onset, R = rhyme,
N = nucleus and M = margin

Bats consists of one syllable. That syllable has two constituents, namely the ONSET which comes at the beginning and the RHYME which follows it. In the first syllable of *e-ver*, the rhyme is simple. It does not BRANCH. It contains just one constituent: the vowel. The rhyme of *bats*, on the other hand branches. It contains a vowel which is followed by a consonant. The examples above show that the rhyme is the HEAD CONSTITUENT (i.e. the only compulsory constituent) of the syllable. The onset is the part that branches off on the left of the rhyme, coming from the same node. Thus, in English, it is possible for a well-formed syllable to contain no onset, as in the case of the first syllable of *e-ver*. But it is not possible for a well-formed syllable to exist without a rhyme.

The binary partition of syllables which we are suggesting is supported by versification practices in English:

> [9.2] Two syllables with the same onset but different rhymes alliterate (e.g. p̲an, p̲et, etc.) while two syllables with the same rhyme, but different onsets, are said to be rhymes (e.g. p̲an, m̲an, etc.). In contrast, the onset and nucleus (e.g. p̲a̲n, m̲a̲n) do not form a significant grouping for verse.

We noted above that the rhyme is the only essential element of the syllable in English. What is true of English is also true of other languages. The rhyme is always obligatorily present in all syllables in all languages. What varies from language to language are the elements that can be part of the rhyme. Typically the nucleus slot in the rhyme is occupied by a vowel but occasionally a consonant may fill that position, as in [9.1c] above where the final [1] of *little* is syllabic.

Find two more examples of syllabic consonants in English or in some other language. What kind of elements can precede or follow the syllabic consonants? Refer back to section 3.3.1 on page 43.

Another model – that of Hyman (1985), has a different slant. Hyman suggests that the core of phonological representations consists of rhythmic WEIGHT UNITS rather than onsets and rhymes or C and V slots proposed by other writers (see next section). Segments have weight units associated with them underlyingly. But only associations between weight units and vowels tend to survive to the surface. Normally consonants lose their weight units and get re-associated with the weight unit of an adjacent vowel by the syllabification rules. Only those segments whose association with a weight unit is preserved to the end of a derivation are syllabic.

9.3 The CV-tier

Most current work in theoretical phonology assumes a model that incorporates a CV-tier (Consonant-Vowel tier) in terms of which the canonical forms of morphemes are stated. Precursors of this approach are Hockett (1947) and Abercrombie (1967). Using a multi-tiered approach in studies of classical Arabic, McCarthy (1979, 1981, 1982) has shown that PROSODIC TEMPLATES (see section 10.5 below) are needed to represent sequences of CV elements which function as morphemes. Though McCarthy's work has great phonological interest, his concerns are primarily morphological.

9.3.1 A generative CV-phonology model of syllable structure

It is Clements and Keyser (1983) who have expounded a CV-model of phonology specifically designed to deal with the syllable. Theirs is the model that I shall use in the rest of the book. Clements and Keyser require the theory of the syllable to perform three tasks:[1]

[9.3] (a) state universal principles governing syllable structure;
(b) state syllable structure TYPOLOGY, i.e. define the range within which syllable structure may vary from language to language;
(c) state language-specific rules governing syllable structure

In order to fulfil function (a), the syllable is assumed to have a THREE-TIERED STRUCTURE consisting of a SYLLABLE NODE 'σ'; a CV-TIER whose C and V elements DOMINATE (i.e. have below them as constituents in the syllable tree) consonantal and vowel segments; and a SEGMENTAL TIER consisting of bundles of distinctive feature matrices which represent consonant and vowel segments (for convenience these features may be abbreviated using letters of the phonetic alphabet):

[9.4]

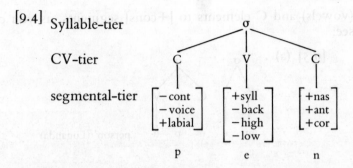

Roughly translated into the terms of the theory in [9.1], a V element of the CV-tier represents a syllable NUCLEUS i.e. peak of sonority (see below) while a C element represents a syllable ONSET or MARGIN, i.e. an element which is not the peak.

Nowadays a CV-phonology model of some sort is assumed by many phonologists. The version proposed by Clements and Keyser has the advantage of being conceptually simpler than the alternatives. Intervening between the syllable node and segmental tier there is a 'flat' CV-tier, lacking internal constituent structure. Contrast this with the more complex syllable models with onsets and rhymes which are illustrated in [9.1].

As in syntax, a tree like [9.4] shows IMMEDIATE CONSTITUENT STRUCTURE. An element is an immediate constituent of a higher element within which it is contained. This is shown by a constituent being IMMEDIATELY DOMINATED by that higher element. Thus, in *pen* the elements CVC of the CV-tier are all immediately dominated by σ while the elements [p,e,n] of the segmental tier are immediately dominated by C V and C respectively.

In a theory where several tiers are posited it is essential to specify how the tiers are LINKED. In CV-phonology, the linking is done using ASSOCIATION LINES which are subject to a WELL-FORMEDNESS CONDITION (this principle is discussed in more detail in the next chapter). To relate the CV-tier to the segmental tier, association lines are drawn following certain universal rules. Normally, these rules link V elements to [-cons] segments (vowels) and C elements to [+cons] segments, as you can see:

[9.5] (a)

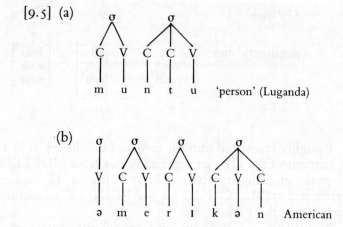

'person' (Luganda)

(b)

ə m e r ɪ k ə n   American

One of the functions of the syllable in all languages is defining syllabicity for segments. Any segment dominated by a C-element of the CV-tier is nonsyllabic while any segment dominated by a V-element is syllabic. An interesting consequence of this model is that it obviates the need for the feature [syllabic] (section 3.3.1): the V element of the CV-tier is the constituent of the syllable that contains the SONORITY PEAK.

The class of segments capable of functioning as syllable peaks is not arbitrary. It has been noted by generations of phoneticians and phonologists that the distribution of segments in syllables follows a clear pattern which can be stated in terms of the SONORITY HIERARCHY in [9.6] below which was suggested by Hooper (1972, 1976). This hierarchy was introduced earlier in section 6.2.1.

[9.6] Sonority hierarchy

least sonority

1	voiceless obstruents
2	voiced obstruents
3	nasals
4	liquids
5	glides
6	vowels

greatest sonority

The phonological sonority hierarchy has the phonetic correlates of openness and propensity for voicing. The more sonorous a sound is, the more audible it is likely to be. The sonority hierarchy is a mirror image of the strength hierarchy (section 6.2): sonority is in inverse proportion to strength (Hooper 1976).

The element dominated by V (which in other approaches is called the NUCLEUS) is relatively more sonorous than the consonants that surround it. (These are recognised as the ONSET and MARGIN of the syllable in other models). In a word like *bat*, the vowel /æ/ is dominated by V and it is more sonorant than the consonantal segments /b/ and /t/ which it is flanked by. The chart in [9.6] correctly predicts that vowels are the most likely and obstruents the least likely segments to be dominated by V, with other sounds occupying intermediate points on the hieararchy.

As the syllabic potential of a sound depends on its propensity to vocalise, it is only to be expected that the more open a vowel is, other things being equal, the more likely it is to be the peak of sonority in its syllable. The algorithm (i.e. formal procedure) that assigns syllabicity works by ranking consonants and vowels on the sonority hierarchy. The most sonorous segment is assigned to the V-element (the nucleus). Less sonorous sounds preceding the nucleus are assigned to the initial C-element (onset) and those following it are assigned to the other C-element (also variously known as the CODA, MARGIN, or TAIL). This principle predicts that the vowel /u/ is dominated by a V-element in [9.5a].

It also predicts that, in [9.7] the vowel /u/ is initially assigned to the V-element because it is higher up the sonority hierarchy than the consonant /m/ which precedes it. But when the fact that it is followed by /a/ is taken into account, association lines need to be re-drawn, making /a/ the only [-cons] dominated by V and linking /u/ instead with the preceding C-element. This makes it a nonsyllabic glide:

Clements and Keyser's model performs the second task of describing syllable typology by including a range of CORE SYLLABLES. Linguistic elements which are part of the CORE GRAMMAR are present in all languages. At the

[9.7] Glide formation

Glide formation

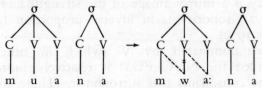

m u a n a → m w a: n a 'child' Luganda

Note: (a) a broken line is an instruction to 'LINK' i.e. insert new association line;

(b) an association line with two lines through it shows DELINKING i.e. termination of an association.

level of the syllable, CV type syllables meet that requirement. So far, no language has been reported to lack CV type syllables. Other syllable types may be seen as modifications of the prototypical CV syllable. Many languages, English included, have syllables containing only V, (see *ever*). Such languages may be assumed to have a rule at the entry to the phonological component which deletes the syllable initial C and thus allows canonical syllables with V only. Languages may also have CVC syllables which are obtained by a rule which adds a C after the V element to form canonical CVC syllables. Languages may have any one of the following canonical syllable types:

[9.8] Type 1: CV   e.g. *ta*
   Type 2: CV, V   e.g. *ta, a*
   Type 3: CV, CVC e.g. *ta, tat*
   Type 4: CV, V, CVC, VC e.g. *ta, a, tat, at*
     (based on Clements and Keyser 1983:29)

Make up two long words (in a real or imaginary language) which have each one of the four syllable types in [9.8].

Further embellishments of the syllable types in [9.8], peculiar to different languages, do occur. To fulfil the third requirement of syllable theory set out in [9.3c] a mechansim is needed to deal with language-specific syllable structure principles. There are languages which allow core syllables to have C★ or V★ (where C★ or V★ represents sequences of C or V elements) so that well-formed core syllables may contain combinations like CCCVCC or CCVVC or V elements. Thus, while [9.5] only shows single C and V elements following each other, languages like English allow syllables with CCCVCC sequences as in the word *strand*. The theory has to provide a mechanism for stating such language-specific facts. We shall explore this in section 9.4.1.

9.3.2 Syllabification

The theory has to provide a way of grouping arrays of CV elements into syllables in situations like this: VCVCCCVC. From the foregoing it is clear that each V-element will be associated with a syllable peak. What is yet to be shown is: to which syllable node are C-elements assigned in ambiguous cases, where they could go with either the preceding or the following vowel? To which syllable, for example, should the middle consonant of *panic* (CVCVC) be assigned?

The ONSET FIRST PRINCIPLE (Kahn 1976, Clements and Keyser 1983) has been proposed to deal with such situations. It is stated in [9.9]:

[9.9] (a) 'Syllable-initial consonants are maximised to the extent consistent with the syllable structure conditions of the language in question.

(b) Subsequently, syllable-final consonants are maximised to the extent consistent with the syllable structure of the language in question.'
(Clements and Keyser 1983:37)

Principle (a) applies before (b) in any derivation. In potentially ambiguous cases initial consonant clusters take precedence over syllable final ones. This means that unless there is an overriding language-specific reason for doing otherwise, given a string like VCV, the Onset First Principle requires that the string be divided up as V-CV rather than VC-V : a word like *ever* [evə] is divided up as [e-və] and not *[ev-ə]. To take another example, English allows CC sequences like [sp]. They can be initial as in *spoon* or final as in *grasp*. In a word like *aspire*, where the [sp] cluster could be regarded as syllable initial or syllable final, the word can be syllabified as either *a-spire* or *asp-ire*. The Onset First Principle predicts that the former is the correct syllabification.

The theory incorporates the following algorithm (formal, step-by-step procedure) for building syllables, with the procedures being applied starting from V outward to successive C-elements in the order specified in [9.10] below, which is based on Clements and Keyser (1983:38):

[9.10] (a) Underlyingly every V of the CV-tier is linked to σ; this merely reflects the fact that no syllable exists without a V element (as nucleus).

(b) Link each C element to the nearest V-element to its right provided the resulting sequence of segments does not violate any language-specific rules. This procedure creates syllable onsets.

(c) Repeat the procedure in (b), this time linking the C-elements to the nearest V to its left. This procedure creates syllable margins.

The effect of this algorithm is illustrated in [9.11]

[9.11] (a)

V-elements are pre-linked with σ by convention [9.10a]

(b)

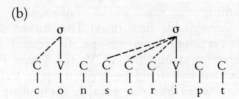

By convention [9.10b], link C-elements to the V on their right, one at a time, provided the resulting sequence is permissible in the language in question. Thus, in this case the procedure creates *scri* but stops short of **nscri* because in English nasals are not allowed to occur at the beginning of a syllable initial consonant cluster (see section 9.4.1 below).

(c)

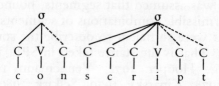

By convention [9.10c] link C-elements to the V preceding them so long as the resulting sequence is allowed in the langauge.

Write rules and produce derivations similar to [9.11] above to account for the syllabification of the following words: *agony* [ægənɪ], *corner* [kɔnə], *December* [dɪsembə], *extinct* [ekstɪŋkt]

You should come up with trees like the following:

(d)

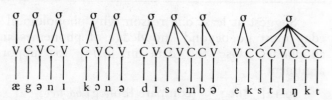

It must be emphasised that any language-specific restrictions on consonant clustering override universal principles. For instance, since *tl-* is not a permissible combination syllable-initially in English, a word like *atlas*, the Onset First Principle notwithstanding, cannot be syllabified as **a-tlas*; rather it must be divided up as *at-las*. Universal principles can be viewed as providing the default state of affairs which applies, unless specific instructions to the contrary are given by the grammar of a particular language.

9.4 Functions of the syllable

In early generative phonology, although the feature [syllabic] was used, the syllable was not given a place in the theory. It was assumed that segments, boundaries and rules stating permissible combinations of segments in morphemes and words were sufficient to describe the sound systems of languages. That is the stance taken in SPE. But subsequent work (e.g. Hooper 1972; Vennemann 1972; Bell and Hooper 1978; Kiparsky 1979; Selkirk 1980) showed that there are good reasons for rejecting that position. Today the place of the syllable is secure. Below I show the central role it plays in phonology.

9.4.1 The syllable as the basic phonotactic unit

One of the most basic functions of the syllable is to regulate the ways in which lower level units (consonants and vowels) of the phonological hierarchy can combine.

Knowledge of the phonological system which speakers of a language have consists in part of a knowledge of the phonemes of that language and their allophones. But this is not all.

Suggest at least one reason why phonological knowledge must go beyond knowledge of phonemes and their allophones. Use the data in [9.12] to support your argument.

[9.12]   *tleg   (compare [butleg] *bootleg*)
         *ndaɪz   (compare [mɜtʃəndaɪz] *merchandise*)
         *bmɪt   (compare [sʌbmɪt] *submit*)
         *psɪŋ   (compare [kəlæpsɪŋ] *collapsing*)

What [9.12] illustrates is the importance of constraints on the combination of sounds. All the starred pseudo-words contain English phonemes; all the consonant sequences at the beginning of the pseudo-words are permissible in English: [tl] occurs in *bootleg*, [nd] occurs in *merchandise*, [bm] occurs in *submit* and [ps] occurs in *collapsing*. But, the sequences in [9.12] are not potential English words. Just as at the level of grammar not all sequences of words produce a well-formed grammatical sentence, so it is in phonology: not all combinations of sounds produce possible words. Some non-occurring nonsense words, like those in [9.12] are beyond the pale, while other non-occurring words could easily be turned into real words if a meaning could be found for them. For instance, if you invented a machine which automatically does phonological analysis, you could call it by any one of these names:

[9.13] [fɒnəlaɪzə]
      [aʊsl]
      [glukə]

As a speaker of English, you know that the non-occurring words in [9.13] are potential words while those in [9.12] are not. The rules which reflect speakers' knowledge of what combinations of sounds are allowed in their language are variously referred to as PHONOTACTIC RULES or MORPHEME STRUCTURE CONDITIONS.

The syllable is the unit in terms of which phonotactic rules are best stated. Thus, for instance, in English the sequence [tl] is allowed so long as the *t* and the *l* belong to different syllables as in *boot-leg* [but-leg], *at-las* [æt-ləs], *part-ly* [pɑt-lɪ] or *litt-le* [lɪt-l̩] (syllabic *l* is the nucleus of the second syllable (see [9.1c]). But the sequence *tl* is not allowed in the same syllable. Hence the impossibility of *tleg as an English word since it has tl as a syllable onset. Likewise, [bm] can occur in English if there is a syllable boundary separating them as in *sub-mit* but [bm] would not be allowed where those two sounds belonged to the same syllable as in our imaginary word *bmit.

Another English example of a phonotactic constraint is the rule which only allows vowels to follow syllable-initial affricates: while *cheap*, *judge* and *adjust* are English words, *chleep, *jpudge and *adjpudge are neither real nor potential words in English.

Supply three examples of your own of:
(a) non-occurring **possible** words in English;
(b) non-occurring **impossible** words in English.
Explain the grounds for your decisions.

Constraints on syllable structure serve as a filter allowing only certain sound sequences to occur. These constraints are specific to a particular language. What is a well-formed syllable in Swahili may not be in English. In Swahili (and in many other African languages) for instance, NC sequences like [nd] as in [ndugu] 'brother' or [ŋg] as in [ŋguruwe] 'pig' are allowed in syllable- (and word-) initial position but they are outlawed in that position in English: *[ndu], *[mpig] and *[ŋget] are not potential words in English. (That is why the names of African leaders like *Nkrumah* and *Nkomo* tend to have a short [ɪ] or [ə] vowel inserted before them to make them pronounceable by English speakers.)

The nativisation of foreign loanwords and the phenomenon of 'foreign accent' provide interesting evidence of how deeply ingrained syllable structure rules are. For the same reason that native speakers of English insert a vowel before a word-initial (and syllable-initial) velar nasal in words like *Nkrumah*, speakers of languages like Walpiri (Australia) and Luganda, which only have syllables ending in V in the phonetic representation, will insert a vowel after a syllable-final consonant in borrowed words such as [wʌn] 'one'. In Walpiri *one* is rendered as [wani] and in Luganda as [wanu]. Likewise, English loanwords in Japanese are normally modified to fit in with the predominantly CV syllable structure of the language. So, 'baseball' and 'milk' become [besuboru] and [miruku] respectively.

9.4.2 The syllable as the domain of phonological rules

The relevance of syllable structure constraints is not restricted to loanwords and mother tongue interference. Syllable structure often plays an important role in conditioning the application of phonological rules internal to a language.

A frequently cited example of the relevance of the syllable in determining whether a phonological rule applies is some form of obstruent devoicing rule which is found in many languages including Russian, German and Turkish. In Turkish it is responsible for alternations like [rengi], (possessive), [renkten] (ablative) and [renk] (nominative) 'colour'; in German for the alternation between [tāk] 'day' and [tāgə] 'days'; in Russian for the alternation between [gorat] 'town' and [garada] 'towns'.

The rule can be written as follows:

$$[9.14] \quad [\text{-sonorant}] \rightarrow [\text{-voice}]/\_\_ \left\{ \begin{matrix} C \\ \# \end{matrix} \right\}$$

This rule correctly states that obstruents are devoiced word-finally or before another consonant. But it misses the point that the environments 'word-finally' and 'before another consonant' are not accidentally related contexts. The two environments share the property of being syllable final.

The makeshift nature of the solution provided by rule [9.14] becomes even clearer when it is appreciated that the environment 'word-finally or before another consonant' turns up frequently not only with respect to obstruent devoicing, but also with respect to other rules. Take the nasalisation rule of French (which is similar to a nasalisation rule found in numerous languages):

$$[9.15] \quad V \rightarrow [\text{+nasal}] / \_\_N \left\{ \begin{matrix} C \\ \# \end{matrix} \right\}$$

Vowels are nasalised when followed by a preconsonantal nasal as in /enfle/ [āfle] *enflé* 'swollen' or word-finally as in /bon/ [bɔ̃] *bon* 'good'.

Account for the nasalisation of the vowel in *grand* [grā] 'big' and *sentiment* [sātimā] 'feeling'.

The same nasalisation rule applies even where on the surface the nasal is not syllable-final in words like *sentiment* [sātimā] (*sentimental* [sātimātal] 'sentimental'); and *grand* [grā] (*grande* (feminine) [grād]). A derivation is worked out for *grand* to show this:

[9.16] UR: /grand/
Rule a
Vowel nasalisation before syllable-final NC:
grand → grānd (see [9.15])
Rule b
Consonant deletion: grānd → grā (see [7.4])
PR [grā]
(Note: rules a and b may apply simultaneously
as the underlying representation satisfies the
structural descriptions of both rules.)

If the relevance of the syllable is not recognised, the fact
that the same environment turns up in various rules in
different languages remains a puzzling mystery. If,
however, the syllable is recognised, it becomes obvious that
these processes are conditioned by the presence of a syllable
boundary.

Furthermore, probably in every language there are
phonological processes whose motivation is the preservation
or the creation of preferred syllables. The function of such
rules can only be understood if they are approached in terms
of the syllable. A classic example in the literature comes
from the Californian language Yawelmani. In this language
consonant clusters are allowed only if they do not exceed
two consonants. When a consonant-commencing suffix
such as the aorist[2] suffix – hin is added to verb roots whose
last two segments are consonants, a vowel is inserted
between the last two root consonants to prevent a triconsonantal sequence from occurring:

[9.17] root – aorist
/ʔilk – hin/ → [ʔilikhin] 'sang'
/paʔt – hin/ → [paʔithin] 'fought'
(t is retroflex)

If a vowel-commencing suffix like the dubitative suffix
-al is added, however, no vowel insertion takes place since
the requirement of a maximum of two consonants in a
cluster is not violated. (The dubitative mood is used to
express doubt.)

[9.18] root – dubitative
/ʔilk – al/ → [ʔilkal] 'might sing'
[paʔtal] → [paʔtal] 'might fight'

9.4.3 The syllable and the structure of complex segments

The syllable not only regulates the combination of segments, it also controls the combination of features which make up segments. In this, current thinking differs from that of early generative phonology which assumed that phonemes were bundles of features with these two characteristics:

(i) the scope of each feature was one segment and no feature could extend over adjacent segments;

(ii) within a single phoneme the features were unordered which meant that there was no subphonemic structure.

Both these assumptions fail in many cases. Frequently articulatory gestures are not started and completed within a single phonological segment (Firth 1948). Obvious examples are words like *guard-room* and *barbarism* in which the feature [+voice] is not restricted to particular segments but extends over the entire word. We need not labour the point that was made in Chapter 4 that since speech organs are not mechanical ratchets, it is only to be expected that articulatory gestures are going to overlap in the transition from one segment to the next.[3]

One of the main functions of the syllable is to provide an analysis of the internal structure of segments and to indicate the number of rhythmic units present in a syllable. This depends on the way C and V elements present on the CV-tier are linked with consonant and vowel segments on the segmental tier (Hyman 1985). Three patterns of internal segmental structure are possible:

(a)   A one-to-one association of V or C with a segment:

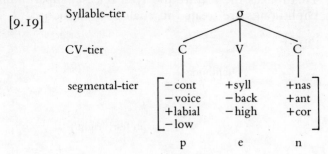

(b) Simultaneous association of one segment with two C or V slots. That is the case when consonants are GEMINATED (i.e. the same consonantal articulation is held for the duration of two consonantal beats) or when a vowel is lengthened (i.e. the same vowel quality is maintained over two V slots). I represent both possibilities with a Luganda example in [9.20]. The word *ttaala* [t:a:la] 'lamp', begins with a geminate *t* followed by a geminate vowel.

[9.20]

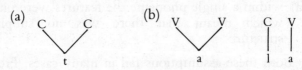

(c) The third possibility is the simultaneous association of a single C slot with two segmental distinctive feature matrices. This is what happens when complex segments like affricates occur. Affricates like [pf], [tʃ] and [dʒ] are described using the feature [+delayed release] in SPE (see section 3.3.6). But they can be more revealingly represented in this way:

[9.21]

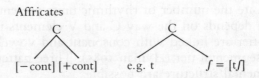

Affricates

This makes the feature [delayed release] superfluous. Diphthongs are treated in analogous fashion:

[9.22]

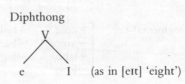

Diphthong

Many languages have prenasalised consonants which, like the complex segments above, do show sequential organization of features at the subsegmental level. An example of a prenasalised consonant is the sound [ⁿd] as in Kikuyu [ⁿdɛgwal] 'bull'. In the light of [9.21], how should pre-nasalised consonants be represented?

A prenasalised consonant can be represented as follows:
[9.23]

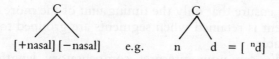

9.4.4 Compensatory lengthening

In addition, the approach to the syllable outlined in the last section accounts in a natural way for some traditional problems in phonology such as COMPENSATORY LENGTHENING. In many languages, if an underlying syllabic segment is deleted or is released as nonsyllabic, an adjacent syllabic gets lengthened 'in compensation'. We shall exemplify this with the data from Luganda in [9.24].

[9.24] /ba+a+lab+a/ [ba:laba] 'they saw'
(but /ba+ku+lab+a/ [bakulaba] 'they see you')
/ba+e+lab+a/ [be:laba] 'they see themselves'
/mu+a+lab+a/ [mwa:laba] 'you saw'
(but /mu+tu+lab+a/ [mutulaba] 'you see us')
/li+ato/ [lja:to] 'boat, canoe'
/ma+ato/ [ma:to] 'boats, canoes'

The rule is that a high vowel is realised as a nonsyllabic glide if it appears followed by another vowel; it is delinked from a V slot and re-associated with a C slot (see rule [9.7] above). But a nonhigh vowel is deleted altogether if it appears followed by another vowel. The motivation for the glide formation and vowel deletion rules in Luganda is to prevent two dissimilar vowels from being adjacent to each other in the phonetic representation. Interestingly, the number of V-elements on the CV-tier remains stable regardless of the fate of the first vowel. How can this be explained?

Let us assume that in the underlying representation each C and each V element of the CV-tier has a certain amount of potential duration. This can be represented as a BEAT or TIMING UNIT (or WEIGHT UNIT). Normally only those timing units which are associated with vowels survive in the phonetic representation. Timing units tend to reflect syllabic peaks because the syllabification rules in [9.10] ensure that only the timing unit of the more sonorous segment is retained when segments are grouped together in a syllable.

We can now interpret compensatory lengthening as follows: when the first vowel is deleted or realised as a nonsyllabic glide, its V-slot (and timing unit) is inherited by the second vowel which becomes simultaneously associated with two V slots and hence has virtually the duration of two vowels in the phonetic representation:

[9.25]

$$\sigma \quad \sigma \quad \sigma \quad \rightarrow \quad \sigma \quad \sigma \quad \sigma$$

C V V C   V C   V   →   C V V C   V C   V
| | | | | | | | | | | | |
b a e l   a b   a   b a e l   a b   a   [be:laba]

[9.26]

$$\sigma \quad \sigma \quad \rightarrow \quad \sigma \quad \sigma$$

C V V C   V   →   C V V C   V
| | | | | | | | |
l i a t   o   l j a t   o   [lja:to]

See if you can find an example of compensatory lengthening in a language that you know.

9.4.5 The syllable as indispensable building block for higher phonological domains

In recent years, phonological research has amassed evidence showing that the syllable is the hub of phonological organisation. In many languages, higher prosodic phenomena like stress, nasalisation, and quantity (length) can only be insightfully described in terms of the syllable because often, in order to determine whether a given rule is applicable, the number of syllables in a word (or part of a word) has to be counted. There are rules which require main word stress to fall on a certain syllable of the word which could be, say, the last syllable or second syllable from the end (penultimate syllable) of a word. We shall preview this kind of rule here and return to it in more detail in Chapter 11.

Which syllable receives stress in the Swahili data in [9.27]?

[9. 27] píga   'hit'
         pigána   'fight',
         piganíʃa   'cause to fight'.
         tutawapíga   'we shall hit them'
         tutawapiganíʃa 'we shall make them fight'

The answer is that stress falls on the penultimate syllable. The relative position of stress remains the same even when the word grows longer with the addition of affixes.

Swahili has another rule which determines whether the noun class 9 nasal prefix is syllabic. This rule also takes the number of syllables in a word into account: if attached to MONOSYLLABIC roots, the nasal prefix is syllabic but if attached to longer roots, it is non-syllabic:

[9.28] (a) ņta   point   (b) mbuzi   goat
           ņtʃi   country   ŋguruwe   pig

The next example is from Luganda. It involves CLITICS. But before we examine the Luganda data we need to digress and clarify the notion of 'clitic'. Typically a clitic is an unstressed particle which is attached to a HOST (i.e. main) word and is incapable of standing on its own.

Often clitics affect the stress pattern of the host word. A clitic attached to the beginning of a word is called a PROCLITIC and a clitic attached to the end of a word is called an ENCLITIC. Some clitics are derived from self-standing words. For example, the French first person pronoun form *je* (as in *je le vois* 'I see him') is an independent word. But in *j'ai* (from *je ai*) 'I have' it is a PROCLITIC. In English *not* is a separate word in *she is not* but it is an ENCLITIC in *she isn't*. Other clitics are not derived from independent words e.g. Latin *-que* 'and' as in *mensamque* 'and the table' (accusative case). The process of adding clitics is called CLITICISATION.

We can now return to Luganda after the digression. In this language there is a vowel length rule which is sensitive to the number of syllables. Some words of more than one syllable end in a long vowel and others in a short vowel. The difference between these two word types shows up when an enclitic (a grammatical particle attached to the end of a word) like the interrogative marker *-ki* is present. A word like *mutawa:na* 'trouble' which underlyingly ends in a long vowel becomes [mutawa:na:ki] 'what trouble'. But a word like *mukozi* 'worker' which underlyingly ends in a short vowel, when cliticised (e.g. when the enclitic interrogative particle *-ki* is attached to it), becomes [mukoziki] 'which worker' not *[mukozi:ki].

Interestingly, in Luganda all monosyllabic roots end in a long vowel in the underlying representation. That long vowel is shortened in most contexts in the phonetic representation. But it is protected and shows up before enclitics like the interrogative marker as you can see:

[9.29] Monosyllabic length

Underlying Representation	Cliticised Form Phonetic Representation	Non-cliticised Form Phonetic Representation
ki-taa 'calabash'	kita: ki 'which calabash'	kita 'calabash'
ki-loo 'night'	ki-lo: ki 'which might'	ki-lo 'night'
ma-taa 'milk'	ma-ta: ki 'which milk'	ma-ta 'milk'

mu-tii	mu-ti: ki	mu-ti
'tree'	'which tree'	'tree'

Swahili and Luganda are not extraordinary in requiring a count of the number of syllables before deciding whether or not a rule applies. Some other languages, for example Spanish, do the same. Jaeggli (1980) has shown that there are Spanish dialects where the form that a diminutive suffix takes depends simply on the number of syllables in the noun to which the diminutive suffix is added: -sita/-sito is added after disyllabic words and -ita/-ito after trisyllabic ones.

[9.30]   (a) *-sita (fem.)/ -sito (masc.)*

Noun		Diminutive
madre	'mother'	madre-sita
cruz	'cross'	cruze-sita
buey	'bull'	bueye-sito

(b) *-ita*

comadre	'midwife'	comadr-ita
dinosauryo	'dinosaur'	dinosaur-ito

Semantically, the addition of a diminutive suffix to a noun has the effect of changing its meaning so that it can be paraphrased in English as 'a little or insignificant somebody or something'.

9.5 Syllable weight

Traditionally the major distinction drawn between syllable types found in languages has been between OPEN SYLLABLES and CLOSED SYLLABLES. An open syllable ends in a vowel while a closed syllable ends in a consonant. In some languages syllables typically end in a vowel, that is to say, they are open. That is the situation in languages like Japanese and Luganda (if syllabic nasals are disregarded). In other languages, like French and English, syllables can end in a consonant. But, even in those languages which allow closed syllables, there is often a clear preference for open syllables. In French, for instance, syllable final consonants suffer a considerable degree of attrition. There is a rule which deletes word final consonants in words like *petit* [pə ti] 'little' and preconsonantal consonants as in *enfant* [ãfã] 'child'. The effect of this deletion rule is to turn what would be a closed syllable into an open syllable.

The consensus today is that more important than the traditional classification of phonological systems in terms of open and closed syllables is their classification in terms of SYLLABLE WEIGHT. In numerous languages a factor that determines the applicability of certain phonological rules is the WEIGHT of the rhyme. Essentially, a syllable is LIGHT if it contains a nonbranching rhyme as in [9.31]. But a syllable is HEAVY if it contains a **branching rhyme** as in [9.32]. The onset seems never to play any role in the computation of syllable weight. Consequently, its internal structure is irrelevant.

Generally, languages in which a distinction between light and heavy syllables is drawn fall into two camps which are shown as type A and type B below. To begin with, for convenience, I assume that the syllables have the structure given in [9.1] at the beginning of this chapter.

Type A Languages

(a) In a light syllable the rhyme contains a short vowel as in [9.31]:

[9.31]

(b) In a heavy syllable the rhyme contains
    either
    (i) a long vowel or diphthong optionally followed by one or more consonants;
    or
    (ii) a short vowel followed by at least one consonant as in (9.32)

[9.32]

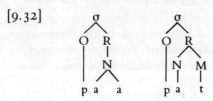

Type B Languages

(a) In a light syllable the rhyme contains a short vowel. As always, the presence or absence of a consonant in the onset is irrelevant. But in this case so is the presence of a consonant in the margin, following the nucleus:

[9.33]

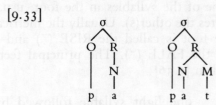

(b) In a heavy syllable the rhyme contains a long vowel or diphthong, the presence or absence of any consonant in the margin being again irrelevant.

[9.34]

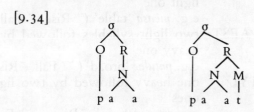

Probably Latin is the best known example of a type A language. Stress placement in Latin was governed by a rule which was sensitive to syllable weight:

[9.35] *Latin Stress Rule*

    (i) In disyllabic words, stress the first syllable, as in [ré-go:] *rēgo* 'I rule'

    (ii) In a word of more than two syllables, stress a heavy penultimate syllable (the second syllable from the end of the word). A syllable is heavy if it contains a long vowel as in [i-ni-mí:-kus] *inimīcus* 'enemy' or, alternatively, if in the margin, following the vowel there is a consonant as in [re:k-sis-tis] *rēxistis* 'you (plural) ruled'.

    (iii) If the penultimate syllable is short and has no consonant in the margin, it is regarded as light and stress in that case is placed on the antepenultimate syllable, as in [in-su-la] *insula* 'island'

Syllable weight is at the heart of Latin METRE. Traditional Latin primers, like Kennedy (1948:203) on whom the account here is based, have taught generations of students that a VERSE (i.e. line of Latin poetry) consists of a certain number of FEET. Each foot is made up of two or more syllables. One of the syllables in the foot, usually the heavy one dominates the other(s). Usually the metrically dominant part of the foot is called the RISE (¯) and the weaker part is called the FALL (˅). The principal feet in Latin poetry are listed in [9.36]

[9.36] IAMBUS: one light syllable followed by a heavy one
e.g. *carō* 'flesh' (˅ Fall, ¯ Rise)

TROCHEE: one heavy syllable followed by a light one
e.g. *mēnsa* 'table' (¯ Rise, ˅ Fall)

ANAPAEST: two light syllables followed by a heavy one
e.g. *patulae* 'broad' (˅˅ Fall, ¯Rise)

DACTYL: one heavy followed by two light ones
e.g. *litora* 'shore' (¯Rise, ˅˅ Fall)

SPONDEE: two heavy syllables
e.g. *hērōs* 'hero' (˅Fall ¯ Rise; or ¯ Rise ¯ Fall)

TRIBRACH: three light syllables
e.g. *temere* 'to fear' (˅Fall, ¯Rise; or ¯ ¯Rise, ˅Fall)

The spondee and tribrach are rare. The common feet all share the characteristic of having strong, dominant syllables which alternate with weak ones.

Let us leave Latin and turn to an example of a type B language. We have borrowed Larsen and Pike's (1949) data from the Mexican language Huasteco for our illustration.

Work out the placement of stress in this language, showing the interaction between stress and syllable weight. Vowel length is phonemic and it is indicated by a colon in the usual way. An apostrophe after a consonant shows that it is glottalised. The accent marks stress.

[9.37] *Disyllabic words*

/ʔátʻem/	'salt'	/cálam/	'shade'
/búːcʼiʔ/	'coward'	/ʔéːjal/	'boss'
/cijóːk/	'chin'	/ʔamúːl/	'rubbish'
/ʔiːláː b/	'seed'	/yaːníːl/	'many times'

[9.38] *Trisyllabic words*

/hílkʼoma/	'leftovers'
/ʔáː u lom/	'field of garlic'
/kʷʼahíːlom/	'window'
/hu: úːkʼ ik/	'blisters'
/ʔalabéːl/	'pretty'
/bíːnomac/	'one who gave'
/ʔubaːtʼláːb/	'game, plaything'
/ʔeːlaː wáːj/	'(they) surely find each other'

I hope you have worked out a statement along these lines for predicting stress placement in Huasteco:

[9.39] (i) If a word contains one or more long vowels, stress falls on the syllable with the last long vowel.

(ii) If a word contains no long vowels, stress falls on the first syllable.

The upshot of this discussion is that while the rhyme plays a role in determining the applicability of stress rules, the onset does not. As a rule, in order to apply rules, it is necessary to know the constituent structure of the rhyme but not that of the onset. The crucial characteristic of rhymes has been formally stated in the literature in terms of the BRANCHING RHYME HYPOTHESIS: a syllable with a nonbranching rhyme is light, while a syllable with a branching rhyme is heavy. The difference between type A languages like Latin and type B languages like Huasteco is accounted for by assuming the tree geometry in [9.40] and [9.41] respectively for these languages.

The metaphor of PROJECTION[4] has been used to express the principle at stake: in quantity-sensitive stress systems, where syllable weight plays a key role, we could say that as far as the stress rules are concerned, the syllable onset is not relevant, it is not 'seen'. What is projected (on

[9.40] *Type A Heavy Syllables*

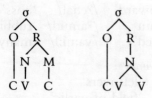

[9.41] *Type B Heavy Syllables*

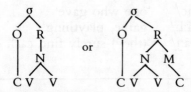

an imaginary screen, as it were) and 'seen' by the stress rules is the rhyme. In type A languages what is watched out for is branching anywhere in the rhyme, be it at the level of the nucleus and margin, or within the nucleus itself. In type B languages, on the other hand, only the nucleus is projected. The question whether branching occurs is only asked about the nucleus.

Let us now return to the CV-tier model and restate syllable weight within that framework. In CV-tier phonology the differences between type A and type B languages can be accounted for by assuming that only V (and the segments it dominates) and any C following the V element are projected. The situation in the two types of language is shown in [9.42] and [9.43] respectively. (I have boxed off the elements that are projected.)

[9.42] *Type A Language*
   (a) *light syllables*

(b) *heavy syllables*

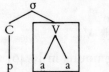

[9.43] *Type B Language*
(a) *light syllables*

(b) *heavy syllables*

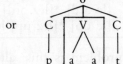

9.6 Abstract segments

The theory of the syllable outlined here also succeeds in throwing some light on one of the most recalcitrant problems in phonology: the problem of *abstract segments*. In many languages phonologists have discovered that 'ghost segments' which do not appear in the phonetic representation may affect the way in which phonological rules apply (see Chapter 8, section 3, pages 145–146).

Consider the facts of French which are shown in [9.44] and [9.45]:

[9. 44] [labe]	l(e) abbé	'the abbot'
[lane]	l(a) année	'the year'
[leta]	l(e) état	'the state'
[lidãntite]	l(a) identité	'the identity'

A rule deletes the vowel of the definite article when the next word begins with a vowel:

[9.45] Vowel truncation
[-cons] → ø/ __# V

The consonant-commencing nouns in [9.46] are unaffected:

[9. 46] [lə bwa]   le bois   'the forest'
[la karaf]   la carafe   'carafe, water-bottle'
[lə pa]   le pas   'step, pace'
[la maladi]   la maladie   'illness'

In the light of the solution provided above, how should words below commencing with the so-called 'H ASPIRÉ' be represented in underlying lexical representations? Justify the rule which you propose. (You might find it useful to review first the discussion in section 3 of Chapter 8.)

[9.47] [le ara] *[lez ara] les haras 'the stud farms'
[le arpist] *[lez arpist] les harpistes 'the harpists'
[le erɔ̃] *[lez erɔ̃] les hérons 'the herons'
[le ɔrd] *[lez ɔrd] les hordes 'the hordes'
[le up] *[lez up] les houppes 'the bunches'

The problem is this: although phonetically they start with a vowel, these words behave phonologically as though they started with a consonant. This raises questions about the nature of that consonant as we saw on page 146.

The solution which the theory of the syllable outlined here enables us to come up with is simple. The theory allows C and V elements to exist at the CV-tier without being linked to consonant or vowel segments. In that event, they do not surface in the phonetic representation – they are not pronounced. But phonological rules affecting the CV-tier would have access to them.

In the case of h-aspiré words, there is an unattached C which inhibits the application of the vowel truncation (deletion) rule although it is not linked to any concrete sound on the segmental tier. The situation can be represented in this way:

[9.48]

haras 'stud farm'

9.7 Extrasyllabicity

The reverse situation also occurs. A segment can be phonetically fully specified without being linked by association lines to a C or V. Such a 'floating' segment is not part of any syllable: it is EXTRASYLLABIC.

Another French example illustrates this. Instead of using the familiar consonant truncation rule (see [7.4] and [9.16]) which deletes syllable-final consonants unless they are followed by a vowel, we can simply attribute the failure of such consonants to surface in the phonetic representation to their being extrasyllabic.
Compare these data:

[9.49] (a) [pəti prɛ̃s] petit prince 'petty prince'
(b) [pəti tɑ̃fɑ̃] petit enfant 'little child'

Where the next word begins with a consonant as in *petit prince* [9.50a], the floating underlying final /t/ of *petit* remains unattached at the end of the derivation and consequently fails to surface. But where the next word begins with a vowel as in *petit enfant* [9.50b], a C-element is inserted at the CV-tier and the floating underlying /t/ is attached to it. The Onset First Principle [9.9] ensures that the inserted C (and the segment it dominates) is attached as a syllable onset. The /t/ is then able to surface phonetically.

[9.50] (a)

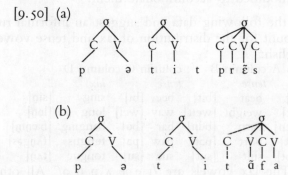

(b)

This analysis implies that French prefers open syllables both in underlying and surface representations.

Syllable-based rules are not extraordinary in ignoring peripheral elements. As we shall see presently, in many languages stress rules also tend to disregard peripheral elements in words (see section 11.2.3).

9.8 Summary

To summarize, the syllable has the following functions:

(i) Phonotactic regulation: constraining the combination of consonants and vowels of a language.
(ii) Regulation of subsegmental structure through the CV-tier.
(iii) Serving as the unit of the phonological hierarchy in terms of which the behaviour of higher units of the prosodic hierarchy such as stress, tone, and duration is stated.

Exercises

1. (a) Make a broad transcription of the data below.
   (b) Divide the words into syllables using the syllabification convention in [9.10].

met	fright	sphere
strict	laughed	scratched
juxtapose	Knesset	Gdańsk

   (c) Comment on any problematic cases. Does [9.10] need to be modified to accommodate them?

2. (a) Study the following data and suggest an informal rule to account for the distribution of lax and tense vowels in English:

column A	column B		column C		column D	
lax	*tense*		*tense*		*lax*	
bit [bɪt]	beat	[bit]	bee	[bi]	sing	[sɪŋ]
get [get]	weight	[weɪt]	way	[weɪ]	long	[lɒŋ]
ban [bæn]	barn	[bɑn]	bar	[bɑ]	banging	[bæŋɪŋ]
pot [pɒt]	port	[pɔt]	paw	[pɔ]	fungus	[fʌŋgəs]
soot [sʊt]	suit	[sut]	sue	[su]	tongue	[tʌŋ]

   Hint: The lax vowels are /ɪ e æ ʌ ɒ ʊ ə/ All other vowels are tense. Syllable structure affects the distribution of lax vowels.

3. (a) The data below exemplify the process known as LIAISON in French. Using the approach to the syllable

proposed in this chapter, formulate a rule to account
for liaison. Specifically, state how the segmental tier,
the CV-tier and the syllable tier are linked.

[le dam]	les dames	'the ladies'
[le fose]	les fossés	'the ditches'
[le primat]	les primates	'the primates'
[le mwa]	les mois	'the months'
[lez animo]	les animaux	'the animals'
[lez ebenist]	les ébénistes	'the cabinet-makers'
[lez idjo]	les idiots	'the idiots'
[lez ordinatœ:r]	les ordinateurs	'the computers'
[lez urs]	les ours	'the bears'
[lez ãfã]	les enfants	'the children'

Notes

1. For a good discussion of the functions of the syllable
   also see Fudge (1969).

2. The term AORIST means simple past tense, e.g. *went*,
   or *walked* as opposed to *had walked* or *had been walking*.

3. We shall return to this point in the next chapter when
   we consider suprasegmental phonological phenomena
   like vowel harmony.

4. The account I have presented is not universally
   accepted. It has been argued by Hyman (1985) that the
   notions of branching rhymes and projection of the
   rhyme only offer a partial explanation of the nature of
   the syllable. This is because they fail to show that the
   units which contribute to syllable weight are also the
   same units which can carry tone, stress and quantity.
   There is nothing in the projection approach that shows
   that this is not mere coincidence. Hyman argues that
   a more illuminating account would be one which incorporated the notion of MORA (timing unit or weight
   unit). Nonbranching rhymes contain one mora while
   branching rhymes contain two.

CHAPTER 10

Multi-tiered phonology

10.1 Introduction to tone languages

Very many of the world's languages are TONE
LANGUAGES. They have morphemes which are at least
in part realised by pitch modulation: pitch differences can
be used to make phonemic contrasts. Pitch depends on the
rate of vibration of the vocal cords. The more taut the vocal
cords are, the faster they vibrate and the higher is the pitch
of the perceived sound.

Linguists usually use tone marking diacritics like those
in [10.1] to represent pitch in tone languages. The diacritics
are to be interpreted as follows:

[10.1] ` = low tone e.g. [àwò] 'star' (Igala, Nigeria)
 ´ = high tone e.g. [áwó] 'guinea fowl' (Igala,
 Nigeria)
 ‾ = mid tone e.g. [àwō] 'an increase' (Igala,
 Nigeria)
 ˆ = falling tone e.g. [mùsànâ] 'sunlight'
 (Luganda, Uganda)
 ˇ = rising tone e.g. [òkpǎ] 'length' (Gwari,
 Nigeria)

In tone languages pitch can be used to distinguish word
meaning or to convey grammatical distinctions. In this
respect they differ from STRESS (nontonal) languages like
English where pitch does not have those functions. (See
section 10.4.1 below.)

The Nigerian language Igala is an example of a
language which uses pitch differences to contrast word
meaning:

[10.2] Igala (Nigeria) Welmers (1973:116)

áwó 'guinea fowl' [‾‾]   àwó 'a slap' [_ ‾]
áwō 'an increase' [‾ –]   àwō 'a comb' [_ –]
áwò 'hole (in a tree) [‾ _]   àwò 'star' [__]

In some tone languages tone has a predominantly
LEXICAL FUNCTION. It is used almost exclusively to
distinguish word meaning. This is generally the case in
oriental tone languages like Chinese. See [10.5] below for
a well-known Chinese example of the use of pitch to
distinguish word meanings. However, in some other
languages the function of tone is primarily GRAMMAT-
ICAL. It is used mainly or exclusively for the signalling of
grammatical distinctions. This is the case in many African
languages. All intermediate possibilities between these two
extremes are also possible.

In [10.3] some data from Longunda (Nigeria) which
illustrate the use of tone to make grammatical distinctions
are presented. In this language, there are three sets of
personal pronouns and in all three sets the difference
between first and second person is expressed tonally:

[10.3] Longunda (John and Bonnie Newman 1974:113)

	Neutral		Future		Continuous	
	Sg.	Pl.	Sg.	Pl.	Sg.	Pl.
1st person	ná	ká	ń	kә́	náná	káa
1st inclusive		kà		kә̀		kàa
2nd person	nà	kà	ǹ	kә̀	nànà	kàa

Now attempt [10.4]. What are the functions of tone in
Luganda? What is your evidence?

[10.4] Luganda
    (a) àtúsómélá   's/he reads for us' (main clause)
        àtùsómèlá   's/he who reads for us' (relative clause)
        àsòmâ   's/he who reads' (relative clause)
        àsómá   's/he reads' (main clause)
    (b) kwésèlá   v. refl. 'to bubble up in boiling'
        kwèsélá   v. trans. 'to water cattle'
        mùsánvú   'seven'
        mùsânvú   'twig'

I hope in working out the answer to [10.4] you established the fact that tone need not have an exclusively lexical or grammatical function. Tone has both lexical and grammatical functions in Luganda. The existence of minimal pairs like those in [10.4b] shows that tone contrasts word meanings while the use of tone to distinguish between main clauses and (subordinate) relative clauses in [10.4a] shows that tone is also used to make grammatical distinctions.

Tone languages can be classified as belonging to one of two categories on the basis of the shape of their 'pitch phonemes': REGISTER TONE LANGUAGES and CONTOUR TONE LANGUAGES. In an ideal register tone language the tones have LEVEL high, mid or low pitch. They are almost pure notes. The pitch hardly goes up or down during the production of a particular tone. That is the case in the Igala examples above.

In contrast, in a contour tone language, many tones have fluctuating pitch as can be seen in the following Mandarin Chinese examples:

[10.5] Chinese
ma	'mother'	(level high tone) [ˉ]
ma	'hemp'	(high rising tone) [ˊ]
ma	'horse'	(falling rising tone) [ˇ] (also referred to as dipping rising or low rising)
ma	'scold'	(high falling tone) [ˋ]

The distinction between contour tone and register tone languages is not absolute. In reality most systems display some mongrel qualities: a register tone language often has a few contour tones, and vice versa. Above, the Mandarin Chinese word /mā/ 'mother' has a level high tone although contour tones are the norm in that language; and the Luganda word /àsòmâ/ 's/he who reads' ends with a falling contour tone although the norm in this language is level low or high tones.

10.2 The nature of phonological representations

Until the mid-1970s the consensus view among phonologists was that phonological representations consist of segmental and suprasegmental representations. The segmental representations were assumed to be made up of consonant and vowel segments, together with empty segments referred to as syllable, morpheme, word and phrase JUNCTURES or BOUNDARIES. Boundaries are included in phonological representations to indicate the domain in which a particular phonological process takes place (see Chapter 12).

Boundaries may have a conditioning or inhibiting effect. Some phonological processes only take place when a certain boundary is present, or absent. For instance, in English voiceless stops are aspirated only if two conditions are satisfied: they must be in a stressed syllable and, in addition, they must be immediately preceded by a SYLLABLE BOUNDARY. Both conditions are met in [pʰen] 'pen' and [dɪtʰeɪn] 'detain'; a voiceless stop preceded by /s/, e.g. /p/ in [spik] 'speak', is unaspirated even when it is followed by a stressed vowel because in that position the stop is not syllable initial.

In SPE it was assumed that super-imposed on the segmental layer were tone and stress, and possibly a few other phenomena such as vowel harmony (i.e. the sharing by vowels within a word of certain phonological features (see [10.6] below)). Both segmental and suprasegmental elements were thought to be arranged in a row one after another. The correctness of the assumption that phonological representations consist of linear segmental and suprasegmental levels was taken for granted for a long time. Moreover, the question of how the two levels related to each other was not raised in a serious way.[1]

In the 1970s a number of studies focused on the relationship between segmental and suprasegmental representations. The findings arrived at revealed that the assumptions that the received orthodoxy was based on were questionable. The questioning initially took place in discussions of the representation of tone. A key question that was raised was whether tonal properties such as [high] [low] or [rising] should be regarded as properties of a vowel, much in the same way that features such as [back] or [round] are, or, rather, were tonal properties to be viewed as distinct from the segmental representation of vowels? Should tone be represented using DIACRITIC MARKS like (´ – `) for high, mid and low tone respectively, to indicate its peripheral status? The answers to these questions have a bearing on how the nature of phonological representations is interpreted. The key issue is whether SPE (and structuralist phonology before it) is right in assuming that phonological representations are linear, with segments, some of them bearing suprasegmental properties, arranged in a neat sequence.

10.3 The representation of tone

Goldsmith (1976) proposed some interesting answers to questions of this kind. He proposed that the division of the speech continuum into 'segments' may proceed in different ways in different languages. Thus, while the parameters of place and manner of articulation, for instance, are normally treated as segmental properties belonging to individual consonants, there are languages where these properties may extend over several segments. Nasalisation is usually a property of nasal consonants only, yet in some languages it can be a property of the syllable or even the word as a whole. The rate of vibration of the vocal cords which determines the pitch of a sound can be a property of an individual segment, of a syllable or even of an entire word.

A central claim of the new theory inaugurated by Goldsmith is that in principle the various articulatory parameters, e.g. aspiration, nasalisation, voicing, and tone are AUTONOMOUS and the articulations that result from them are, in principle, independent. One of the main tasks of phonological theory is to establish the language-specific as well as universal principles which regulate the linking of these autonomous parameters. Goldsmith called this model AUTOSEGMENTAL PHONOLOGY, a name intended to highlight the fact that, in this theory, the potential independence of the various phonological parameters is regarded as crucial, for the reasons outlined below.

10.3.1 Contour tones

Contour tones, like rising and falling tones, pose theoretical difficulties for what was the standard generative approach to phonology until the mid-seventies. This approach incorporated a principle which Goldsmith (1976) refers to as the ABSOLUTE SLICING HYPOTHESIS. This is the claim that speech can be exhaustively sliced into segments which consist of unordered bundles of features which are linearly ordered. In an SPE inspired model a word like 'mad' would be represented as in [10.6]:

$$
[10.6] \quad
\begin{bmatrix}
+\text{cons} \\
+\text{nas} \\
+\text{lab} \\
-\text{cor} \\
-\text{cont} \\
\cdot \\
\cdot \\
\cdot \\
m
\end{bmatrix}
\begin{bmatrix}
-\text{cons} \\
-\text{nas} \\
-\text{lab} \\
-\text{cor} \\
+\text{cont} \\
\cdot \\
\cdot \\
\cdot \\
\text{æ}
\end{bmatrix}
\begin{bmatrix}
+\text{cons} \\
-\text{nas} \\
-\text{lab} \\
+\text{cor} \\
-\text{cont} \\
\cdot \\
\cdot \\
\cdot \\
d
\end{bmatrix}
$$

While the assignment of the various features to discrete segments in [10.6] might look plausible, the same procedure could not be extended to the feature [+voice] in this word since [+voice] is a property of the entire word. Nor could it be extended to the analysis of pitch here because it too could not be vertically sliced and allocated to a single segment, without any leakage into adjacent segments. This evidence undermines the fundamental claim of the 'slicing hypothesis'. As we saw earlier in [4.1], even apparently segmental features can often extend over more than one segment.

In the discussion of complex segments in the last chapter we saw another counter-example to the SPE position of regarding all segments as minimal, unordered bundles of features. Not all segments are unordered feature bundles. Segments can have internal structure involving the linear ordering of some features. That is true of affricates, prenasalised consonants and diphthongs (section 9.4.3).

The same can be demonstrated to be true of contour tones. A contour tone is a combination of two more basic tones. For example, a falling tone is made up of a high tone followed by a low tone, while a rising tone consists of a low tone followed by a high tone.

I shall illustrate this point using data from Gwari

(Nigeria). The source is Hyman (1973). In Gwari there is a rule which spreads the tone of the first syllable onto the following syllable creating a contour rising tone or falling tone:

[10.7] *UR*   *PR*

     (a) L H   →   L LH

        /òkpá/   →   [òkpǎ]   'length'

     (b) H L   →   H HL

        /súkNù/ →   [súkû̃]   'bone'

Even where a contour tone cannot, on the face of it, be broken into a sequence of two tones, inspection of its phonological behaviour shows that it acts like two consecutive tones. This will be shown by considering the phenomenon of DOWNDRIFT which is found in many African tone languages. When an underlying high tone is preceded by a low tone it is usually automatically lowered and becomes phonetically indistinguishable from a mid tone. Downdrift is an example of partial assimilation: a high tone is somewhat lowered and becomes more like a low tone which precedes it:

[10.8] *UR*   *PR*

$$\begin{bmatrix} \text{H} & \text{L} & \text{H} \\ \_ & \_ & \_ \\ \_ & \_ & \_ \end{bmatrix} \qquad \begin{bmatrix} \_ \\ \_ \\ \_ \end{bmatrix}$$

Thus, in Luganda an underlying high tone preceded by another high tone remains high. However, a high tone preceded by a low tone or a falling tone gets lowered. The later part of a falling tone thus behaves just like a simple low tone.

[10.9] (a) nábáddé sígúlâ   'I was not buying'

$$\begin{bmatrix} \text{-} & \text{-} & \text{-} & \text{-} & \widehat{} \\ & & & & \_ \end{bmatrix}$$

    (b) twábáddé túgùlá 'we were buying'

$$\begin{bmatrix} \text{-} & \text{-} & \text{-} & \text{-} \\ & & & \_ \\ & & & \_ \end{bmatrix}$$

    (c) kìkúúkúùlú   'crowd'

$$\begin{bmatrix} & \text{-} & \text{-} & \text{-} & \text{-} \\ \_ & & & \text{-} & \\ & & \_ & & \_ \end{bmatrix}$$

(d) bánêttá   'They will kill themselves'

$$\begin{bmatrix} \bar{} & \bar{} \\ & \underline{} \end{bmatrix}$$

In a theory which insists on regarding segments as unordered feature bundles the facts which we have surveyed are simply accidental. There is no apparent reason why [+low] and [+falling] tones should both trigger off downdrift. If, however, falling tones are treated in a way analogous to that proposed for complex segments like affricates in section 9.4.3, the reason for the similarity between low tones and falling tones becomes obvious. A falling tone, even when it is borne by a short vowel, is not an unordered bundle of features. It is a sequence of a high tone followed by a low tone and naturally it will cause the same perturbations as a simple low tone. In view of this, contour tones should be represented as complex tones which have internal structure:

[10.10] [+high]   [−high]

$$\begin{bmatrix} -cons \\ +syll \end{bmatrix}$$

The implication of this is that the simple slicing hypothesis should be replaced with a model that recognises that there need not be a one-to-one mapping between elements at various levels. As [10.10] shows, the tonal features [+high] and [−high] are both simultaneously associated with a single vowel.

However, it is not a free-for-all that is being advocated. There are restrictions on the ways in which tones can be associated with segments. The theory incorporates the OBLIGATORY CONTOUR PRINCIPLE (OCP) which prohibits two identical tones from being adjacent (Leben 1973, 1978). Adjacent identical tones are simplified:

[10.11]   *UR*   *PR*
            LH H   →   LH
            HLL   →   HL

A rising tone (LH) is simplified to L before a high tone and a falling tone (HL) is simplified to high before a low tone.

This can be seen in the Mende examples below which are cited by Leben (1978). The high toned definite singular suffix -í causes the simplification of the underlying rising tone of *mba* but has no effect on the falling tone of *mbu*.

[10.12]   *UR*   *PR*

(a)   HLH →   HLH

       mbû-í   mbûí'owl'

(b)   LH H →   LH

       mbǎ-í   mbɛ̌í'rice'

(The change in the vowel is not relevant.)

Likewise, the underlying low tone of the indefinite plural suffix -ngà: causes the simplification of a falling tone but has no effect on a preceding rising tone:

[10.13] *UR*   *PR*

(a) H L L   H L

    mbû-ngà: mbúngà: 'owl'

    L H L   L H L

    mbǎ-ngà: mbǎ-ngà: 'rice'

It has been proposed by some that the OCP applies not only to tone but also other tiers, including the segmental tier (see McCarthy 1986).

10.3.2 Tone stability

In many languages when an underlying tone-bearing segment (normally a vowel) is either deleted or becomes nonsyllabic and loses its ability to bear tone, the tone still survives and surfaces on an adjacent syllable. Tone shows a kind of STABILITY which cannot be accounted for if it is assumed to be an integral part of the phonological segment on which it appears in the phonetic representation.

Consider the following examples from Margi (Nigeria) and see what happens to tone when a vowel is deleted:

[10.14] Margi (Hoffmann 1963)

    Indefinite   *Definite*

(a) sál   'man'   sálári

(b) fà   'farm'   fàri

(c) tì   'mourning'   tyǎri

In [10.14a] when the definite suffix -ari, with its HL tones is added, no phonological process takes place. But in [10.14b] when the same suffix is added, one of the vowels is deleted so that the phonetic representation is *fǎri* and not *fàári*. Note, however that the underlying LHL tone pattern is preserved although that means the LH being squashed on to a single vowel. Similarly, in [10.14c], when glide formation turns an underlying high vowel into a nonsyllabic glide incapable of bearing tone, the tone does not disappear. It merely gets shunted on to the next syllabic segment. Once again the underlying LHL tone pattern is preserved by having a rising tone on the first available vowel.

Normally, when a phonological rule deletes a consonant or vowel it wipes it out in its entirety. The fact that tones can survive either the deletion or loss of syllabicity of the segments that bear them is further evidence of their autonomy.

Note however, that tone stability is not a universal phenomenon. There are many cases where deletion of the tone-bearing element spells doom for the tone which it carries. This is particularly true of languages where only heavy syllables can bear complex contour tones. This is because many such languages have a requirement that there can only be one-to-one association between tones and tone-bearing units. We shall return to this point presently.

10.3.3 Melody levels

A further type of argument for the autosegmental approach is the existence of MELODY LEVELS. There are languages where a given pitch configuration is linked to certain morphemes or words or grammatical constructions regardless of the number of consonant and vowel segments which they contain. A classic example of this is Mende (Sierra Leone) (Leben 1973, 1978). Most words containing one morpheme in this language have the following tone patterns: H, L, HL, LH and LHL irrespective of the number of syllables they contain:

[10.15] Mende

H:	kɔ	'war'	pélé	'house'	háwámá	'waistline'
L:	kpà	'debt'	bèlè	'trousers'	kpàkàlì	'tripod chair'
HL:	mbû	'owl'	ngílà	'dog'	félàmà	'junction'
LH:	mbǎ	'rice'	fàndé	'cotton'	ndàvúlá	'sling'
LHL:	mbâ	'companion'	nyàhâ	'woman'	nìkílì	'groundnut'

Leben suggests that if we regard the tone pattern as phonologically separate from the consonant and vowel segments in these words, we can capture the fact that a given melody is realised on each class of words regardless of the number of segments present.

To summarise, at the abstract level of lexical representation, tones do have a separate existence. But at some point in a derivation, which differs from one language to the next, tone gets segmentalised so that phonetically it is realised as a feature of a tone-bearing unit in much the same way as segmental properties like [± coronal] or [± back] are.

10.4 The autosegmental model and the representation of tone

In the last section the arguments in favour of the autosegmental model were presented. How does autosegmental phonology differ from SPE phonology?

The main concerns of autosegmental phonology differ from those of SPE. In the SPE model (the spirit of which is reflected in the first eight chapters of this book), the main preoccupation was with rules that modify feature specifications in different ways; with the ways in which rules mapping underlying onto surface representations interact and with the degree to which underlying representations may differ from surface representations.

In autosegmental phonology the focus shifts to ways in which phonological rules can change the ORGANIS-ATION of phonological representations. In autosegmental phonology phonological representations are no longer seen as simple rows of segments, with all phonological processes taking place at one single level. Rather, they are regarded as complex arrays of (in principle independent) elements arranged on different levels or TIERS.

Various metaphors can be used to express this insight. Phonological representations can be compared to a multistoried building, with the syllables as the structural pillars and beams which support the weight of different levels of the building. In this building various events can take place at the different levels (e.g. the stress level, the tonal level, etc.) without necessarily having any effect on what goes on

at another level. The different levels, though inter-
connected, are in principle autonomous.

Alternatively, following Morris Halle, we can use the
analogy of a book with many pages to describe the autosegmental model of the organisation of phonology. Imagine
a book with many pages, with each page standing for a
different phonological tier. All languages have the consonant and vowel segments page (tier). But there is some
variation as to what other pages (tiers) are selected by any
one language. The possibilities include a page each for
stress, tone, nasalisation and vowel harmony. Whatever
selection is made, however, the binding or the core that
makes the various pages of the book hold together is the
syllable. In the last chapter (which was in effect a practical
introduction to autosegmental phonology) we saw the
central role of the syllable in phonology. We are going to
build on that in this chapter.

In this model, establishing the principles that govern
the ways in which elements on different tiers are ASSO-
CIATED becomes a central task of phonology. ASSOCI-
ATION LINES are the apparatus used to LINK elements
on different tiers. Phonological rules may not only have the
effect of modifying segments, they may also alter the way
in which elements on different tiers relate to each other.
Phonological theory has to establish universal principles of
association and descriptions of particular languages have to
show any idiosyncratic aspects of the ways in which association between different tiers takes place.

The notation used in writing rules is presented below:

[10.16] Autosegmental notation

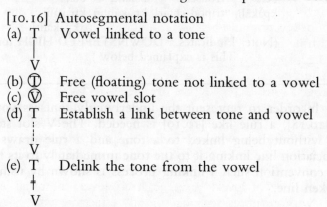

(a) T   Vowel linked to a tone
    |
    V

(b) Ⓣ   Free (floating) tone not linked to a vowel
(c) Ⓥ   Free vowel slot
(d) T   Establish a link between tone and vowel
    ⋮
    V

(e) T   Delink the tone from the vowel
    ╪
    V

As you can see in the Margi example below, underlying tone association may be different from surface association. Phonological derivations may involve deleting or redrawing association lines. You will also observe that both the possibility of a one-to-one MAPPING of tone onto tone-bearing units (vowels in this case) and that of a one-to-many mapping are both envisaged.

[10.17]

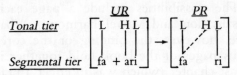

It is not expected, given the autonomy of the different levels, that every tone will be necessarily associated with a tone-bearing unit. Thus, Leben shows that in Mende there exist both tone-bearing suffixes like the definite marker –í and toneless ones like the post-position -*hu* 'in'.

Examine the data in [10.18] and suggest a rule to account for the realisation of tone in these Mende suffixes:

[10.18] Citation form		-*hu*	-*í*
kɔ́	'war'	kɔ́hú	kɔ́í
mbû	'owl'	mbúhù	mbú! í
mbǎ	'rice'	mbàhú	mbɛ̀í
pɛ́lɛ́	'house'	pɛ́lɛ́hú	pɛ́lɛ́í
bɛ̀lɛ̀	'trousers'	bɛ̀lɛ̀hù	bɛ̀lɛ́í
kpàkàlì̀	'tripod chair'	kpàkàlihù	kpàkàlì̌í
			([kpàkàli:])

(Note: ! indicates a DOWNSTEPPED HIGH tone. This is explained below.)

In order to represent the underlyingly toneless vowel in [10.18], a rule like [10.19] is needed. The V slot starts off without being linked to a tone and a rule draws an association line linking it to the tone immediately to its left. By convention such a linking process is shown by using a broken line.

[10.19]

The converse of [10.19] is not only theoretically possible, it is also a practical reality. Many languages have tones
which are underlyingly unlinked to any tone-bearing
element. Such tones are referred to as FLOATING tones.
The word [mbú!í] in [10.18] above contains an example
of a floating tone. As you can see, the root has an underlying falling tone. But when it is followed by the high tone
of the definite singular suffix, the falling tone (HL) is
simplified to high (H) (i.e. $\widehat{HL}$ → H). After the deletion of
the low part of the falling tone there should be two high
tones next to each other and they should have the same high
pitch in the phonetic representation. The surface representation should be *[mbúí] ($^-$ $^-$). But that is not the case.
This is because before it is deleted by the tone simplification
rule, the underlying low tone (the second part of the falling
tone) brings about the lowering to mid of the high tone of
the suffix. The correct surface representation has the high
tone of the suffix -í lowered so that it is like a mid tone.
We assume this derivation:

[10.20]   *UR*   *PR*
/mbû í/   ⟶   [mbú!í] ($^-$ _)

DOWNSTEP is the name given to this process
whereby a high tone is lowered in the absence of any
preceding low tone in the phonetic representation. A downstepped high tone is represented by ('or 'H).

It is necessary to distinguish between downdrift and
downstep. Downdrift is automatic lowering induced by the
presence of a low tone immediately before a high tone in
the phonetic representation. But downstep is phonetically

nonautomatic lowering. The underlying low tone that causes the lowering does not occur in the phonetic representation. The nonsurfacing low tone which causes downstep is referred to as a FLOATING tone.

Our next example of a floating tone comes from Mbui, a language of Cameroon and is borrowed from Hyman and Tadadjeu (1976: 61):

[10.21] (a) bàkɔ́ɔ 'crabs'   bə̀ndúm 'husbands'
         (b) bàkɔ́ɔ bə́ sə́ŋ   'the crabs of the bird'
             bə̀ndúm !bə́ sə́ŋ 'the husbands of the bird'

In isolation both 'crabs' and 'husbands' have L-H tone. However, when these words come together in the associative construction, with high tone [sə́ŋ] as the second noun, the associative marker [bə] is realised with its underlying high tone after 'crabs' but is downstepped to ¹H after 'husbands'. Since in Mbui, as in many other languages a downstepped high (¹H) only arises when a high tone is preceded by a low tone, we can infer that although no low tone is actually phonetically present, there is one at the underlying level. We can therefore set up these two different underlying representations for [10.21]:

[10.22] a. /bàkɔ́ɔ + bə́ + sə́ŋ/   'the   crabs   of   the bird'

        b. /bə̀ndúmˋ + bə́ + sə́ŋ/ 'the husbands of the bird'

The lexical representation of 'husbands' is given in [10.23] where the final low tone of the word is floating (i.e. not linked to any tone-bearing segment in the underlying representation):

[10.23]
$$\left[\begin{array}{ccc} \text{L} & \text{H} & \textcircled{\text{L}} \\ | & | & \\ \text{b ə n du m} \end{array}\right]$$

In Mbui we have recognised a FLOATING LEXICAL TONE tone (i.e. a floating tone that is part of the underlying representation of a noun, verb, adjective or adverb). This is a somewhat rare phenomenon. Much more common are FLOATING GRAMMATICAL TONES[2] (i.e. floating tones that are part of the representation of grammatical morphemes like tense, number, definiteness, possession etc.).

Study the following data and work out the evidence in favour of a floating grammatical tone. Having done that show how it could be represented in autosegmental notation.

[10.24] Etsako (Nigeria) (Elimelech 1976a:56)
    (a) /àmè èθà/ → àmèèθà → [àmêθà]
       water father   'father's water'
    (b) /àmè òké/ → àmèòké → [àmôké]
       water ram   'a ram's water'
    (c) /àmè ɔ́mɔ̀/ → àmèɔ́mɔ̀ → [àmɔ́mɔ̀]
       water child   'a child's water'
    (d) /ódzí ɔ́mɔ̀/ → ódzíɔ́mɔ̀ → [ódʒɔ́mɔ̀]
       crab child   'a child's crab'
    (e) /ɔ̀té ɔ́mɔ̀/ → ɔ̀téɔ́mɔ̀ → [ɔ̀tɔ́mɔ̀]
       cricket child   'a child's cricket'

The associative construction is marked with a floating high tone which occurs between the nouns. Where as in 'a child's crab', the first noun ends in a high tone and the next noun begins with a high tone, the floating high tone cannot be detected. However, where in isolation the two nouns in the construction respectively begin and end in a low tone, the detection of a floating high tone is easy: it is linked to the low tone at the beginning of the second noun. The result of the combination of high and low tone on the same syllable is a falling tone as in [àmêθà] 'water of father'.

[10.25]

$$\begin{bmatrix} L & L & \textcircled{H} & L & L \\ | & | & \ddagger & | & | \\ am & \varepsilon & & e\ \theta\ a \end{bmatrix} \rightarrow \begin{bmatrix} L & L & H & L & L \\ | & | & \diagdown & | & | \\ a & m\textcircled{e} & & e & \theta a \end{bmatrix}$$

/àmè èθà/   [àmêθà]

In autosegmental phonology, given the starting assumption of the autonomy of tone, the existence of such free, unassociated tones is not surprising. But the same facts cause severe embarrassment in a theory of linear phonology where tone features are assumed to be an integral part of the segmental representation of tone-bearing units such as vowels because the prediction that tone is always a segmental feature is not borne out by the evidence. The existence of floating tones was one of the original arguments used to justify autosegmental representations.

The Etsako data in [10.24] are also interesting for another reason. They show that contour falling tones arise from underlying sequences of HL which happen to surface on the same tone-bearing segment. We shall not labour this point as it has already been made above.

Besides linking tone to tone-bearing units by drawing new association lines, rules may also DELINK tones. That is to say, the association line between a tone and a tone-bearing unit can be severed. Thus, in Hausa (Nigeria), an underlying rising LH tone is SIMPLIFIED and becomes a simple high tone when preceded by a high; the L tone of the rise is deleted as you can see in the first example, meaning 'I took (unspecified object)':

[10.26] (a) Hausa (Schuh 1978: 243)
/náa ɗăukàa/ [náː ɗáukàː] 'I took
(unspecified object)'
/náa ɗàukée tà/ [náː ɗàuké: tà] 'I took it'
(b) /náa tàmbáyàa/ [náː tàmbáyàː] 'I asked
(unspecified object)'
/náa tàmbàyée tà/ [náː tàmbàyé: tà] 'I
asked her'

The delinking of the association line between the tone and the vowel can be formalised as in [10.27] (and as before, the broken association line indicates tone spreading (see [10.16]) above).

[10.27]

(a) [H L H L] na a ɗa u ka a   'I took'

(b) [H L H L L] na a ɗa u ke e ta   'I took it'

We have now seen the case for a multi-tier approach to phonological organisation. But how are the tiers related? The principles governing the linking or association of elements on different tiers have been articulated in what is called the WELL-FORMEDNESS CONDITION (WFC). This convention exists in a number of slightly different versions. The version below is based on Goldsmith (1976):

[10. 28] *Well-formedness Condition (WFC)*

      (i) Each vowel must be associated with at least one tone.

     (ii) Each tone must be associated with at least one vowel.

    (iii) No association lines may cross.

This convention lies at the heart of autosegmental phonology. It has the effect of adding and deleting association lines as appropriate at any point during a derivation. Its function is not to police phonological representations; it is not a filter that only lets through representations which meet certain pre-set criteria; rather, it is to be seen as a statement of the unmarked, neutral, normal state of affairs. Aberrations from the unmarked situation are sorted out by tone rules.

The discussion above has implicitly used the WFC. In our earlier Mende examples in [10.19], which is repeated below as [10.29] for convenience, tone spreads from the first syllable of the root to the toneless vowels that follow it so that no vowel surfaces without tone:

[10.29]

$$\begin{bmatrix} H \\ p\varepsilon\ l\varepsilon\ +\ hu \end{bmatrix} \rightarrow [p\acute{e}l\acute{e}h\acute{u}]$$

$$\begin{bmatrix} L \\ b\varepsilon\ l\varepsilon\ +\ hu \end{bmatrix} \rightarrow [b\grave{e}l\grave{e}h\grave{u}]$$

$$\begin{bmatrix} L \\ kpakali\ +\ hu \end{bmatrix} \rightarrow [kp\grave{a}k\grave{a}lih\grave{u}]$$

Likewise, the floating (unassociated) tone of Etsako in [10.25] (repeated below as [10.30]) becomes associated by the WFC:

[10.30]

$$\begin{bmatrix} L & L & \textcircled{H} & L & L \\ \vert & \vert & & \vert & \vert \\ am & \varepsilon & & e & \theta a \end{bmatrix} \rightarrow \begin{bmatrix} L & L & H & L & L \\ \vert & \vert & & \vert & \vert \\ a & m\textcircled{ε} & & e & \theta a \end{bmatrix}$$

The WFC is assumed to be a universal constraint on the structure of phonological representations.

Use the WFC to perform tone mapping in the following example from an imaginary language:

[10.31]

$$
\begin{bmatrix}
& & \overset{\textstyle H}{\underset{\textstyle |}{}} & & & & \overset{\textstyle L}{\underset{\textstyle |}{}} & \\
\text{ta} & \text{li} & \text{la} & \text{lu} & \text{ku} & \text{ma} & \text{zi} & \text{sa}
\end{bmatrix}
$$

When doing the tone mapping we must remember that association lines are not allowed to cross. Obviously, in this case that means that the high tone which is linked to -la- in the underlying representation has to be mapped onto the toneless first two syllables of the word and the low tone linked to -ma- has to be mapped onto the last two syllables:

[10.32]

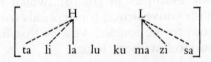

The problem is determining how tone mapping should proceed in the case of the syllables /lu-ku/ which are flanked by high and low tone-bearing vowels. They could be both high, with tone spreading from left to right; they could be both low, with tone spreading from right to left; or they could acquire the adjacent low and high tones respectively. As it stands, the statement of the WFC in [10.28] is not explicit enough to show which of these three alternatives should be chosen. What is needed is a more explicit statement of the mapping principles.

In order to cope with situations like this where the requirements of the WFC can in principle be met by implementing a variety of procedures, the following supplementary principles have been appended to the WFC (Clements and Ford 1979; Clements and Goldsmith 1984):

[10.33]   (i) Associate free tones to free tone-bearing units going from left to right.

(ii) The association of free (unassociated) segments takes precedence over that of already linked (associated) segments; furthermore, (a) give precedence to segments linked to unaccented elements, if there are any; (b) give precedence to segments on the left.

(iii) Add the minimal number of association lines required to undo the violation of the WFC.

Once we adopt [10.33], there is no more ambiguity as to which tones should be mapped onto -luku- in [10.32]. The second principle of [10.33] states that the association goes from left to right. So the high tone is mapped on to luku- :

[10.34]

$$\begin{bmatrix} & & & H & & & L & \\ ta & li & la & lu & ku & ma & zi & sa \end{bmatrix}$$

In most cases, applying these principles in this order eliminates any uncertainty about the application of the WFC.

In the remainder of this chapter we shall see how the insights into the nature of phonological representations gained from the autosegmental study of tone have been extended to other aspects of phonology.

10.5 Tone and intonation

Sometimes TONE LANGUAGES are contrasted with INTONATION LANGUAGES. But they should not be. Tone languages also have intonation. One common intonation effect found in many register tone languages is TONE TERRACING. Terracing involves several related phenomena: DOWNDRIFT, DOWNSTEP and UPSTEP.

As we saw in (10.3), downdrift refers to the automatic lowering of pitch in a PHONOLOGICAL PHRASE whenever a high tone is preceded by a low tone. A phonological phrase is an utterance, often coterminous with the sentence at the syntactic level, which can be said in one breath and can naturally be followed by a pause. Downdrift creates a falling intonation contour in a phonological phrase. Because every high tone is lower than the preceding high each time there is an intervening low, a phonologically high tone can be phonetically lower in pitch than a low tone appearing before it in a phonological phrase. Thus downdrift creates a 'terracing' effect:

[10.35]

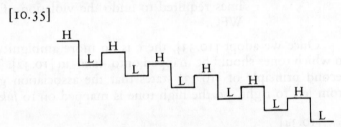

Downdrift only obtains within a phonological phrase. Pitch is reset at the beginning of each phonological phrase. A Luganda example of downdrift is given in [10.36].

[10.36]

tètúlábyé mùntú álímá mù mmwànyí

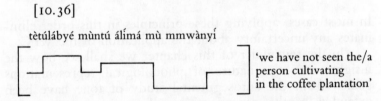

'we have not seen the/a person cultivating in the coffee plantation'

Recall that in our discussion of floating tones we noted that that the term DOWNSTEP is used to describe situations where tone lowering occurs which is not automatically triggered off by the presence of a low tone immediately before a high tone. Sometimes, for no apparent surface phonetic reason, a high tone may be lowered (ᴵH) when it is preceded by another high tone as in Akan (Ghana) (Schachter & Fromkin 1968):

[10.37] /mí ɔ́ -bú/ [míᴵbú] 'my stone'

The noun /ɔ́-bú/ contains the vowel /ɔ́/ which bears a low tone prefix. The vowel is deleted in the possessive construction following the possessive morpheme /mí/; but the tone is not. Rather it is left floating. The presence of this floating low tone is responsible for the tonal downstep. While the phonetic motivation of downdrift is present on the surface, that of downstep is not. Yet from the point of view of intonation, downstep is similar to downdrift in that it causes the pitch of the utterance to go down.

UPSTEP is the converse of downstep. It is the raising of the pitch of a tone so that it is phonetically a step higher in pitch than the preceding token of the same tone. Upstep produces rising intonation over part of the utterance.

Cope (1970) reports that in Zulu (South Africa), low tones between highs become high and that in a series of successive high tones, each high tone is higher than its predecessor:

[10.38]   'the boys who do not want it'

/áɓàfánà àɓáyìfúnì/ → [áɓáfáná   áɓáyífúní]

While in Zulu a high tone is raised if preceded by another high tone, creating a crescendo effect, in Engenni (Nigeria) (Thomas 1974), there is automatic upstepping of a high when it is followed by a low in the same phonological phrase:

[10.39]   'I saw you'   'I did see you'

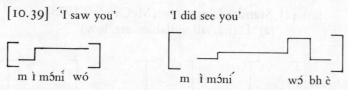

m ì móní wó   m ì móní   wó bh è

Sometimes intonation contours are associated with particular sentence types. In many languages falling intonation (due to downdrift) is associated with declarative sentences while rising intonation resulting from a mitigation or total undoing of the effects of downdrift is associated with interrogative sentences.

Thus in Hausa in questions downdrift is suspended towards the end of the phonological phrase. The last high tone is upstepped and acquires extra-high pitch with a sharp fall (Hombert 1974 cited in Schuh 1978):

[10.40]

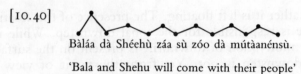

Bàláa dà Shéehù záa sù zóo dà mútàanénsù.

'Bala and Shehu will come with their people'

[10.41]

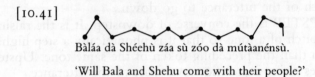

Bàláa dà Shéehù záa sù zóo dà mútàanénsù.

'Will Bala and Shehu come with their people?'

10.6 Pitch-accent

The impression might have been given that all languages are either tone languages or stress languages. The reality is somewhat more complex. Some languages are not clearly one thing or the other. A classic example of a language that does not fit neatly into either category is Japanese.

In Japanese pitch is used contrastively as in a tone language. But it is subject to the constraint that there can only be **one pitch drop per word.** Pitch can go up or down only once in a word. An illustration of this is given in [10.42] below. You will observe that there are only four basic melodies: L, HL, LH and LHL:

[10.42] Standard Japanese (McCawley 1978)

(a) L (i.e. all syllables are low)

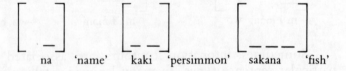

na 'name'   kaki 'persimmon'   sakana 'fish'

(b) HL (i.e. the first syllable is high and subsequent syllables, if any, are low)

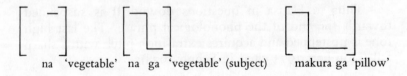

na 'vegetable'   na ga 'vegetable' (subject)   makura ga 'pillow'

(c) LH (i.e. the pitch starts low and goes up)

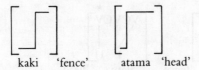

kaki 'fence'   atama 'head'

(d) LHL (i.e. the pitch starts low, goes up, and goes down again)

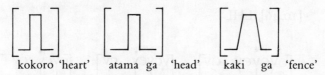

kokoro 'heart'   atama ga 'head'   kaki ga 'fence'

(Note: the particle *ga* which follows the noun here is the subject marker. It is always low.)

As you can see, all the syllables of the nouns in (a) are assigned low tone; there is no pitch drop in the word. In the rest of the examples, however there is a pitch change. An abstract ACCENT, which is represented by an asterisk or star (*), marks the syllable where the change in pitch occurs:

[10.43] L (i.e. no asterisk and hence no pitch change)

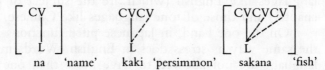

na 'name'   kaki 'persimmon'   sakana   'fish'

> The well-formedness condition ensures that low tone spreads to all the syllables of this class of word.

[10.44] H or HL

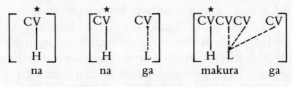

na   na ga   makura ga

A HL melody is assigned, with H going to the first syllable and L to the remainder, if any.

[10.45] LH

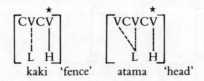

kaki 'fence'   atama 'head'

Conversely, a LH melody is assigned, with H on the last syllable and L on the rest.

[10.46] LHL

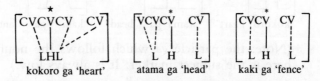

kokoro ga 'heart'   atama ga 'head'   kaki ga 'fence'

A specified starred high toned syllable is flanked by low toned syllables. Low is the DEFAULT or neutral tone assigned when there is no instruction (in the form of an asterisk) to assign a high tone.

Japanese is called a PITCH ACCENT language. It shares some of the characteristics of both STRESS languages like English (which are the subject of the next chapter) and those of tone languages like Chinese.

On the one hand, in Japanese pitch functions in much the same way as stress does in English. Words in a stress language are not allowed to have more than one peak of prominence (in English it is not possible to place two main stresses on a word like *disinformátion*). Similarly, in a pitch accent language there can be at most one peak of prominence in a word. A Japanese word can have only one of the following patterns: L, H, HL, LH or LHL [see [10.42]. High tones cannot alternate with low tones.

On the other hand, however, Japanese is like a true tone language in that pitch contrasts are used phonemically. In this it differs from a stress language like English which does not have minimal pairs distinguished by pitch differences alone.

Study [10.42] and identify words distinguished by pitch differences.

The following are minimal pairs distinguished by pitch:

> *na* (L) 'name'   *na* (H) 'vegetable'
> *kaki* (L) 'persimmon'   *kaki* (LH) 'fence'

10.7 Vowel harmony

Vowel harmony is a process whereby within a certain designated domain, usually the word, all vowels are required to share one or more phonological properties. The vowels of a language are divided into two mutually exclusive sets and all vowels within a stipulated domain must be, say, either front or back, high or low, rounded or unrounded, etc. Thus, in classical Mongolian all the vowels in a word are either front as in [købegyn] 'son, boy' and [køtelbyri] 'instruction' or alternatively, they are all back as in [uɣuta] 'bag' (Lightner 1965).

Welmers (1973:34) reports that in Igbo (Nigeria), vowels belong to either set A, which is [+ATR] or set B, which is [-ATR]. Normally, all the vowels used in a word come from just one of these two sets:

> [10.47] Set A: [i e u o]   Set B: [ɪ a ʊ ɔ]
>   ó rìrì 'he ate'   ɔ́ pìrì 'he carved'
>   ó mèrè 'he did'   ɔ́ sàrà 'he washed'
>   ó gbùrù 'he killed'   ɔ́ zʊ̀rʊ̀ 'he bought'
>   ó zòrò 'he did'   ɔ́ dɔ̀rɔ̀ 'he pulled'

Vowel harmony differs in a significant way from archetypical suprasegmental properties like tone and stress. While these are always located on a separate tier from that where vowels and consonants are found, harmonising phonological features like [back], [round], [high] and [ATR] are normally part of the segmental representation of individual vowels. But they are extracted from the segmental tier and are placed on a distinct harmony tier and cease functioning as properties of individual segments. They SPREAD to all vowels within a specified domain. This domain is usually the word.

Vowel harmony constitutes a theoretically fascinating phenomenon which can throw light on the nature of phonological representations because of the way in which it functions partly as a segmental and partly as a suprasegmental property.

Vowel harmony can be described in the framework of autosegmental phonology by using these principles:

[10.48] (i)   identify the set of harmonising features which are suprasegmentalised and placed on a separate tier;

(ii) identify the class of elements (vowels) which bear the harmonising feature;

(iii) identify the set (possibly empty) of OPAQUE SEGMENTS. Opaque segments are vowels which ought to obey the vowel harmony rules but fail to do so because they are specified in the lexicon for the harmonising feature and are therefore exempt from vowel harmony rules which fill in blanks for the harmonising feature during a derivation;

(iv) *mutatis mutandis*, harmonising features are associated with vowels in accordance with the requirements of the WFC [10.28, 10.33]

In [10.49] these principles are used in the mapping of the feature [ATR] in the derivation of the Igbo forms in [10.47]:

[10.49]

(a) *Vowel harmony tier*   [+ATR]

Segmental tier   O   zOrO → [o zoro] 'he did'

(b) *Vowel harmony tier*   [−ATR]

Segmental tier   O   dOrO   → [ɔdɔrɔ] 'he pulled'

Note: Capital letters are used in underlying representations for vowels specified for all features except the harmonising feature, in this case, [ATR].

Attempt writing an autosegmental rule for the Mongolian example [købegyn] 'boy, son' which we referred to earlier.

For Mongolian, the feature [back] is the one that is placed on the vowel harmony tier. A rule like [10.50] is needed:

[10.50]

Vowel harmony tier:	$\begin{bmatrix} [-\text{back}] \\ \\ kO \quad bEgUn \end{bmatrix}$ → købegyn
Segmental tier:	

Now write a rule to account for the Akan vowel harmony data in [10.51] which are borrowed from Clements (1985):

[10.51] (a) *All vowels are* [+ *ATR*]
  [o-fiti-i] 'he pierced (it)'
  (b) *All vowels are* [− *ATR*]
  [ɔ -cɪrɛ -ɪ] 'he showed (it)'

Your rule should be like [10.52]:

[10.52]

(a) $\begin{bmatrix} [+\text{ATR}] \\ \\ O\text{-fl } tI - I \end{bmatrix}$ → [ofitii]   (b) $\begin{bmatrix} [-\text{ATR}] \\ \\ O\text{-cl } rE - I \end{bmatrix}$ → [ɔcɪrɛɪ]

Unfortunately for the phonologist, all Akan forms are not so well behaved. There are words which have a mixture of vowels from the two harmonising sets. That is the case in [o-ɲinsɛɲɪ-ɪ] 'she became pregnant'. This is an instance of OPAQUE ASSOCIATION, i.e. some of the vowels are linked to harmonising features in the underlying representation. The infinitive form of this verb is:

[10.53]
$$\begin{bmatrix} [+\text{ATR}] & & [-\text{ATR}] \\ | & & \nearrow \\ \text{ɲ} & \text{i} & \text{n} & \text{s} & \text{ɛ} & \text{ɲ} \end{bmatrix}$$ 'to become pregnant'

The derivation of [o-ɲinsɛɲɪ-ɪ] proceeds as in [10.54]:

$$\begin{bmatrix} [+\text{ATR}] & & [-\text{ATR}] \\ | & & \nearrow \\ \text{O-ɲ} & \text{i} & \text{n} & \text{s} & \text{ɛ} & \text{nɪ} - \text{ɪ} \end{bmatrix} \rightarrow \begin{bmatrix} [\text{ATR}] & & [-\text{ATR}] \\ \wedge & & \wedge \\ \text{o-ɲi} & \text{n} & \text{s} \text{ɛ} \text{ɲ} \text{ɪ} - \text{ɪ} \end{bmatrix}$$

Vowel harmony is of theoretical interest because of what it reveals of the 'slicing' phenomenon. A phonological parameter may be selected for different degrees of suprasegmentalisation: it may be put on an entirely separate tier, like stress or tone in many languages; or it may be only partially suprasegmentalised, like vowel harmony in those languages where certain features are sometimes put on a separate tier and sometimes treated as an integral part of vowel phonemes.

10.8 Nasalisation

Like vowel harmony, NASALITY, is another phonological parameter that can be suprasegmentalised. Normally, the specification [+nasal] is an integral part of nasal consonants (and possibly nasal vowels). However, in some languages this feature is extracted from the segmental tier and placed on the suprasegmental tier so that it characterises several syllables or morphemes or even entire words.

Desano, a Colombian language of the Amazon basin, is a standard example of a language which treats nasalisation as a suprasegmental element. Native Desano words consist of morphemes which are either all oral or all nasal:

[10.55] Desano (Kaye 1971)

nasal		oral	
[wãĩ]	'name'	[wai]	'fish'
[nõhsõ]	'kind of bird'	[johso]	'kind of lizard'
[sẽnãnũ]	'pineapple'	[goru]	'ball'
[mĩnĩnũl]	'a small round thing'	[wyariru]	'a large round thing'

The voiceless segments /p t k s h/ are NEUTRAL. They are neither capable of bearing the property of nasalisation, nor of inhibiting its spread. They are 'invisible' to the nasalisation rule. But voiced segments are all capable of bearing nasalisation: they have both oral and nasalised versions:

[10.56]

Oral	Nasal
v	ṽ
b	m
d/r	n
g	ŋ
j	ɲ
w	w̃

In Desano, nasalisation is not simply a property of certain consonants. It is extracted from the segmental tier and placed on a separate suprasegmental tier. To represent the Desano situation rules like [10.57] are needed:

[10.57]

$$\begin{bmatrix} [+\text{nasal}] \\ \nwarrow \uparrow \nearrow \\ w \quad a \quad i \end{bmatrix} \rightarrow [\text{w̃ãĩ}] \qquad \begin{bmatrix} [-\text{nasal}] \\ \nwarrow \uparrow \nearrow \\ w \quad a \quad i \end{bmatrix} \rightarrow [\text{wai}]$$

Where there are neutral voiceless consonants, the mapping proceeds in the same way, only this time being blind to the presence of voiceless consonants:

[10.58]

$$\begin{bmatrix} [+\text{nasal}] \\ \nwarrow \uparrow \\ \text{johso} \end{bmatrix} \longrightarrow \text{ɲõhsõ}$$

In the discussion of both vowel harmony and nasalisation I have used the concept of SPREADING. Originally spreading was seen as a unique property of tone. In recent years, however, it has been suggested by a number of linguists (Steriade 1982; Hayes 1986; Archangeli and Pulleyblank 1986; Hyman and Pulleyblank 1987) that all assimilation should be treated as spreading. That includes processes like voice assimilation, palatalisation and place of articulation assimilation which were dealt with by feature copying rules in the past. This is in conformity with the view of speech outlined in Chapter 4.

10.9 Morphemic tier

Students of Semitic morphology have extended the theory of autosegmental phonology in other directions. McCarthy (1979, 1981) has proposed the setting up of a morphemic tier for languages like Arabic and Hebrew. Usually in a Semitic language words are formed by adding vowels to a SKELETON root which consists of three consonants.

Thus, in Egyptian Arabic the root meaning 'write' is *ktb*, and the root meaning 'understand' is *fhm*. Various word-forms are derived by adding vowels (and in some cases consonants) to these skeletal consonantal roots:

[10.59] (a) katab 'he wrote' fihim 'he understood'

(b) katbu 'they wrote' fihmu 'they understood'

(c) kattib 'he caused to write' fahhim 'caused to understand' (i.e. he explained)

McCarthy's proposal is that the verb is made up of co-existent representations on three separate tiers. There is a CV-SKELETON which is the consonantal root. Two other tiers are linked to this: a consonantal tier and a vowel tier containing the vowel pattern of the word which is mapped in a manner reminiscent of tone melodies in Mende.

[10.60]

Now provide a derivation similar to [10.60] for *katab, katbu* and *kattib*.

Your solution should be essentially the same as that given in [10.60] except for the root consonants which in this case are *ktb* instead of *fhm*.

We have seen that Arabic regular verbs have a triconsonantal root to which various vowel melodies are added, depending on the grammatical form required. Interestingly, wherever there are more slots for C or V segments on the skeletal tier than there are vowels or consonants on the vowel or consonant tier, a phenomenon akin to tone spreading takes place. A single vowel or consonant is linked to two C or V slots as is required by the WFC. Such a segment is realised as geminate in the phonetic representation (section 9.4.3).

Thus notions of nonlinear phonology, originally proposed in order to deal with tone, turn out to make correct predictions for totally unrelated phenomena like vowel harmony, nasalisation and Semitic concatenative (infixing) morphology. This has encouraged linguists to believe that significant principles of linguistic organisation have been unearthed.

In the next chapter we shall consider another non-linear approach to phonology which has been very successful in the analysis of stress and is inspired by principles similar to those of autosegmental phonology.

Exercises

1. Bekwarra (Nigeria) (SIL *Introduction to Phonemic Analysis*, 1980 page 159)
    Study the data below where high, mid and low tones are respectively marked by the diacritics ´ ¯ and `.

ókú	'match'	ápī	'cow'	úkò	'parrot'
īké	'baboon'	īgē	'water yam'	ījè	'mother'
ùbú	'goat'	ùpù	'vulture'	áwù	'measuring bowl'
idē	'father'	inē	'gun'	àlà	'bird'
ùsī	'snake'	àbì	'charcoal'	ūbì	'gun powder'

(a) What is the function of tone in Bekwarra?

(b) Is Bekwarra a register tone or a contour tone language? What is your evidence?

2. Kombe (based on Elimelech 1976b)
   In Kombe, a Bantu language spoken in Rio Muni (Equatorial Guinea) there are only two underlying phonemic tone oppositions, namely high and low. But five phonetic tones occur phonetically. Thus nouns in isolation exhibit the following five tones in the phonetic representation:

H	(high)	[V́]	[⌐]
L	(low)	[V̀]	[⌐]
L°	(unreleased low)	[V°]	[–]
F	(falling)	[v̂]	[⌐]
D	downstep high	[V]	[—]

   In the examples in (a) below the tones L, L°, D and F are shown on the final syllable of nouns:

(a) tàbà   [_ _]   'goat'
    L L

    èlè°   [_ _]   'tree'
    L L°

    célé   [⁻ ⁻]   'sand'
    H D

    kûbà   [⌐]   'chicken'
    F L

    èbô   [⌐]   'hand'
    L F

It is interesting to note that nouns in isolation never end on a high tone.

(b) Kombe shows an interesting distinction between nouns occurring in *isolation* or *prepause position* and those nouns which occur *within a phrase*.

isolation		*inside a phrase* (e.g. identification)		
tàbà	'goat'	tàbà	ndîrà	'that's a goat'
		goat	is that	
èlè°	'tree'	èlé	ndîrà	'that's a tree'
		tree	is that	
célé	'sand'	célé	ndîrà	'that's sand'
		sand	is that	

kû6à	'chicken'	kú6à	ndîrà	'that's a chicken'
		chicken	is that	
ìbûmù	'belly'	ìbùmù	ndíɟîrà	'that's a belly'
		belly	is A that	
		(where A = agreement)		
ɓìɲɔ̀nì°	'bird'	ɓìɲɔ̀ní	ndíɓîrà	'that's a bird'
		bird	is A that	
ìkáyí	'leaf'	ìkáyí	ndíɟîrà	'that's a leaf'
		leaf	is A that	
ìlâlì	'stone'	ìláli	ndíɟîrà	'that's a stone'
		stone	is A that	
ìlɔ̂	'ear'	ìlɔ̂	ndíɟîrà	'that's an ear'

isolation		*in phrase final position*	
kû6à	'chicken'	à tóyèndì kûbà	'he saw a chicken'
ìlâlì	'stone'	à tóyèndì ìlâlì	'he saw a stone'
èlè°	'tree'	à tóyèndì èlè°	'he saw a tree'
ɓìɲɔ̀nì	'bird'	à tóyèndì ɓìɲɔ̀nì°	'he saw a bird'
célé	'sand'	à tóyèndì célé	'he saw sand'
ìkáyi	'leaf'	à tóyèndì ìkáyi	'he saw a leaf'

Attempt the following problems:

(i) List all the tonal alternations in nouns observed in comparing the left and right columns.

(ii) Suggest rules to predict the occurrence of:
   (a) F i.e. falling tones (ˆ)
   (b) L° i.e. unreleased low (L°)
   (c) D i.e. downstep high tones (')

Notes

1. Firthian prosodic analysis rejects the structuralist phonemicist's position presented here. Prosodic analysis assumes a more complex view of phonological structure. Phonological representations are said to consist of PHONEMATIC UNITS (roughly equivalent to consonants and vowels) and PROSODIES like tone, stress, vowel harmony, voicing and nasalisation (Palmer 1970).

2. Where a floating tone does surface in some realisations of a morpheme (as is the case in the Mende example

in [10.19]), the idea of floating tones is not very controversial. However, there is considerable disagreement as to whether it is justifiable to posit an abstract floating tone (which never surfaces anywhere phonetically) the existence of which can only be detected from the tonal perturbations which it causes.

The analysis of the Etsako associative marker as a floating high tone is an example of an abstract floating tone. The validity of this analysis is disputed by those who object to underlying representations which are distant from phonetic representations. The essence of the criticism is similar to that made against abstract segments at the level of segmental phonology (see section 8.2). Critics of very abstract underlying representations would prefer to interpret problematic tonal alternations like that in Etsako in terms of lexical or grammatical conditioning. They would argue, for instance, that instead of a rule like [10.25] the grammar of Etsako should contain a statement to the effect that the associative marker conditions the change of a low tone into a falling tone on the first syllable of the second noun in an associative construction if that noun begins with a low tone.

CHAPTER 11
Stress and intonation

11.1 Introduction: stress

This chapter is in two sections. The first section introduces
you to the description of STRESS using a non-linear
approach known as METRICAL PHONOLOGY. The
second part is devoted to intonation.

11.1.1 What is stress?

Linguists have an intuitive understanding of the phonetic
properties of stress although they find formulating a precise
description of these properties problematic. Stress is
primarily a matter of greater AUDITORY PROMI-
NENCE. It is essentially a perceptual phenomenon, with
ill-defined articulatory correlates. An element that is stressed
is highlighted so that it becomes auditorily more salient than
the rest of the elements in the string of which it is a part.
The main phonetic ingredients of stress are PITCH,
LENGTH and LOUDNESS. Stressed syllables tend to have
higher pitch and longer duration than their non-stressed
counterparts. In addition, they may be somewhat louder
than unstressed syllables; but loudness is a much less
important parameter than pitch or length. There may be
also increased respiratory energy in the production of a
stressed syllable although this is by no means essential.
Additionally, in some languages, vowels in stressed syllables have clear or full vowel quality while vowels in
unstressed syllables are reduced and have a somewhat
'muffled' quality like that of schwa (/ə/) in English. The
phonetic properties of stress will not be explored in this
book. Rather it is the phonological properties that will be
investigated.

From a phonological angle, several different kinds of stress can be recognised. One kind is WORD STRESS. In English, for instance, every lexical item is entered in the dictionary with word stress. A particular syllable of a word is pronounced in a way that makes it more prominent than the rest. If you say words like *mother, better, cotton* and *pity*, you will notice that the first syllable in all these words is much more salient than the second. The first syllable is said to be *stressed* and the second one *unstressed*.

In longer words, there is often not just one stressed syllable and a host of unstressed ones. Besides the syllable that receives the *main* or *primary* stress, there are other syllables which receive *secondary* stress. Such syllables are more prominent than the weakest syllables of the word.

If you say the word *radiator* very carefully, you will notice that the first syllable receives primary stress and that the third syllable has secondary stress; it is more prominent than the second and fourth, though not as prominent as the first. Trager and Smith (1951) introduced the convention of recognising four levels of stress in English, marked as ' ^ ` ˇ to indicate decreasing order of prominence.

The authors of SPE continue this tradition. Their view is that at least five degrees of stress can be easily detected in English. They use the integers 1–4 to mark stress, with 1 as the strongest and 4 the weakest stress. They suggest that unstressed syllables i.e. [-stress] are 'representable as [5 stress] in this case' (SPE, page 116). In practice, for convenience, unstressed syllables are not assigned any integer, as you can see from the examples below which are taken from SPE:

[11.1]
1 3	1 3
absolute	survey (noun)
1 3	1 3
kaleidoscope	advocate
3 1	3 1
intercept	interlock
2 1	2 1
mentality	gestation
2 3 1	2 3 1
relaxation	deportation

3   4 1   3   4 1
instrumentality   complementarity
3   4 1   3   4 1
documentation   experimentation

Mark the most prominent syllable in the following words:

[11.2a] market   water   chemistry   little
         analyse   equality   antagonise   indemnify

The task set above involves assigning the appropriate integer to each stressed syllable (and nothing to any unstressed one). You were expected to work out an answer along these lines:

[11.2b] 1   1   1   1
      market   water   chemistry   little
      1 3   3 1   1 3   1   3
      analyse   equality   antagonise   indemnify

The analysis of English stress presented in [11.2b] might give the impression that stress is a matter of absolute prominence attached to each syllable and that it can be indicated by unambiguously placing the appropriate diacritic on the syllable in question. Disputes, to a large extent sterile, have arisen in the past as to the precise number of degrees of stress which a language like English has. Are all the weak syllables left unmarked (which could be assigned degree 5 of stress) equal in prominence? For instance, is the final syllable of *chemistry* not somewhat more salient than the middle one? And, furthermore, is the final syllable of *chemistry* not stronger than the last syllable of

                            3 1   1   3
water? And are the vowels of *equality* and *indemnify* which are given degree 3 of stress equal in prominence? Reaching agreement on the exact number of degrees of stress has turned out to be almost impossible. The problem is that the syllable that is most heavily stressed in a word (and is therefore assigned degree 1 of stress) is easy to identify. But there is often some uncertainty as to the degree of stress of the less heavily stressed syllables. It is difficult

to determine whether or not a given non-primary stress is equivalent to some other non-primary stress in prominence.

Fortunately, research has shifted in a more fruitful direction in recent years. Following Liberman and Prince (1977) many linguists today recognise that a theory of stress must take on board the fact that prominence is a RELATIONAL concept. What matters is that a stressed syllable is more salient than its unstressed counterparts.

Examine some familiar noun-verb pairs in [11.3] which are distinguished by stress.

[11.3] *verb*	*Noun*
project	project
reject	reject
conduct	conduct
protest	protest
refuse	refuse

Add three examples of your own to the list in [11.3]. Underline the syllable that receives primary stress in each example in [11.3].

One of the things which these data show is that stress is not an integral part of a vowel. In many disyllabic words in English the location of stress depends on whether the word appears as a noun or as a verb: stress falls on the first syllable when the word is used as a noun and on the second when it is used as a verb. This shows in a simple way that stress is an autosegmental property of the entire word.

The words in [11.3] are in no way extraordinary. There are numerous examples of English words in which stress shows a considerable degree of mobility. Say the following, noting the syllable with the main or primary stress:

[11.4] (a) nation national nationalist nationalise
(b) nationality nationalistic nationalisation

Underline the syllable which receives the main stress on each occasion.

This should be enough to convince you that stress is not an inherent property of any vowel. In [11.4a] the first syllable receives the main stress regardless of the presence or absence of suffixes. But when certain suffixes are present, as in [11.4b] stress shifts from the first syllable to the syllable immediately preceding the suffix. Stress is not an inherent vowel feature. It is an autosegmental property of the word. Its location in the phonetic representation of a word may depend on the presence of certain affixes or grammatical information such as whether the word is realised as a noun or as a verb.

11.1.2 Metrical phonology

METRICAL PHONOLOGY is an approach developed within the generative phonology framework in recent years to handle stress phenomena. It complements AUTOSEGMENTAL PHONOLOGY which, as we saw in the last chapter, was primarily designed for the description of tone although it was used later to account for other aspects of phonology.

We have seen that stress is a relational concept: a stressed syllable is more prominent than an unstressed one. This fact is regarded as crucial in metrical phonology. Relative prominence is expressed using BINARY BRANCHING TREES, which are labelled STRONG (s) and WEAK (w). The more prominent syllable is dominated by s (i.e. it lies below s on the tree) and the less prominent one is dominated by w.

[11.5]

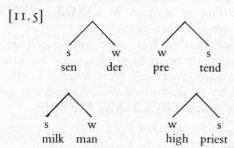

Strong and weak syllables are paired together by a procedure called FOOT FORMATION. What is proposed is that stress is assigned to strings which have constituent structure consisting of two elements, one of which is strong (i.e. dominant) and the other weak (i.e. subordinate). The dominant one is the HEAD. The head governs its immediate neighbour to the left or right. In [11.5] a number of metrical feet are exemplified, with the head coming first or second.

The structure of metrical feet plays an important role in English poetry. Find examples of poems where right-headed and left-headed metrical feet are used. What are the literary terms for these feet?

This short passage from Shakespeare illustrates right-headed metrical feet:

Hĕ cán | nŏt líve, | Ĭ hópe, | ănd múst | nŏt díe
Tĭll Geórge | bĕ páck'd | wĭth póst-| hŏrse úp | tŏ heáven.
Ĭ'll ín, | tŏ úrge | hĭs hát | rĕd móre | to Clárénce
Wĭth lies | wĕll steél'd | wĭth weigh | tў ár | gŭménts . . .
          (William Shakespeare *Richard III*, I.I. 145–8)
(Note: V̆ indicates a weak syllable and V́ a strong syllable.)

The above lines of blank (i.e. non-rhyming) verse typically contain five feet. Each foot in turn tends to contain an unstressed (weak) syllable which is followed by a stressed (strong) one. As you will recall from the discussion of Latin metre in (9.5) this pattern is called IAMBIC METRE. (To be precise, this extract is written in IAMBIC PENTA-METRE i.e. there are five feet in each line.)

A variety of left-headed feet were introduced in our brief account of Latin metre in (9.5). Examine an English example of left-headed metrical feet where a stressed syllable is followed by an unstressed one. As in Latin verse, this verse pattern is called TROCHAIC METRE:

Hoẃ thĕ | Chímnĕy | sweépĕr's | crý
Éverў | bláckn'ing | Chúrch ăp | páls;
Ánd thĕ | háplĕss | sóldier's | sigh
Rúns ín | bloód dŏwn | Pálăce | wálls.
          (From William Blake *London, Songs of experience*)

The account of relative prominence given in [11.5] only deals with disyllabic words. Initially, I was careful to avoid longer words for clarity's sake. But in fact, such words can be comfortably handled by assuming that phonological systems are HIERARCHICAL and that the concept of relative prominence is applicable at various points in the hierarchy. The rank which we considered in [11.5] is that of the FOOT. Adjacent syllables were grouped together and one of them was identified as being more salient than its neighbour. Where a word contains more than two syllables, the same manoeuvre can be repeated, with adjacent feet being grouped together in order to establish which one of them is more salient. Consider

[11.6]

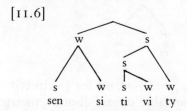

This procedure is known as WORD-TREE FORMATION. We can identify the antepenultimate syllable -ti- as the one receiving primary stress. By inspecting the tree, we can establish that it is dominated by more s's than any other syllable. Degrees of stress are read off the tree by counting the number of s nodes that dominate a particular syllable: the more s nodes there are above a syllable in the tree, the more heavily stressed that syllable is.

Unfortunately, the model just outlined does not always yield the correct results. It fails to capture some prominence distinctions in English. For instance, it would lead us to construct the following trees for *radio, rabbi, racer* and *racy*:

[11.7] (a)

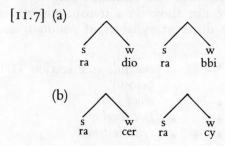

(b)

The trees in [11.7] are identical. But we know that the final syllable of the words in [11.7a] is more prominent than the final syllable of the words in [11.7b]. To solve this problem, Liberman and Prince (1977) proposed the retention of the SPE segmental feature [± stress] in their metrical theory of stress. If that is done, [11.7] can be re-written as [11.8], bringing out clearly the differences in the relative prominence of the final vowel:

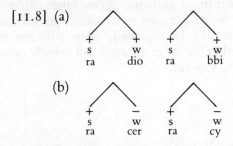

[11.8] (a)

	+	+	+	+
	s	w	s	w
	ra	dio	ra	bbi

(b)

	+	−	+	−
	s	w	s	w
	ra	cer	ra	cy

(Here + stands for [+stress] and − stand for [−stress])

There is some understandable unease about a metrical, nonsegmetal theory of stress which sets out to show the relational nature of stress allowing binary segmental feature [±stress] to play a role in metrical trees. A simpler way of showing the relative salience of syllables which overcomes this problem is proposed by Prince (1983). He advocates the construction of a METRICAL GRID. This is done by representing information of the kind contained in a metrical tree as an array of asterisks. One asterisk is assigned to each syllable at the syllable tier, an additional asterisk is assigned to the stronger syllable in each foot, and if necessary, at word level a further asterisk is assigned to the strongest foot which is nearest the beginning or the end of the word, depending on the preference of a particular language.

Using a grid we can show in a transparent way the relative stress of the different syllables of *sensitivity* as in [11.9]

[11.9]

```
                *              end rule (see section 11.1.3
                               below)
       *        *              word level
       *        *        *     foot level
       *    *   *    *   *     syllable level
     sensitivity
```

Although trees and grids can convey the same information, grids are preferable because they do so in a more perspicuous manner.

Convert the metrical trees in [11.5] into metrical grids.

11.1.3 Metrical trees and grids

If you cast your eye back to [11.5], you will observe that in words like *sender* the left syllable is stronger than the right one in the same foot while in a word like *pretend* the right-hand syllable is the stronger of the two. Trees like those in [11.5] where one syllable functions as the HEAD and governs the syllable that immediately precedes or follows it are said to be BOUNDED.

In addition to bounded trees, there exist UN-BOUNDED trees where a head governs not just one adjacent syllable, but all the syllables that precede or follow it. This is the situation in a language where primary stress always falls either on the initial or final syllable of a word.

Hayes (1981) provides a typological classification of metrical systems. He shows that in some languages, such as Maranungku (Australia), primary stress falls on the first syllable, and secondary stress on alternate syllables to its right:

[11.10]

tíralk	'saliva'
mérepèt	'beard'
yángarmàta	'the Pleiades'
lángkaràtetì	'prawn'
wélepènemànta	'kind of duck'

An unbounded tree with a dominant left node [11.11] is needed to describe the facts of Maranungku:

[11.11]

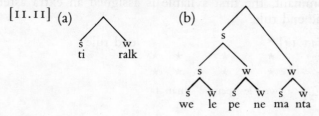

Contrasting with a language of this kind, are languages like French which have unbounded trees with a dominant right node. In French stress falls on the last syllable of a word:

[11.12] pe*tit* 'little'
encoura*ger* 'encourage'
télécommunica*tion* 'telecommunication'

Draw an unbounded tree to represent stress in French *télécommunication*.

The tree required is [11.13]

[11.13]

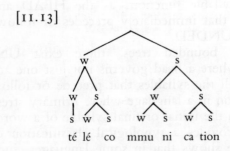

té lé co mmu ni ca tion

The head is on the right and it can have an indefinite number of subordinate syllables preceding it.

Maranungku and French are not unusual. In many languages, primary stress falls at or near the periphery of a word. Metrical grid theory reflects this fact by incorporating the END RULE convention. This convention is responsible for the addition of extra salience (shown by an extra asterisk on a metrical grid) to the most prominent left-hand or right-hand column of a word, depending on whether a language favours the beginning or the end of the word as the locus of primary stress.

In Maranungku where the left-hand edge of the word is dominant, the first syllable is assigned an extra asterisk by the end rule:

[11.14]

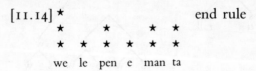

we le pen e man ta

end rule

In Weri (Papua–New Guinea) (Hayes 1981) the situation is reversed. The final syllable is dominant and alternating secondary stress is put on the syllables preceding it in a word.

[11.15]

```
                    ★
            ★   ★   ★
        ★ ★ ★ ★ ★
        akunetepal  →  àkunètepál        'times'
```

11.1.4 Extrametricality

In some languages, such as Finnish and Hungarian, primary stress normally falls on the initial syllable while in other languages, such as Cambodian and Modern Hebrew, it is the final syllable that gets primary stress. In systems of this kind all syllables are taken into account in deciding where to put stress.

However, in many other languages syllables at word fringes are ignored by stress assignment rules. Such syllables are said to be EXTRAMETRICAL. They are completely 'invisible' to the rules which assign stress (see extrasyllabicity in (9.7)). The concept of extrametricality is useful in the treatment of languages which have their main stress on the PENULTIMATE syllable of the word. In these languages, the last syllable is 'not seen' by the algorithm which proceeds to put stress on the second last syllable. Swahili is a typical example of such a language (the extrametrical final syllable is put in parentheses):

[11.16]	pí(ga)	'hit, beat'
	pigá(na)	'fight, hit each other'
	pigani(sha)	'cause to fight'
	tutawapí(ga)	'we shall beat them'

While in Swahili, which has penultimate main stress, it is the final syllable of a word that is extrametrical, in Native American languages like Dakota, Northern Paiute and Southern Paiute, where main stress falls on the second syllable of the word, it is the first syllable that is extrametrical.

11.1.5 Quantity sensitivity

We have seen above some of the typological parameters used in the study of stress: languages may have bounded as opposed to unbounded trees; the left or the right end of the word may be dominant; either all syllables in a word may be taken into account by stress placement rules or some of them may be extrametrical. Typological considerations of this kind are important because linguistic theory is concerned not only with the description of particular languages, but also with an exploration of the parameters within which languages can differ. For, as I have stressed at various points in the book, differences between languages occur within certain pre-set limits.

In this section we are going to examine a further typological parameter, namely whether stress placement in a given language is sensitive to the internal structure of the syllable that bears it. In particular we shall consider the role of SYLLABLE WEIGHT in stress placement. In the examples discussed above, no mention was made of syllable weight because in the languages which were cited, the internal structure of syllables is not taken into account in determining where to put stress. Syllables are treated in the same way irrespective of whether they are light or heavy.

The languages described in the last few paragraphs have SYLLABLE QUANTITY INSENSITIVE STRESS RULES. You will recall that we broached the subject of SYLLABLE QUANTITY SENSITIVE STRESS rules when examining Latin syllable structure in Chapter 9. Like the Swahili rule, the Latin stress rule treats the last syllable as extrametrical, and ignores it. But there the resemblance ends. While the Swahili rule puts primary stress on any penultimate syllable, the Latin rule is choosy. It puts stress on a penultimate syllable only if it has got a branching rhyme (i.e. it has either a long vowel or is closed by a consonant). The Latin stress rule can be re-stated as [11.17]:

[11.17] (i) ignore the final syllable: it is extrametrical;
(ii) construct an unbounded right-headed tree;
(iii) put primary stress on the first heavy syllable at the right-hand side of the word if it is in penultimate position (excluding the final syllable which is extrametrical);

(iv) if the penultimate syllable is light, put primary stress on the ante-penultimate syllable.

Use [11.17] to predict the syllable which gets primary stress in [11.18]:

[11.18] (a) amō   'I love'
     (b) amāmus   'we love'
     (c) amābāmus 'we loved'
     (d) amābimus 'we shall love'
     (e) amāverās   'you had loved'
     (f) amābantur 'they will be loved'

Your solution should be along these lines (V́ indicates primary stress):

[11.19] (a) á(mō)

Since the final syllable is always extrametrical and therefore irrelevant for stress placement purposes, in disyllabic words primary stress must be on the first syllable regardless of its structure.

     (b) amá(mus)

The penultimate syllable contains a long vowel and therefore counts as heavy. It receives the stress.

     (c) amābá(mus)

The penultimate syllable is stressed again because it is heavy.

     (d) amábi(mus)

The penultimate syllable only has a short vowel in the rhyme; it is light. Stress skips it and lands on the ante-penultimate.

     (e) amáve(rās)

The statement made for (d) above covers this.

     (f) amābán(tur)

The penultimate syllable has a branching rhyme consisting of a vowel followed by a consonant. It is heavy. It receives the stress.

11.1.6 English stress

I shall now illustrate the theory of metrical phonology by sketching an outline description of aspects of stress in English. The stress system of English is extremely complex. Here I can only give you a flavour of a metrical analysis of the system. To come to grips with the intricacies of English stress, you will need to study the works cited in the bibliography.[1]

As a rule, unless they are long or complex, grammatical words like prepositions and conjunctions do not receive primary word stress. (But long grammatical words, e.g. the preposition *underneath* and the conjunction *notwithstanding* receive primary word stress.) All lexical words, i.e. nouns, adjectives, verbs and adverbs must have one syllable which receives primary stress; obviously, in monosyllabic words like *dog, look* and *bag*, the only syllable that there is must be stressed. Word stress rules are needed in the grammar to account for the location of stress in words of two or more syllables. Only one syllable receives primary stress and the rest are subordinated to that syllable.

First consider stress placement in a few disyllabic verbs:

[11.20] (a) order   ferry cover   carry   dither copy
        (b) open   lollop hiccup lavish covet   pocket

[11.21] (a) compare delay endow   enjoy   survey prefer
        (b) corrode avoid refine design amuse   presume
        (c) concoct enlist protect attend assent announce

Suggest a rule (or rules) to account for the placement of primary stress in these words.

Your rule needs to be quantity sensitive. It must make crucial reference to syllable weight. What is needed is an algorithm which constructs a right-headed bounded tree over the word and places main stress on the first heavy syllable, counting from the right-hand end of the word. Where disyllabic verbs contain no heavy syllables, stress falls by default on the first syllable. But otherwise stress falls on the right-handmost heavy syllable.

Thus, in [11.20a] there is no heavy syllable. So, primary stress falls by default on the first syllable in words like *copy* and *ferry*. In [11.20b] the second syllable contains a short vowel and a consonant. On the face of it, the second syllable should count as heavy. But it does not. This is because the last consonant of a verb is extrametrical, i.e. it is 'not seen' by stress rules. A word like *lavish* [lævɪ(ʃ)] is only scanned up to the vowel [ɪ]. Consequently its final syllable is classed as light and primary stress goes on the first syllable.

In [11.21a], on the other hand, in each case the second syllable contains a long vowel or diphthong. This makes it heavy and capable of bearing primary stress. In [11.21b] too the final consonant is extrametrical but this does not prevent primary stress falling on the second syllable. This is because the part of the syllable that is seen contains a long vowel or diphthong (see *avoid* [əvɔɪ(d)]). Finally, in [11.21c] stress once more falls on the second syllable. In these words the second syllable has two consonants following the vowel. Even though the last consonant is extrametrical, it is the second syllable which is nevertheless stressed. This is due to the fact that the part of that syllable which is 'seen' by the stress rule counts as heavy because it contains a short vowel followed by a consonant (see *enlist* [enlɪs(t)]).

Note in passing, however, that the rule stated above is not exceptionless. Words ending in [əʊ] (like *follow* and *sorrow*) are stressed on the first syllable although the second syllable contains a diphthong and 'ought to be' regarded as heavy.

Disyllabic adjectives are subject to the same rule as verbs. Adjectives like *tender, tiny* and *holy* which contain no heavy syllables are stressed on the initial syllable. Adjectives like *evil, timid* and *livid* whose second syllable ends in a consonant and therefore 'ought to be' heavy are, in fact, stressed on the first syllable because the final consonant is extrametrical. The part of the syllable that is 'seen' by the rule is light (a consonant followed by a short vowel). Lastly, adjectives like *robust, morose* and *alive* are stressed on the second syllable because their second syllables are heavy.

Next, let us turn to disyllabic nouns.

Begin by marking the syllable which receives primary stress in the words below:

[11.22] (a) pity   baby   sugar   river
            picture ferry   panda   butter
        (b) magic   tulip   mason   foetus
        (c) almond contact subject dentist
        (d) canoe   bamboo   bazaar   settee
        (e) police alert   debate   cartoon

In [11.22a–c] primary stress falls on the first syllable while in [11.22d–e] it falls on the second syllable. As before, a right-headed tree is constructed for each word. Where there is no heavy syllable, a disyllabic word is stressed on the first syllable. But if a word contains a heavy syllable, stress goes on the heavy syllable nearest to the end of the word.

Note, however, this crucial difference between nouns on the one hand and verbs and adjectives on the other: for the purposes of this rule, a heavy syllable in a noun must contain a long vowel or diphthong. While in verbs and adjectives only the final consonant is extrametrical, in nouns, any consonants following the final vowel are extrametrical. This means that the presence of consonants after a vowel does not contribute to syllable weight in nouns.

Thus, in [11.22a] nouns like *pity*, whose second syllable is light are stressed on the first syllable. Similarly, the first syllable is stressed in both [11.22b and c] because of the extrametricality of any consonant following the vowel in the second syllable. Consequently, the part of the second syllable that is 'seen' contains a short (lax) vowel and therefore cannot be stressed.

However, nouns like *police* [11.22e] whose second syllable contains a long vowel (followed by one or more extrametrical consonants), are stressed on the second syllable just like nouns such as *canoe* [11.22d] which end in a long vowel or diphthong. All that matters is whether or not the second syllable contains a long vowel or diphthong. In other words, with regard to the disyllabic noun stress rule, only the nucleus of the second syllable is projected. The noun stress rule only 'sees' the syllable nucleus: if the nucleus branches (i.e. contains a long vowel or diphthong), stress is on the final syllable. Otherwise, stress is on the initial syllable.

We can now move on to longer words. We shall observe that the stress rule that applies in longer words is reminiscent of the Latin stress rule.

Study the data in [11.23] and work out the rule that determines location of primary stress:

[11.23] (a) cinema   Agatha   effigy   Malibu
            jeopardy overture calumny   Salisbury
        (b) Galapagos Antigone America   rhinoceros
            epitome
        (c) tornado   rhododendron   aroma
            psychosis bronchitis   Theresa
            brontosaurus

As in Latin, the stress placement algorithm creates a right-hand headed tree, ignoring the final syllable, which is extrametrical. Stress lands on the penultimate syllable if it is heavy [see 11.23c], but if the penultimate is light, stress goes on the ante-penultimate syllable (see [11.23a, b]).

Up to this point we have only considered stress in simple words. We have not examined yet the problem of stress placement in complex words which consist of a root and one or more affixes, which may be prefixes or suffixes. Interestingly, in English the addition of a prefix tends not to affect the placement of stress. Usually words are stressed in the same way with or without prefixes:

[11.24] write   rewrite   políte   impolíte
        exámine   re-exámine grátitude ingrátitude
        polítical apolitical móral   amóral

The effect of the addition of suffixes is much more fascinating because different suffixes affect stress placement in different ways. First, there are suffixes whose presence has no effect on the primary stress of the root to which they are attached. A good example of this can be seen by observing what happens when the suffix -ment is added to a verb stem like góvern to yield the noun góvernment. The position of stress remains unchanged. Likewise, the suffixes *-ness* as in *kíndness* and *-ful* as in *fáithful* have no effect on stress.

Another class of suffixes attract stress to themselves as though they were magnets. When they are attached to a word they always get the main stress. They include *-étte* as in *maisonétte* and *kitchenétte*, *-ésque* as in *picturésque* and *grotésque*. (These suffixes are borrowed from French and obey the French stress rule.)

Add two more examples to this list.

A third class of suffixes make the primary stress move to the syllable immediately preceding them. That is the case when a suffix like *-ic* is added to a stem like *démocrat* to derive the adjective *democrátic* or when the suffix *-ity* is added to the stem *públic* to produce *publícity*.

(a) Write down three examples of words containing each of the suffixes *-some*, *-hood*, *-ity* and *-ic*.
(b) Contrast the effect on stress placement of the presence of the suffixes *-some* and *-hood* on the one hand and *-ity* and *-ic* on the other.

You will have discovered that *-some* and *-hood* have no effect on stress. A word is stressed on the same syllable with or without these suffixes. However, the suffixes *-ity* and *-ic* do affect stress placement in the base to which they are attached: they attract stress to the syllable immediately before them. Interestingly, the rule, which attracts stress to the syllable before the suffix is a QUANTITY INSENSI-TIVE rule – it puts stress on that syllable regardless of whether the syllable is light or heavy. Suffixes like *-ity* and *-ic* which attract stress to the syllable immediately preceding them are called STRONG MODE SUFFIXES.

There is a fourth category of suffixes which are similar to the strong mode suffixes in that they also affect stress placement in the base form to which they are attached although they are not stressed themselves. But unlike strong mode suffixes, this class contains QUANTITY SENSI-

TIVE suffixes which put stress on the immediately preceding syllable only if it is heavy either because it has a long vowel or a diphthong:

[11.25] adjectíval   arríval   homicídal
        betráyal   refúsal   recítal

or because it is closed by a consonant:

[11.26] departméntal   ornaméntal   detriméntal
        accidéntal

If the preceding syllable is light, stress misses it out and falls two syllables before it:

[11.27] problemátical   práctical   condítional
        munícipal   séasonal   proféssional

Sufffixes of this kind which only manage to attract stress to the syllable immediately before them if it is heavy, and otherwise attract stress to the second syllable to their left are called WEAK MODE SUFFIXES.

11.2 Intonation

All languages use pitch. This, in part, is an automatic consequence of the fact that any time a voiced sound is produced, the vocal cords vibrate at a certain rate. The rate of vibration corresponds closely to the pitch perceived by the hearer: the higher the rate of vibration the higher is the perceived pitch. The fact that pitch differences can be observed in the utterances of any language is in itself of no great linguistic interest.

What linguists are interested in are the ways in which pitch differences are functionally harnessed. In broad terms, pitch differences can be exploited in two distinct ways. Within the domain of the word, pitch can be used to contrast lexical meaning or to mark grammatical properties, as we saw in the last chapter. In that case we speak of *tone*. Alternatively, the domain of pitch can be an entire utterance, in which case we speak of *intonation*. It would be wrong to classify languages as either tonal or intonational because all languages have intonation. That includes tone languages, as the discussion of downdrift in Chapter 10 showed. One of the issues that has rightly received a good deal of attention from phonologists is the way in which intonation meshes together with stress in a stress language, and with tone in a tone language.

In the next section we shall outline some of the main features of English intonation. This sketch is not meant to be a comprehensive description. Rather it is merely intended to give us a glimpse at the workings of intonation in a stress language.[2]

11.2.1 The form of English intonation

Just as the syntactician focuses on the sentence as the key unit of grammatical analysis, the phonologist focuses on the TONE UNIT (also called the PHONOLOGICAL PHRASE) as the most significant domain in terms of which intonation contours reflecting the pitch of utterances are assigned.

For the purposes of intonation analysis, the English tone unit has the following internal organisation:

$$[11.28] \quad (pre\text{-}head) \quad head \quad \begin{array}{c} tonic \\ or \\ nucleus \end{array} \quad (tail)$$

The nucleus is the central element in a tone unit. It contains the syllable in an utterance which undergoes significant pitch movement – and is consequently more prominent than the rest. That syllable is the NUCLEUS or TONIC SYLLABLE. The tonic syllable is normally preceded by a HEAD. The head is the part of the tone unit extending from the first stressed syllable to the syllable immediately preceding the tonic syllable. Optionally, a head can be preceded by a PRE-HEAD. This consists of any unstressed syllables that occur in front of the first stressed syllable of the head. Again, optionally, a tonic syllable can be followed by a TAIL. The tail contains any syllables (which may or may not be stressed) following the tonic syllable.

Say the sentence in [11.29] noting the way pitch fluctuates. Produce two analogous examples of your own and state verbally the pitch movements which you observe.

[11.29]

|| He will | phone you when | *all* | the children are back. ||
Ph　　　　　 *H*　　　　　 *Ts* 　　　　　　 *T*

key: *Ph* = pre-head; *H* = head; *Ts* = tonic syllable; *T* = tail

---

Normally pitch is low in the pre-head, more or less level high in the head and falling on the tonic; in the tail the pitch pattern established on the tonic is simply continued.

The most common direction of pitch movement on the tonic is downward. As we saw in section 10.5, linguists talk of DOWNDRIFT in tone languages when they describe the tendency for high tones to be somewhat lowered when preceded by a low tone, a phenomenon which results in falling intonation. In many stress languages like English the same downdrift (also called DECLINATION LINE) can be observed. Frequently pitch moves down on the tonic syllable and remains down until the end of the utterance. Pitch tends to be much lower at the end of an utterance than it is at the beginning. FALLING INTONATION, which is exemplified by [11.30], is the unmarked intonation pattern in English.

[11.30]

'James Thurber was born in O`hio.

The widespread tendency to drop pitch as the end of an utterance approaches might have a physiological explanation. Possibly, as the speaker gradually runs out of breath, there is less and less air to cause the vibration of the vocal cords and consequently they vibrate more sluggishly and the pitch of the utterance goes down. (At the same time, in some languages like Luganda, the intensity of the signal also declines, so that the end of the utterance is auditorily less salient than the beginning.)

It is reasonable to ask what the functions of intonation are. Does pitch fluctuation serve any linguistic purpose? Some answers to this question are outlined below.

11.2.2 Accentuation function

Word stress interacts with intonation. One of the words in a sentence has a syllable which stands out above the rest. This is the syllable which has SENTENCE STRESS – also called TONIC STRESS. Such a syllable is sometimes referred to as the TONIC SYLLABLE. In unmarked cases, tonic stress goes on the syllable which carries primary word stress in the last lexical item of the tone unit. Such a lexical item is often a noun, an adjective or a verb. The tonic syllable is underlined in the examples below:

[11.31] They are _working_.
Joan has not _seen_ him.
The children are in the _playground_.

In marked cases, the above rule is superseded by a rule which allows CONTRASTIVE (or EMPHATIC) STRESS to fall on grammatical (function) words such as pronouns, prepositions and conjunctions if the speaker wishes, for some communicative reason, to draw attention to such words or alternatively, contrastive stress may occur on non-final lexical items:

[11.32] (a) _She_ is studying linguistics.
She _is_ studying linguistics.
She is _studying_ linguistics.
(b) _She_ travelled from London.
She travelled _from_ London.
She travelled _to_ London.
She _travelled_ to London.

How does the location of the tonic syllable affect the ways in which these sentences can be interpreted?

The accentual function is the most basic function of intonation. In unmarked cases tonic stress is often used to make a syllable in the lexical word containing new information stand out. But in marked cases, the tonic syllable can be the most prominent syllable of virtually any word which the speaker chooses to highlight.

11.2.3 Intonation and illocutionary force

The choice of intonation pattern is not entirely free. In a language such as English certain ILLOCUTIONARY ACTS (= acts of speaking) such as making statements and asking questions, are typically performed using certain intonation patterns. I use the word 'typically' advisedly. The deployment of intonation contours is not determined by rigid, exceptionless rules. A given illocutionary act may be performed without using the intonation pattern indicated here. But nevertheless, certain intonation patterns are much more likely to be used to perform certain illocutionary acts than others.

The tone unit type with a level head and a falling nucleus (' *h* ` *n*), which is the only one introduced so far, is unmarked. It is the intonation pattern that is assigned when there is no good reason for doing otherwise. For example, it is normally used in statements, in imperatives and in *wh-* questions (i.e. questions beginning with the words *why, where, when, what, which* etc.). You can verify this by reading the sentences below in a neutral way and observing the intonation contour which you use:

[11.33] (a) *Statements*: ' *h* ` *n*
'Mary lives in ` *Lancaster.*
'The shops are ` *closed.*

(b) *WH questions*: ' *h* ` *n*
'When did Mary ` *go* there?
'What is your ` *name*?

(c) *Imperatives*: ' *h* ` *n*
Just 'eat up your ` *dinner!*
`*Sit!*

Note: the head and tail are both optional. They can both be omitted from a tone unit, as in the last example. Only the nucleus is obligatory.

Besides falling intonation, another common (but somewhat marked) type is the LOW RISE ('h,n) where the head is level and the nucleus rises slightly. This pattern is often found in YES/NO QUESTIONS where the speaker queries an item and expects simple confirmation or denial:

[11.34] Are your 'friends going to the ,*party*?
Will you re'tire next ,*year*?

I will mention just one more tone unit type, HIGH RISE (' ' N). This has a level head and a high rising nucleus. The head may be optionally omitted. This is common in elliptical questions like:

[11.35] ' coming? ('Are you 'coming)
        ' tea anybody?
        ' taxi?

Optionally, the pitch of questions may be raised generally so that the upper range of the speaker's voice is employed.

11.2.4 The grammatical function of intonation

The interpretation of the meaning of a sentence in part involves knowing which words should be syntactically bracketed together. In writing, punctuation is used to group together words which grammatically and semantically form coherent units. In the spoken language intonation serves a similar purpose.

Clear evidence of this can be seen by observing the way in which intonation is used to resolve syntactic ambiguity. Many sentences which are potentially ambiguous on paper are not ambiguous in their spoken form. For a long time linguists have been aware that the syntactic bracketing of potentially ambiguous constructions like *old cars and buses* can be clarified by intonation. The whole phrase is said as one unit if both the *cars* and *buses* are *old*. But it is said with an intonation break after cars if it is only the *cars* that are *old*. Effectively, intonation is used to indicate whether the adjective modifies just the first noun or both nouns.

Say the sentences in [11.36] using in each case the intonation contour which reflects the syntactic bracketing. How do the sentences in each pair differ in meaning?

[11.36] (a) Rioting [young men] and [women] were arrested.
Rioting [young men and women] were arrested.
(b) They are [cooking apples].
They [are cooking] apples.

The syntactic functions of intonation can also be considered from the angle of language processing. We have seen that tone groups usually mark off major syntactic constituents like noun phrases and verb phrases. That is what enables them to disambiguate sentences. In addition, the syntactic units marked by intonation seem to have some kind of psychological relevance in language processing. Thus, it is decidedly odd to place a tone group boundary inside a syntactic constituent. Pauses and any hesitations tend to coincide with syntactic boundaries.

(a) Parse the sentences below and show their major syntactic units.

(b) Where could you hesitate in each one of these sentences? Where are the potential intonation breaks?

[11.37] (a) The man to whom John was talking gave him the book.

(b) Frank and David or Helen went to the party.

(c) When she left the dog started barking.

I hope you have discovered that the natural way of marking intonation boundaries and the places where hesitation is likely to occur involves identifying major syntactic divisions:

[11.38] (a) *subject (noun phrase)*
|| The man to whom John was talking |
predicate (verb phrase)
gave him the book.||

(b) *subject (noun phrase)*   *predicate (verb phrase)*
|| Frank and David or Helen | went to the party. ||

(c) *subordinate clause   main clause*
|| When she left | the dog started barking. ||

'GARDEN PATH' sentences like [11.38c], for which one of the most obvious parsings is wrong, are often assigned the wrong intonation before the speaker works out the correct syntactic analysis. You were probably momentarily tempted to parse c. thus:

[11.38] *|| When she left the dog | started barking.||

with an intonation break after *dog*, before you realised that
the principal division here is between the main clause and
the subordinate clause: *dog* is the subject of the verb *started*
in the main clause and not the object of the verb *left* in the
subordinate clause.

11.2.5 Attitudinal functions

Intonation also has an attitudinal function. Inferences can be
drawn from intonation about the speaker's ATTITUDE.
We all have heard someone say 'It was not what he said,
but the way he said it . . .' or 'It is the tone of voice she
used that really upset me'.

We can all mean different things with the same words
by modulating our intonation. Utterances may perform
different illocutionary acts depending on the speaker's attitude as it is revealed through intonation. An utterance like
sit down or *come back* can be a command, a polite invitation
or a threat.

The meaning of an utterance depends on many factors.
Most obviously it depends on the semantic content of the
words as well as the grammatical and logical relationships
between the words used in an utterance. Less obviously, it
depends on the CONTEXT OF UTTERANCE (the
linguistic context in which the words are uttered and the
background situation known to be relevant by both the
speaker and hearer); it depends on the PARALINGUISTIC
features, e.g. gestures, facial expression and voice quality
employed; and it depends on the intonation used by the
speaker. Intonation seems to play a role in conveying attitudinal meaning. But the contribution made by intonation
per se is not easy to isolate with any certainty. It is therefore
not feasible to establish a simple, direct correlation between
intonation and attitude.

One area where a clear link has been established is in
QUESTION TAGS. Normally, falling intonation in the
tag indicates a quest for confirmation:

[11.39] 'George is a ' lawyer, ' isn't he?

But rising intonation indicates a greater degree of uncertainty, with the speaker not merely seeking confirmation
but rather wanting to have a real doubt cleared:

[11.40] 'George is a ' lawyer, ,isn't he?

Elsewhere the link between intonation and attitude is obscure. At best what we can do is outline various factors affecting attitudinal judgements. But it would be rash to claim that these factors **determine** attitudinal judgements.

One important factor affecting attitudinal judgements is VOICE QUALITY. Phoneticians have become increasingly aware of the importance of voice quality as a factor influencing attitudinal judgements (Laver 1980; Knowles 1987: 211–14). Some of the properties of a speaker's voice are INDEXICAL in the sense that they convey some information about the speaker to the hearer. Some indexical features are relatively permanent. A speaker's sex, age, membership of a social group, regional origins or social class membership can often be inferred from voice quality. These indexical features cannot be easily changed by the speaker. Other indexical features of voice quality such as laryngitis or a cold or being drunk are more transient. The addressee can make various favourable or unfavourable judgements about the speaker on the basis of voice quality features of the kind that I have listed.

A speaker can also deliberately attempt to convey attitudinal information by combining a voice quality trait with a purposeful use of pitch. We observed above that the commonest intonation contour in English is a level head followed by a falling nucleus. The SLOPE (or gradient) of the fall is variable. In unmarked circumstances the fall is gentle. If a speaker opts for a very steep slope, this is likely to convey a peremptory, abrupt or domineering attitude, especially when accompanied with harsh voice quality.

Try saying 'Come here !' varying the slope and harshness of the voice quality. Describe the circumstances in which each version of the sentence would be appropriate.

A further variable which has to be considered is PITCH RANGE. There is some correlation between pitch range and emotion.

Say this sentence varying pitch range:

[11.41] (a) I am so glad to see you
(b) Hello!

If a total stranger ran up to you in the street and said

[11.42]

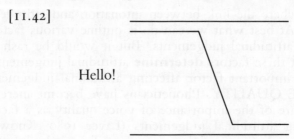

You would probably think it was a case of mistaken identity. If, on the other hand, when a long lost friend turns up at your door you say:

[11.43] I am so glad to see you again.

that would be interpreted as a frosty welcome.

When people are excited they use the upper part of their speech range much more than they do normally. This is usually accompanied by an increase in LOUDNESS and TEMPO. When depressed or sad, on the other hand, people tend to use mostly the lower part of their pitch range and to talk more slowly and more quietly.

There are no cast iron rules which govern the use of intonation to signal attitude. There are only tendencies. The right interpretation of an utterance depends only in part on intonation. As we saw above, there are many other variables which need to be considered. It would be naive to attempt to establish a simple, one-to-one correlation between attitude and intonation.

11.2.6 Discourse function

Talk rarely consists of isolated utterances. The norm is for utterances to be strung together, and in conversation for the roles of speaker and hearer to be swopped frequently. Intonation plays a crucial role in the structuring and gluing together of discourse.

Intonation is normally used to indicate NEW INFORMATION (which the addressee is assumed by the speaker

not to already possess) as opposed to GIVEN INFOR-
MATION (which is known or assumed to be already
known to the addressee). Given information is kept in the
background. It is not in FOCUS. But new information is
foregrounded. It is in focus. One of the words conveying
new information is highlighted by making one of its syllables the tonic syllable.

Imagine an exchange like [11.44] in a butcher's shop:

[11.44] John: Do you 'like ` tripe?
        Mary: I ` loathe tripe. (or *I ` loathe it*)

When John asks the question, *tripe* is new information and
receives tonic stress (the word 'information' is being used
in a very broad sense). But when Mary replies, *tripe* is
already established as the topic of the conversation and
needs no highlighting. So, tonic stress falls on *loathe*. It
would be very odd if in Mary's reply tonic stress was on
tripe (* *I 'loathe ` tripe*).

Furthermore, intonation plays an important role in
turn-taking in dialogue. A fall usually indicates a completed
turn, without the expectation of one's interlocutor replying.
But a rise gives a strong indication that the speaker intends
to continue, or that a response from one's interlocutor is
expected. A simple example of this can be seen in VOCA-
TIVES and in YES-NO QUESTIONS:

[11.45] (a) Vocative
            ` ' Janet (in fact the fall rise is often levelled
            to ¯Ja¯net)
        (b) Yes-No question
            Have you 'lived here for a long ,time?

It is possible to use falling intonation when calling a
person's name e.g. when a school teacher shouts at a
naughty boy: `Smith rather than ` ' Smith. What is the
difference between these two utterances?

A fall-rise calling nucleus (coupled with generally raised
pitch) is the intonation pattern normally used to attract the
addressee's attention. However, a falling nucleus can also
be used for this purpose – with somewhat different prag-

matic force. In our example, (especially if the teacher has a stern look and uses loud and harsh voice quality) this 'call' will in fact probably be interpreted as meaning:

[11.46] ' *pay attention* ' *Smith.*

One of the things that have emerged from this chapter is the fact that phonology has to be placed in a wider context. The discussion of the attitudinal functions of intonation showed the way in which phonology overlaps with verbal paralinguistic properties such as voice quality, pitch-range and tempo. These paralinguistic properties are not part of the linguistic system proper although they impinge on it.

The relationship between language and paralanguage (which includes not only verbal non-linguistic properties such as voice quality and pitch-range but also non-verbal features like eye-contact and posture) is an interesting topic and has attracted considerable interest in the literature (see Argyle (1974); Laver and Hutcheson (1972); Laver (1980) and Lyons (1977)). Unfortunately, we do not have the space to pursue it here.

What we shall explore is the relationship between phonology and the other core components of the linguistic system. At several points in the book we have seen that phonology impinges on grammar and meaning. In the concluding chapter we shall focus on this interaction.

Exercises

1.(a) Study the data below and state verbally the placement of stress in Arabic.

  (b) Draw metrical trees to show where stress falls in the following words: *kátab, kátabu, kátabit, katábt, katábti, lamúuna* and *lamunáat.*

kátab	he wrote
kátabit	she wrote
katábt	you (m.) wrote
katábti	you (f.) wrote
katábna	we wrote
katábtu	you (pl.) wrote
kátabu	they wrote

lamúuna	lemon
lamunáat	lemons
móoza	banana
mozáat	bananas
xóoxa	peach
xoxáat	peaches

2. Ngiyamba (Australia) (Based on Donaldson 1980)
   Study the data below.

(a) Referring to syllable weight, state in general terms the constraints on stress placement in roots and suffixes in Ngiyamba. Which syllables receive primary stress? Which syllables receive secondary stress? And which syllables are unstressed?

(b) Illustrating your answer with examples show how
   (i) primary stress is assigned in roots;
   (ii) secondary stress is assigned in suffixes;
   (iii) secondary stress is assigned in roots;
   (iv) secondary stress is assigned in monosyllabic suffixes with short vowels.
   Note: In the data below, 1 indicates primary stress, and 2, 3 and 4 indicate secondary stress. Unmarked syllables are unstressed.

```
 1
girala              'star'

 1   3
giralaŋ-ga          'on star'

 1      2
girlam-bidi         'big star'

 3    1
gabada:-ga          'on moon'

 3    1
gabada:-bidi        'big moon'

    1
girbadja-gu         '(grey) kangaroos'

 1         2
girbadja-bidi       'big kangaroo'

 1      4      2
yana-wa-y-gara:-dha 'go along all day'
```


$\overset{\text{I}}{\text{yana}}$–wa–y–$\overset{2}{\text{gaː}}$–dha   'go along a bit'

$\overset{\text{I}}{\text{yana}}$–wa–y–$\overset{2}{\text{gaː}}$–giri   '(Let's) go along a bit'

$\overset{\text{I}}{\text{yana}}$–$\overset{2}{\text{buna}}$–wa–$\overset{4}{\text{dha}}$ 'go along back'

$\overset{3}{\text{binjdju}}$–$\overset{\text{I}}{\text{binjdjuːri}}$–nji   '(I) half-recovered (my) balance'

$\overset{\text{I}}{\text{girbadja}}$–gu–$\overset{2}{\text{bagaː}}$–dhi: 'But the kangaroo scented me'

$\overset{\text{I}}{\text{budhaːni}}$–nji   'scent-past tense'

$\overset{\text{I}}{\text{ŋiyam}}$–$\overset{2}{\text{baː}}$ 'Ngiyamba'

$\overset{\text{I}}{\text{gadawu}}$–ga   'on large-leaved sandalwood'

$\overset{\text{I}}{\text{bayirga}}$–gu   'leech -dative case'

$\overset{\text{I}}{\text{maliyan}}$ 'eagle hawk'

$\overset{\text{I}}{\text{mayim}}$–$\overset{2}{\text{buwan}}$ 'with person'

Notes

1. There is a very rich literature on stress in English. SPE is the classic generative work on the subject and any serious student of English stress ought to be familiar with its contents. For an introductory textbook which explores English stress in an accessible way from a non-metrical, non-generative point of view see Knowles (1987). Fudge 1984 is another recent non-metrical, well-exemplified general survey of English stress. Hogg and McCully (1987) is an advanced introductory textbook on metrical phonology. It examines English stress in considerable detail.

The account given here is based on the work of metrical phonologists like Hayes (1982, 1983, 1984) Liberman and Prince (1977) and Prince (1983).

2. Knowles (1987) is an introductory book which deals with English intonation extensively. There are numerous advanced studies of English intonation e.g. Halliday (1967, 1970); Ladd (1980); Pierrehumbert (1980); Cruttenden (1986) which you can consult for more detailed discussion.

CHAPTER 12

Phonology in the Wider Context

12.1 The role of the lexicon

Linguistic theory is interested in sound not just for its own sake, but because it is the medium in which speech is realised. Phonology has to be put in a wider context so that its interaction with the other components of the grammar can be understood. At the beginning of the book, we saw how sounds are used phonemically to contrast word meaning; in the last two chapters we have considered the grammatical and semantic/pragmatic and discourse functions of tone, stress and intonation. In this final chapter we are going to continue with the theme of the relationship between phonology and the rest of the grammar, but this time from a different perspective. We shall highlight the ways in which phonology interfaces with the lexicon and morphology on the one hand, and with syntax on the other.

I think the most promising analysis of the relation between phonology, morphology and the lexicon is the model of LEXICAL PHONOLOGY AND MORPHOLOGY (normally referred to as LEXICAL PHONOLOGY for short). Although it is a recent development, this trend already boasts a substantial amount of literature (see Kiparsky 1982a, 1982b, 1985; Halle and Mohanan 1985; Mohanan 1985; Kaisse and Shaw 1985; Rubach 1985; Pulleyblank 1986).

As its name suggests, lexical phonology gives the LEXICON a key role. This represents a significant departure from previous models. Traditionally, all regular processes were dealt with by rules of the grammar. The lexicon was seen as being no more than an appendix to the grammar, containing unpredictable idiosyncratic phonological, grammatical, semantic and lexical information about morphemes and lexical items. These different kinds of information would be included in the lexicon because of their relevance to the application of semantic, syntactic, morphological and phonological rules.

Phonological information is relevant because speakers need to know how words are pronounced. A lexical representation must contain a distinctive feature matrix showing the representation of the 'segments' which make up the word. In addition, it must contain any idiosyncratic information concerning the association of phonological elements at different phonological tiers. For instance, in a tone language, it must show any syllables which are underlyingly linked with a tone in the lexicon and which do not get assigned tone by regular association principles. In a stress language like English, the lexicon may have to show the special effects which a particular suffix has on the stress pattern of the base to which it is attached. As we saw in the last chapter, some suffixes like *-ee* (in detain*ee*) attract stress to themselves while others, like *-ity* (in electric*ity*) attract stress to the immediately preceding syllable.

Furthermore, the lexicon must contain a list of forms which are exceptions to particular rules as well as a statement of sub-regularities in the language. For example, it needs to show that *sheep* is exceptional in having no overt marking of plural while words like *memoranda, memorabilia, agenda* and *data*, which are borrowed from Latin, form a minor subsystem, where the plural ending *-a* is used.

The lexicon needs to show the various subclasses to which words belong because some morphological and phonological rules only apply to certain subclasses of words. This is most obvious in the differential treatment of loanwords in many languages. In English, for instance, word-formation rules are sensitive to the distinction between native forms and forms borrowed from Latin or French. Thus, except for the word *oddity*, only foreign words of Latin or French origin take the noun-forming suffix *-ity* as in *banality, ferocity* and *community*. The same is true at the phonological level. To take one example, the phoneme /ʒ/ only occurs in English words of French origin. Some of these words are fairly recent borrowings such as *genre, rouge* and *beige* while others, such as *vision,*

usual, occasion and *pleasure* were borrowed from Old French
during the Middle Ages.

It is also necessary to include in the lexicon grammatical properties of words like [+noun], [+adjective] or
[+verb], not only because they are, obviously, relevant to
the application of syntactic rules but also because they may
be important for certain word-formation and phonological
rules. For instance, in English *-ly* can only be attached to
adjective bases to form adverbs (e.g. the adverb *wisely* from
the adjective *wise*). To take another example, /f/ can be realised
as [v] when an *-s* suffix is added after it only where the *-s*
in question represents the noun plural ending (as in *wife*
(singular) and *wives* (plural). Where the *-s* suffix represents
the genitive ending as in *wife's*, the final /f/ of the noun is
unaffected by the suffix.

Finally, the reason for including semantic information
in the lexical representation of words hardly needs
explaining. To the lay person, listing word meanings is *the*
function of the dictionary. But semantic information must
be included for an additional reason: namely, because it can
have a role in both morphological and phonological
processes. It has been noted by students of English word-
formation, for example, that the negative prefix *un-*, which
occurs in words like *uninteresting*, is not freely attachable to
adjectives at the negative end of an implied evaluative scale.
We can form words like *un-happy, un-well* and *un-exciting*
but not **un-sad*, **un-ill* or **un-boring*.

Our last illustration of a semantic constraint on the
applicability of a phonological rule comes from Luganda.
Although Luganda allows nasal plus glide clusters e.g.
[mwa:na] 'child', [mja:lo] 'ports', [ɲwa] 'drink', the cluster
[nj] with an alveolar nasal followed by a palatal glide,
though not outlawed, is severely restricted in its use. This
is because it occurs almost exclusively in taboo words which
belong to the semantic area of defecation – words such as
[kunja] 'defecate', [kinjo] 'anus' and [munjoßoßo] 'dysen-
tery'. Because [nj] has taboo connotations, nowadays
speakers tend increasingly to optionally palatalise underlying /n/ wherever it is followed by a palatal glide so that
words like [kanja:la] 'immature banana' or [munjongo]
'miserable foreigner' are realised as [kaɲa:la] and [muɲo:ŋgo]
respectively, with a palatal nasal. Thus the offending [nj]
sequence is avoided.

12.2 Lexical phonology

We noted in the last section that traditionally, the lexicon has been regarded as nothing more than an appendix to the grammar which contains the idiosyncratic properties of lexical items and morphemes.

Lexical phonology takes a different stance: the lexicon is recognised as a central component of the grammar which contains not only idiosyncratic properties of words and morphemes, but also regular word-formation and phonological rules. It is assumed that word-formation rules of the morphology are directly paired with phonological rules grouped together at various levels. The output of each morphological rule is cycled through the phonology so that the relevant phonological rules of that level are applied to it. One of the main claims of lexical phonology is that both inflectional and derivational word-formation processes can be displayed on a series of linked LEVELS (also called STRATA). This is shown in the diagram in [12.1] which is adapted from Kiparsky 1982a:

[12.1]

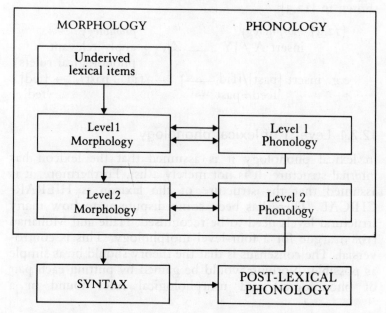

LEXICON

The rules of morphology and phonology applying within the lexicon are essentially CYCLICAL. This is because, as we shall see presently, rules are made to apply in a CYCLE first to the root, then outward to the affixes nearest to the root and then again outward to the outer layer of affixes. In other words, in this theory the word can be likened to an onion with the root of the word as the core and LEVEL 1 as the inner layer, LEVEL 2 as the outer layer and POST-LEXICAL PHONOLOGY as the skin on the outside.

During a derivation there is a constant cycling of data through the interlocking phonological and morphological rules at each level:

[12.2]

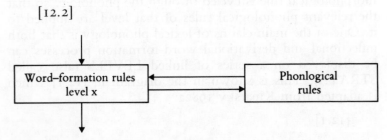

The rules themselves are assumed to have the structure shown in [12.3]:

[12.3] *morphology*   *phonology*
    insert A / [Y _____ Z]$_x$ → apply relevant
                                        phonological rule(s)
  e.g. insert [past]/[fid _____]$_v$ → /fid +past/$_v$ → [fed]
        'feed+past' →   'fed'

12.2.1 Level 1 of lexical phonology

In lexical phonology it is assumed that the lexicon has internal structure. It is not merely a list. Furthermore, it is assumed that the structure of the lexicon is HIERAR-CHICAL. There has been some dispute as to how many structural levels need to be recognised. Halle and Mohanan (1985) argue for a four-level morphology. This is contro-versial. The consensus is that the theory should be as simple as possible. Nothing would be gained by putting each pair of phonological and morphological rules found in a language on a level of their own. But determining the minimal number of strata that is sufficient to account for all the wrinkles in the data is not easy. It is a problem which is still being intensively researched. My preference for the simple model with two lexical strata and one post-lexical stratum is not meant to prejudge the outcome of these investigations.

The onion metaphor captures succinctly the essentials of lexical phonology. At the centre of the word there may be an UNDERIVED lexical item [12.1]. Underived lexical items consist of a single morpheme. They are forms such as *big, boy, girl, talk* and *soon*. No word-formation rule of any kind is used to produce such words. They appear in the lexicon with the phonological, grammatical and semantic properties with which they surface.

Level 1 contains BOUND MORPHEMES like *ab-* and *-duct* in *abduct* or *con-* and *-ate* in *conjugate* which cannot occur independently but must always be attached to some other form.

Some more words containing level 1 bound morphemes are given in [12.4] below. They show one of the important characteristics of level 1 affixes: they tend to be semantically opaque (i.e. their meaning is difficult to pin down):

[12.4] (a) pertain   contain   detain
     (b) perceive   conceive   deceive

     (i) Identify the bound morphemes occurring in the words above.
    (ii) Identify the base and the affix in each example.
    (iii) Does each morpheme you identify have a constant meaning in all the words in which it occurs?
    Note: You are not expected to find *the* answer. This is an open ended question. For further discussion see Aronoff 1976:10 –17.

It is easy to identify the bound morphemes in [12.4], which are all borrowed from Latin. They are the prefixes *per-, con-* and *de-* which were prepositions, and the bases *-tain* and *-ceive*. None of these forms can occur in isolation.

The difficulty is in establishing their exact meaning, independent of some other morpheme with which they combine. For instance, in Latin *per-* was a preposition meaning 'by, through, by means of' but it is doubtful whether any one of these meanings is always relevant to contemporary English speakers' use of words like *pertain* and *perceive*. *Com-* (of which *con-* is a variant) meant 'with, together with' but it is doubtful whether modern English speakers using the words *contain* and *conceive* are normally in any sense aware of these meanings. Finally, *de-* meant 'from' or 'concerning' in Latin. Here again it is debatable if these meanings are salient in the minds of English speakers who have not had a classical education.

Most of the affixes put on level 1 are the ones which, in studies inspired by SPE, were associated with the + boundary. These affixes have a much more intimate relation with the root to which they are attached than level 2 affixes, as we shall see below.

Let us begin by considering inflectional morphology (i.e. grammatically determined alternation in the shape of a word involving categories like number and tense). We shall consider past tense formation in English for our first example. There are several ways of forming the past tense. In the second exercise at the end of Chapter 5 we saw the regular rule which suffixes [d], [t] or [ɪd] to the verb stem. Verb morphology is not altogether regular. Instead of adding that ending, so-called STRONG VERBS undergo changes in the root itself of the kind shown below (ignore the consonants):

[12.5]

	Present		*Past*		*Perfective*
(a)	[ɪ]	~	[æ]	~	[ʌ]
	sing		sang		(has) sung
	ring		rang		(has) rung
(b)	[aɪ]	~	[ɔ]	~	[ɔ]
	fight		fought		(has) fought
(c)	[aɪ]	~	[əʊ]	~	[ɪ]
	drive		drove		(has) driven
	write		wrote		(has) written

(d) [i]   ~ [e]   ~ [e]
    read   read   (has) read
    meet   met   (has)met

The forms in [12.5] show different sub-regularities which a grammar of English needs to capture. Level 1 rules would be used to state the vowel changes which are informally shown above. This illustrates another important property of level 1 rules: they tend to cause drastic changes in the root to which they are attached.

By allowing the verb affixation rules responsible for the alternation in the root itself to apply at level 1, we are able to clear the way for the regular affixation processes which apply to verbs like *walk* ~ *walked* ~ *(has) walked*. Having received their past tense and perfective affixes at level 1, the verbs in [12.5] cannot undergo the more regular verbal affixation processes which apply later at level 2. The theory stipulates that all level 1 rules must precede all level 2 rules which, in turn, precede all post-lexical rules. If a particular rule applies at level 1, it will always have precedence over those rules which are at level 2; if a particular rule is at level 2, it will always precede any rules which apply post-lexically. Thus the ordering of levels has serious implications for the way in which rules interact.

Let us now take another batch of examples:

[12.6] *Noun*   *Verb*
       blood   bleed
       food   feed
       tooth   teethe
       bath   bathe
       house   house

In [12.6] to derive verbs from nouns, two level 1 rules are applied. One rule, which is applicable to all the examples, changes the vowel. In addition, where the final consonant is a voiceless fricative, another level 1 rule operates, changing it into a voiced fricative.

Interestingly, the voicing of a final fricative is a phonological rule which applies elsewhere in level 1 morphology: besides figuring in the derivation of verbs from nouns, it also plays a role in the formation of plural forms of certain nouns such as the following:

[12.7] *Singular*   *Plural*
       [f]   ~   [v]
       hoof   hooves
       wife   wives
       leaf   leaves
       loaf   loaves

First, state the level I word formation process going on in the examples below. Next state the phonological processes that are accompany it.

[12.8] long   length
       strong   strength
       broad   breadth
       wide   width

The morphological process involved is the derivation of nouns from adjectives. Phonologically the *-th* suffix is added, triggering off a change in vowel quality from /ɒ/ to /e/, /ɔ/ to /e/ and /aɪ/ to /ɪ/.[1]

Not all level I affixes are restricted to affecting the segmental phonology of the forms to which they are attached. They can also affect stress. The discussion of some English stress rules in section 11.1.6 highlighted on the one hand strong mode suffixes like *-ity* which attract stress to the immediately preceding syllable and on the other hand weak mode suffixes like *-al* which attract stress to the immediately preceding syllable, only if it is heavy; if the syllable preceding *-al* is light, stress is placed on the second syllable to the left of *-al*:

[12.9] (a) Strong mode suffix *-ity*
           *e*lectric   elec*tri*city
           *ti*mid   ti*mi*dity
           ac*count*   ac*coun*table   accounta*bi*lity
           im*par*tial   impar*ti*ality
       (b) Weak mode suffix *-al*
           *me*dicine   me*di*cinal
           *con*gress   con*gre*ssional
           *ad*jective   adjec*ti*val
           *ac*cident   acc*i*dental

In the light of what has been said above, describe the effect of the following suffixes on stress placement:

[12.10] (a) -ic   as in *phonemic*   and *academic*
        -cide as in *patricide*   and *insecticide*
        -ious as in *acrimonious* and *fallacious*
    (b) -ate   as in *accommodate* and *arrogate*
        -an   as in *American*   and *Franciscan*

The suffixes in [12.10a] are STRONG MODE ones: they place stress on any syllable preceding them while those in [12.10b] are WEAK MODE suffixes and only put stress on the preceding syllable if it is heavy; otherwise they shunt it onto the second syllable to their left.

Certain level 1 suffixes can both affect stress and lead to the modification of the segments in a word. A classic example of this is the suffix *-ity*:

[12.11]   *Adjective*   *Noun*
      (a) sane   /eɪ/   sanity   /æ/
          profane   profanity
      (b) serene   /i/   serenity   /e/
          obscene   obscenity
      (c) virile   /aɪ/   virility   /ɪ/
          senile   senility
      (d) profound /aʊ/   profundity /ʌ/
          pronounce   pronunciation

Find one more pair exemplifying the same vowel alternation as that displayed by the pairs in each group above.

Observe that not only does the presence of the strong mode suffix *-ity* make stress move to the immediately preceding syllable (if it is not already in that position), it also causes the shortening (or laxing) of the diphthong or long (tense) vowel of the root which, as a result, is then realised as the corresponding short (lax) vowel. This vowel shortening rule is called TRISYLLABIC LAXING (SHORTENING) since it only applies to forms with at least three syllables (see section 8.2 page 139).

Trisyllabic laxing which is a level 1 rule, only applies to words formed at level 1. A non-derived form, to which no morphological processes of affixation have applied, is exempt from trisyllabic laxing even when it has three or more syllables and on the face of it appears to satisfy the structural description of this rule. A word like *nightingale* [naɪtɪŋɡeɪl] would be pronounced as *[nɪtɪŋɡeɪl] if it were subject to trisyllabic shortening. But it is not. *Nightingale* /naɪtɪŋɡeɪl/ is an underived lexical item entered as such in the lexicon before any level 1 rules can apply. It is not eligible to undergo trisyllabic laxing which comes later at level 1.

This example is worth dwelling on for it illustrates an important principle, namely STRICT CYCLICITY. In this model, a phonological rule can only affect those strings of sounds that are put together by a word-formation rule applying at the same level. Thus level 1 rules may only modify structure created by level 1 morphological processes and level 2 rules may only change structure created by level 2 morphological processes. The strict cyclicity principle ensures that rules only apply to one layer at a time. The output of a morphological rule at level 1, for instance, cannot undergo a level 2 phonological rule, and vice versa. A rule is not allowed to peep back at a state of affairs preceding arrival at the stratum where it applies, nor is it allowed to glance forward to what might happen at a later stage in a derivation. In a word, strict cyclicity results in a constrained theory which prohibits phonological rules from applying globally. The purpose of imposing restrictions of this kind on the theory is to ensure that we do not allow the grammar to have more power than is absolutely needed to describe the facts of natural language.

Strict cyclicity ensures that phonological rules only have access to morphological information at the same level. When rules referring to grammatical information (which by convention is associated with brackets as in [deny/]$_{verb}$|al]$_{noun}$) apply in the lexicon, the brackets get automatically erased so that subsequent rules at later levels are debarred from referring to that grammatical information. This principle, which is known as the BRACKET ERASURE CONVENTION, means that in order for a rule to apply, it is not necessary to delve into derivational history.[2] For instance,

the regular plural formation rule in English applies in the
same way to an underived noun like *bird* as it does to a
derived noun like *denial*.

In lexical phonology, the ordering of levels serves
another function. It reflects DEGREES OF
PRODUCTIVITY.[3] Level 1 contains the most idiosyncratic
morphological and phonological elements. Many level 1
rules are phonologically idiosyncratic: they tend to have
many exceptions; they are rarely used in the formation of
new words; the class of items they affect and the ways in
which they affect them are usually messy.

We have already noted that strong mode suffixes like
-*ity* and weak mode suffixes like -*al* which cause stress shift
when they are attached to a form all belong to level 1. Level
1 affixes tend to cause more drastic modifications of the base
to which they are attached than level 2 affixes. Thus, unlike
the level 1 suffixes -*al, -ic* and -*ity*, level 2 suffixes like -*er*
and -*ness* do not have any effect on stress: words are stressed
in the same way regardless of the presence or absence of
these suffixes. Thus, in words such as *entertain* ~ *entertainer*
and *aware* ~ *awareness* no stress shift is caused by the
addition of the level 2 suffixes -*er* and -*ness*.

At the segmental level too, level 1 rules tend to show
little regard for the integrity of the base form to which they
are added. As we have seen, the suffix -*ity* frequently causes
a modification of the segments of the base by triggering off
trisyllabic laxing [12.11]. In fact, the disruption caused may
be even more drastic. It may include the deletion of part of
the root:

[12.12] frivol*ous*   frivolity   (*frivol*ou*sity)
        anonym*ous*   anonymity   (*anonym*ou*sity)
        credul*ous*   credulity   (*credul*ou*sity)

In [12.12] when -*ity* is attached to a form ending in -*ous* in
the lexicon, deletion of -*ous* takes place so that -*ity* surfaces in
the phonetic representation next to the segment which
preceded -*ous*.

But this deletion process is sporadic. It fails in [12.13]:

[12.13] relig*ious*   religiosity   (*relig*iou*sity)
        cur*ious*   curiosity   (*cur*iou*sity)
        prec*ious*   preciosity   (*prec*iou*sity)

Here the addition of -*ity* changes the pronunciation of -*ous* from [əs] to [ɒs]. Clearly, the phonological effects of the addition of this suffix are messy (Aronoff 1976).

The -*ity* suffix is not unique in having idiosyncratic phonological properties. Look back at [12.5], [12.6], [12.7] and [12.8] and see the changes in the base form due to the presence of various level 1 suffixes. Describe the phonological effects of each suffix.

Not only do level 1 affixes tend to be phonologically irregular, they also often tend to have idiosyncratic semantic properties. Many level 1 affixes are semantically difficult to pin down. For instance, it is difficult to be specific about the meaning of the suffix -*ity per se*. True, in [12.11] it seems to derive from an adjective a noun which has the general meaning 'the quality/state of being X', e.g. *serenity* is the state of being *serene; divinity* is the quality/state of being *divine*, etc. However, in many other cases it is not possible to identify a common thread of meaning which is shared by words containing that suffix:

[12.14] am*ity*   'friendship'
annu*ity*   'yearly income'
commun*ity*   'group of people living in one
                   locality'
credul*ity*   'readiness to believe'

Perhaps because of their phonological and semantic irregularity, many level 1 affixes are nothing more than historical relics. They are not productive. And others, though still productive, are only used infrequently to form new words. Thus, the suffix -*th* in *length, width, depth* is not used to form new nouns from adjectives in contemporary English, while the suffix -*ity* discussed above, though still used in word-formation is less productive than the level 2 suffix -*ness* which it partially overlaps in meaning. The explanation, according to Aronoff (1976), might be that speakers are more confident to use -*ness* rather than -*ity* because they are unlikely to get things wrong (and make a fool of themselves) as -*ness* does not cause any phonological changes in the base to which it is attached. More-

over, unlike the semantically elusive -*ity*, the meaning of
-*ness* is unproblematic. Its presence consistently produces a
noun meaning 'the quality/state X specified by the adjective' (e.g. *kindness, illness*, etc.).

Likewise, another level 2 suffix, the nominalising suffix
-*er* that derives nouns from verbs (as in *writer* or *maker*)
causes no phonological complications and has an obvious
and uniform meaning of 'person who does whatever X is
specified by the verb'.

Study the words in [12.15]. Divide them into
morphemes and state the meaning of each morpheme.
Comment on any semantically problematic cases which you
encounter.

[12.15]	(a)	(b)	(c)
	adultery	employ	denial
	artillery	embalm	arrival
	machinery	embrace	betrayal
	refinery	embody	recital
	finery	enlarge	trial
	nunnery	ennoble	*teachal
	greenery	endure	*writal
	treachery	engrave	*arrestal
	cannery	engender	*announcal
	fishery	encash	*appointal
	mockery	encase	*sendal

If all morphemes are by definition 'meaningful units',
it should be possible to state unequivocally the meaning of
morphemes like -*ery, en-* and -*al* in [12.15]. But I suspect
that you did not find that task altogether straightforward.
The suffix -*ery* has no consistent meaning which recurs in
all its occurrences in [12.15]. In *cannery, fishery* and *nunnery*
it seems to have a locative meaning, but that meaning is
absent from *treachery, adultery*, etc. Although the prefix *en-*
often has the meaning 'to put into or enclose within' as in
to *encase*, attempting to extend that analysis to a word like
employ would be questionable. (Note in passing the
homorganic nasal assimilation process affecting the prefix
in [12.15b]). Finally, the nominalising suffix -*al* typically has
the meaning 'an act of doing X': an act of **arriving** consti-

tutes an *arrival*, an act of **denying** constitutes a *denial*, etc. But this interpretation is not always valid – an act of **appointing** does not constitute an **appointal* any more than an act of **writing** constitutes a **writal*. There seems to be no good reason for the fact that certain verbs will take a given derivational suffix while others will not.

The problem of erratic semantic behaviour is not restricted to affixes. Many roots to which affixes are attached do not have their own specific and consistent semantic content. It is not possible to say for instance what the roots *-trib-*, *-duce* and *-tend* mean below (unless you happen to know their original Latin meanings: *tribut-* 'allot, grant', *duc-* 'lead' and *tend-* 'stretch'). As English morphemes, they are bound forms which never occur in isolation. Their meaning on any one occasion seems to depend on the meanings of the other morphemes with which they co-occur in the word:

[12.16] (a) contribute   (b) conduce   (c) contend
         attribute   adduce   attend
         distribute   deduce   distend
         retribution   reduction   portend
         tributary   produce   pretend
         tribute   reduce   intend

The upshot of this discussioin is that we must abandon the view that the morpheme *per se* is the minimal meaningful unit. The meaning of a root or affix is often unclear until it is put together with other morphemes in a word. The morpheme may be meaningful, as in the case of *-er* or in the case of a mono-morphemic word like *dog*, but it need not be. There are many bound roots like *-trib-* ,*-duce* and *-tend* which have no clear, identifiable meaning that remains constant when different affixes are attached to them. Similarly, there are many affixes, as we have seen already, to which no steady meaning can be attributed. It is prudent to regard the morpheme primarily as a DISTRIBUTIONAL UNIT. What occupies centre stage, as far as signalling word meaning is concerned, is the word rather than the morpheme. Every word found in the lexicon of a language must be meaningful but every morpheme need not be (Aronoff 1976).

12.2.2 Level 2 of lexical phonology

In the last section we established that level 1 rules are normally more idiosyncratic than level 2 rules. We saw that often the meaning of level 1 affixes is unclear, their phonological effects unsystematic and their very applicability erratic, with many forms which on the face of it ought to undergo a particular level 1 rule failing to do so for no apparent reason. Level 2 rules on the other hand have fewer exceptions and their phonological effects and semantic properties are more predictable. Consider again -*er*, a typical level 2 affix. By suffixing -*er* to it, we can turn virtually any verb base into an agentive nominal meaning 'doer of activity X designated by the verb':

[12.17] read-*er*   mind-*er*
          paint-*er*   speak-*er*
          teach-*er*   join-*er*
          lead-*er*   cook-*er*

I say 'virtually' because even very regular level 2 rules can have occasional exceptions. For instance, there are agentive nominals which are not formed by suffixing -*er*. Some agentive nominals are formed by a process known as CONVERSION or ZERO SUFFIXATION whereby morphological derivation is achieved without the overt addition of an affix, as in the case of *judge* (n) which is derived from *judge* (v) or *bore* (n) from *bore* (v) or *cook* (n) from *cook* (v).

Yet other agentive nominals are formed by adding a suffix other than -*er*. That is the case in the formation of the nouns *applicant* and *defendant* from the verb *apply* and *defend*. These irregular nominalisations take place at level 1 and block the regular level 2 process of adding -*er* to form agentive nominals.

Another kind of irregularity is exemplified by the word *cooker*. It takes the regular ending -*er*, but its meaning is not the expected one of 'a person who cooks', rather it refers to an appliance used to perform the activity of cooking. *Joiner* is another problematic example. This word normally refers to a craftsman who constructs things by joining pieces of wood but it can also refer to a machine for doing various kinds of work in wood. This second meaning is less common.

Find more examples of semantic irregularity in word formation. Suggest a way in which the irregularity could be dealt with by the grammar. We shall come back to this problem in the next section.

From a phonological point of view, the presence of the *-er* ending has no repercussions: it does not affect stress placement nor does it affect the segments of a word in the way that a level 1 suffix like *-th* [12.8] or *-ity* [12.12] and [12.13] can do.

The same applies to other level 2 derivational suffixes such as *-ful*, *-ly*, and *-ness* in [12.18]. There are almost no arbitrary restrictions on the class of forms to which they can be suffixed and they have no quirky phonological or semantic properties:

[12.18] (a) handful   (b) kindly   (c) kindness
        cupful   sadly   illness
        plateful   happily   tiredness
        spoonful   badly   loudness

12.2.3 The elsewhere condition

The ordering of levels in lexical phonology implicitly deals with the problem of rule interaction which was discussed in Chapter 7 by incorporating the ELSEWHERE CONDITION (Kiparsky 1973, 1982b; Koutsoudas *et al.* 1974). This principle can be stated informally thus:

If two rules compete for the same territory,
the more specific rule applies first,
blocking the more general rule.

Normally, a more specific rule applies first and later the general rule applies *elsewhere*. So, putting an inflectional or derivational process at level 1 means that it is subject to a restricted rule which can pre-empt the application of a more general level 2 rule. In inflectional morphology, for instance, the elsewhere condition ensures that the formation of the past tense forms of strong (irregular) verbs like those in [12.5] belongs to level 1 while the more general rules deriving the past tense forms of weak (regular) verbs belong to level 2:

[12.19]

    (a) [sing + past] → (sæŋ] (level 1)
        (pre-empts regular past tense formation at level 2)
    (b) [love + past]
        (i) (no access to level 1 morphology: so miss any level 1 word-formation rules)
        (ii) [lʌv + d] → [lʌvd] (level 2 regular past)
        (love+ed → loved)

The effect of level ordering can be seen more clearly by examining the phenomenon of CONVERSION (or ZERO SUFFIXATION) whereby a word changes its category without the overt addition of an affix, as in a *chair* (n) and *to chair* (v) or *a man* (n) and *to man* (v).

Begin by noting that many strong verbs ending in *-ing* or *-ink* follow the pattern of *sing* ~ *sang* ~ *sung* (viz. *ring* ~ *rang* ~ *rung; sink* ~ *sank* ~ *sunk*, etc. Find two similar examples). However, when a verb is derived from a noun ending in *-ink* or *-ing*, the expected irregularity is lost. Thus, whereas we say '*ring* ~ *rang* ~ *rung*' of ringing a bell, we say the town is '*ringed by mountains*' not ★ ' *rung by mountains*'.

Lexical phonology offers a simple explanation for these facts. The strong verb past tense formation takes place at level 1. The derived verb *ring*, which comes from a noun and has the meaning 'encircle' does not exist at the point when level 1 morphology takes place because the derivation of verbs from nouns occurs at level 2. Verbs derived from nouns can only undergo level 2 past tense inflection in the form of the regular *-ed* ending.

The elsewhere condition is also useful in describing the formation of the plural of nouns. The regular plural formation rule which adds *-s* to form the plural of nouns is a level 2 rule while irregular plural formation whereby nouns take endings like *-ren* as in *children* or *-i* as in *cacti* or *-a* as in *addenda* is a level 1 process. The addition of these irregular plural endings at level 1 blocks the application of the regular plural formation rule. When forms such as [cact+ $i_{pl.}$] or [addend+ $a_{pl.}$] are produced at level 1, it is not possible for the regular level 2 plural formation to apply later, yielding *[cact+$i_{pl.}$+$s_{pl.}$] or *[addend+ $a_{pl.}$ + $s_{pl.}$]

How can we extend our analysis to cover nouns such as *equipment, accommodation, news* and *mumps* which are **inherently** singular, or nouns like *people, police, cattle, scissors* and *trousers* which are **inherently** plural?

The case of inherently singular nouns is not problematic. They have to be marked explicitly with a diacritic or a [-rule n] feature which shows that they are invisible to the rules that assign plural number. So, a word like *equipment* would have a mark on it saying that it is not available to any plural formation rule.

More interesting is the treatment of the inherently plural nouns. What we want to say is that certain words are unavailable for plural formation rules of any kind because they occur as plural underived lexical items in the lexicon. Kiparsky (1982b) suggests that each lexical entry be deemed to be a 'rule' – a special kind of lexical identity rule where the non-derived lexical item is the input and that same non-derived lexical item emerges as the output. Then the derivation of *cattle* or *police*, etc. could be handled as in [12.20]:

[12.20] *Structural description*   *Structural change*

$$[[police] _{N + pl.}] \rightarrow \quad [[police]_{N + pl.}]$$
$$[[cattle]_{N + pl.}] \rightarrow \quad [[cattle]_{N + pl.}]$$

When the output of [12.20] reaches levels 1 and 2, no plural formation rule can affect it since it already bears the mark of plural. The elsewhere condition correctly predicts that being more specific, the idiosyncratic plural rules peculiar to certain nonderived lexical items like *police* take precedence over any more general level 1 or level 2 plural formation rule.

We have seen how level ordering and the elsewhere condition offer a natural way of dealing with rule interaction in situations where one rule blocks another. Now we are going to see how the theory also provides a mechanism for dealing with rule interaction in cases where rules are in a feeding relationship (i.e. where one rule creates the input to another rule (Chapter 7, page 125)).

The theory predicts that the irregular inflection derived at level 1 can form the input to more regular word-formation processes taking place at level 2. This is borne out by [12.21]:

> [12.21](a) paw-marks (*paws-marks)
>   (b) lice-infested (*louse-infested)
>   (Find two similar examples.)

The possibility of level 1 irregular plural formation appearing in compounds suggests that level 1 rules can feed level 2 rules. Having undergone plural formation at level 1, *lice* is still available for compounding later at level 2 in the formation of *lice-infested*. Unfortunately, the facts do not always give unequivocal support to this analysis. We would expect other irregular plurals formed at level 1 such as *feet* and *teeth* to appear in compounds as *feet-steps* and *teeth-brushes* but instead we find *foot-steps* and *tooth-brushes*. Some more investigations are needed to deal with the problem.

12.2.4 The order of affixes

In (12.2) we used the onion metaphor to describe word structure in lexical phonology. We return to that metaphor now and see how it sheds light on rule interaction in word formation by capturing the generalisation that level 1 affixes are placed nearer the root than level 2 affixes:

> [12.22] [[level 2 aff.] [level 1 aff.] root [level 1 aff.]
> [level 2 aff.]]

Consider the nominalising suffix *-ian* as in *politician, electrician, grammarian* and *librarian*, (and also the adjective-forming suffix *-ian* as in *Olympian, Aeolian, Bavarian, Edwardian, Dickensian* and *sesquipedalian*) as well as the nominalizing suffix *-ant* as in *applicant, inhabitant, attendant* and *communicant*. These are all level 1 suffixes. Each one of them attracts stress to the syllable immediately preceding it in the same way that the level 1 suffixes *-ic* and *-ity* described earlier do. On the other hand, the suffix *-ism* as in *baptism* and *communism*, is a level 2 suffix. It does not modify the stress of the base to which it is attached.

The theory predicts that a level 1 affix will be nearer
to the root than a level 2 suffix in cases where both occur
in the same word:

[12.23] Shakespear-*ian-ism*   *Shakespear-*ism-ian*
          antiquar-*ian-ism*   *antiquar-*ism-ian*
          protest-*ant-ism*   *protest-*ism-ant*

A suffix at a given level can be followed by other
suffixes at the same level as in [12.24a] where all the affixes
in question are at level 1, or [12.24b] where all the suffixes
are at level 2 :

[12.24] (a) publ-*ic-ity*
               pur-*if-ic-at-ion*
          (b) re-*re-make*
               care-*ful-ness*

Determine which of the suffixes in [12.25] are at level
1 and which are at level 2. Does this have a bearing on the
ordering of suffixes in a word?

[12.25] electrification
          leaderless

In *electrification* the suffixes -*if(y)* -*ic-(at)ion* are all level
1 suffixes. This can be verified by seeing the way in which,
like numerous level 1 suffixes, they all attract stress: e`lectrify;
e`lectric and electrifi`cation. But in *leaderless* both suffixes are
at level 2. They have no phonological effect on the base.
Moreover, their meaning is reasonably clear and consistent
as is the norm for level 2 affixes.[4]

12.2.5 Post-lexical rules

After all lexical rules have applied, words can be inserted
in syntactic representations to form sentences. Once
sentences have been formed, level 1 and level 2 rules of
lexical phonology cannot apply any more. But that does not
necessarily render words secure from all phonological
modification. The sounds of individual words can still be
modified by rules which apply in CONNECTED

SPEECH, affecting phrases or longer chunks of utterances. In this model such rules are called POST-LEXICAL RULES. They are late rules which apply **after** all lexical rules (see figure [12.1]). Unlike lexical rules, post-lexical rules are not intrinsically cyclic. The output of a lexical phonological rule is not submitted to the morphology or vice versa. Nor do they respect the strict cyclicity principle (section 12.2.1). Unlike lexical rules, post-lexical rules are not restricted to forms derived at the same stage in a derivation. They can affect forms derived at an earlier stage.

For our first illustration of a post-lexical rule we shall consider the floating tone in associative constructions in Mbui described by Hyman and Tadadjeu (1976: 61) which was introduced in [10.21]. The data are repeated here for convenience as [12.26].

[12.26] Mbui:
  (a) bək5ɔ 'crabs' bəndúm 'husbands'
  (b) bək5ɔ bə́ sə́ŋ 'the crabs of the bird'
    bəndúm !bə́ sə́ŋ 'the husbands of the bird'

In isolation both 'crabs' and 'husbands' have L-H tone. When, however, in the associative construction these words come together with a high tone word like [sə́ŋ] as the second noun, the associative marker [bə́] is realised with its underlying high tone after 'crabs' but is downstepped to 'H after 'husbands'. Obviously, this downstepping is a post-lexical rule since it only occurs in an associative phrase and is not present in words in isolation.

For our next example of a post-cyclical rule we shall turn to Chi-mwini, a Bantu language of the Horn of Africa. Kenstowicz and Kisseberth (1977: 86) report that in this language all words have a short final vowel when they occur in isolation:

[12.27] xpala 'to scale' ŋguwo 'clothes'
   kuja 'to eat'   chisu 'knife'
   navaːle 'that he dress' mashuːŋgi 'hair'
   hujo 'one who eats'
   husoːmo 'one who reads'

But all word final short vowels are lengthened if they occur in phrase medial position in a sentence:

[12.28] xpalaːnsi	'to scale fish'
kujaː nama	'to eat meat'
navaleːŋguwo	'that he put on clothes'
hujoːzijo	'one who eats *zijo*'
husomoːchuwo	'one who reads'
ŋguwoːmphiya	'new clothes'
chisuːchile	'knife'
mashuŋgiːmale	'long hair'

Suggest a rule to account for the alternation in vowel length in the words: *navaːle, husoːmo* and *mashuːŋgi* when they occur phrase medially.

A long vowel is shortened when it is followed by another long vowel within the same phonological phrase (marked by a tall bracket) as in *navaleːŋguwo*:

$$[12.29] \quad V \rightarrow [-\text{long}]/\!\!-\ C_0 \left[\begin{array}{c} V \\ [\text{long}] \end{array}\right]$$

In addition to rules which apply only either lexically (within lexical items), or only post-lexically (across word boundaries), there exist other rules which apply anywhere their structural description is satisfied. Such rules are purely phonetically motivated. They get automatically triggered off wherever auspicious phonetic circumstances occur. An example of such a rule is the flapping rule in American English:

$$[12.30] \quad /t/ \rightarrow [\mathfrak{r}] / \ V \underline{\quad} [- \text{stress}]$$

/t/ is realised as [ɾ] (a voiced consonant which sounds like a very short [d]) whenever it occurs intervocalically at the beginning of an unstressed syllable.

This automatically happens within a single word like [pɪɾɪ] 'pity' or across a word boundary as in [geɾɪt] 'get it'.

The glottalisation rule that applies in broadly similar environments in non-standard British English, producing a glottal stop allophone of /t/, is equally unrestricted. The phoneme /t/ has allophone [ʔ] when it occurs either in intervocalic position followed by an unstressed vowel or in word-final position. Glottalisation applies lexically (within a single lexical item) as in [pɪʔɪ] 'pity', and post-lexically (i.e. across a word boundary) as in [geʔɪʔ] 'get it'.

The typical fast casual speech phenomena of elision and assimilation which occur in many languages are mostly post-lexical. For instance, English consonants, in particular alveolar ones, tend to assimilate to the place of articulation of the following consonant, even across a word boundary:

[12.31] (a) bad boy   (b) [bæb bɔɪ]
            good girl   [gʊg gɜl]
            nice shoe   [naɪʃ ʃʊ]

Elision of word final consonants is also common post-lexically, especially where a word which ends in an alveolar consonant is immediately followed by a another word beginning with a consonant. This can be seen by contrasting the lexical and post-lexical forms in [12.32]:

[12.32] (a) *lexical representation*
         best man   /best mæn/
         round peg   /raʊnd peg/
         hand grenade /hænd grəneɪd/
    (b) *post-lexical (connected speech) representation*
         [bes mæn]
         [raʊn peg]   (→ [raʊm peg]
                     if elision optionally feeds assimilation)
         [hæn grəneɪd] (→ [[hæŋ grəneɪd]
                     if elision optionally feeds assimilation)

An important difference between lexical and post-lexical rules is that the former can take into account lexical bracketing: they are sensitive to word boundaries. We saw in the last chapter that lexical rules which assign stress to words may refer to the first or last or penultimate syllable as the case may be. Lexical rules can also look at word internal morphological bracketing introduced at the same pass through the lexicon – see the trisyllabic laxing rule in section 12.2.1 and Dahl's law in Kirundi which only applies when a prefix is immediately followed by a root (section 5.4).

But post-lexical rules cannot do that. They cannot refer

to word internal bracketing: they cannot refer to elements like 'stem' or 'affix' because each time lexical rules apply morphological bracketing relevant to their application is erased by the bracket erasure convention. Consequently, once we leave the lexicon we cannot have any access to the internal organisation of words.

Another interesting difference between lexical and post-lexical rules is that while the former always preserve the canonical morpheme structure of a language, post-lexical rules need not always do so. For instance, in a language where in the underlying representation all syllables and words end in vowels the output of a rule of lexical phonology must be an open syllable. However, a post-lexical rule may create syllables which violate that condition. Syllable structure found in casual fast speech in many languages differs substantially from canonical syllable structure.

Thus in English 'prohibited' consonant sequences may occur in the phonetic representation in these circumstances: underlying voiced consonants which occur in unstressed syllables may assimilate to an adjacent voiceless consonant and become voiceless when a weak [ə] or [ɪ] vowel following them is deleted. This process, which is especially common where grammatical words like *the* and *of* are present, may combine with consonant elision where appropriate, to create syllable structure which is radically different from the normal syllable structure of English. Consider these examples from Brown (1977: 69):

[12.33] UR   PR
/'səʊld   tə   ðə   ['səʊltθ 'pʌblɪk]   'sold to the
pʌblɪk/   public'
/'bæŋk əv 'ɪŋglənd/ ['bæŋkf 'ɪŋglənd]   'Bank of
                                               England'
/ðə 'fɜst 'raʊnd/   ['θfɜs 'raʊnd]   'the first round'
/'ðæts ðənjuz/   ['ðætsθ 'njuz]   'that's the news'

The consonant sequences *ltθ*, *ŋkf*, *θf* and *tsθ* found in [12.33] are not typical of English. They are not allowed to follow a vowel in the same syllable in the underlying representation.

Now take Luganda, a language where in lexical representations all canonical syllables are open and where the only consonant sequences allowed are those where a nasal is followed by another consonant, as in *mbwa* 'dog' or *nte* 'cow'. Notwithstanding the fact that all canonical syllables are open, in fast, casual connected speech vowels can be optionally dropped, giving rise to a number of consonant clusters disallowed at the underlying level:

[12.34] (a) *lexical representation*

situka	'stand up'
fukamila	'kneel down'
kasikonda	'hiccough'
mafuta	'oil'

(b) *post-lexical (connected speech) representation*

[stuka]	'stand up'
[fkamira]	'kneel down'
[kaskonda]	'hiccough'
[mafta]	'oil'

The required rule states that vowels are optionally dropped between a voiceless fricative and a following voiceless consonant.

$$[12.35] \quad V \rightarrow \emptyset \, / \begin{bmatrix} +\text{cont} \\ -\text{son} \\ -\text{voice} \end{bmatrix} \underline{\hspace{1cm}} \begin{bmatrix} -\text{cont} \\ -\text{voice} \end{bmatrix}$$

Finally, note that while lexical rules are exception ridden, post-lexical rules are free from exceptions. Post-lexical rules apply across the board wherever their structural description is met, without being subject to various restrictions. You can witness this by considering glottalisation of /t/ in non-standard British English or flapping of /t/ in American English (see [12.30] above).

12.2.6. Summary

I shall end ths part of the chapter with a summary based on Pulleyblank (1986):

[12.36] (i) At each level (stratum), morphological rules are paired with phonological rules.

(ii) Lexical rules are cyclic: the output of each set of word-formation rules is submitted to the phonological rules of that level. Furthermore, lexical rules only apply to words formed at the pass through the lexicon at which they apply.

(iii) The ordering of strata (levels) determines the sequencing of morphological processes in word-formation: level one rules precede level two rules; lexical rules precede post-lexical rules.

(iv) The output of each lexical stratum of derivation is a word.

(v) The inventory of lexical items of a language is the output of the morphological and phonological rules of the different levels put together.

(vi) Post-lexical rules are not cyclic.

(vii) A sharp distinction is drawn between LEXICAL and POST-LEXICAL rules. The former have access to word-internal structure, are structure preserving, cannot apply across word boundaries, apply cyclically and have exceptions; the latter have none of these properties.

12.3 Prosodic domains

We said above that post-lexical rules apply to the output of the syntax after words have been put together to form sentences. A key theoretical issue that arises concerns the precise nature of the syntactic information which post-lexical phonological rules need to have access to. In SPE the assumption was that phonological rules apply to the output of the syntactic component without being sensitive to syntactic information; these two components of the grammar were thought to be independent of each other and to function without referring to each other closely. In recent years, however, that position has been called into question.

Evidence has been amassed showing that there exists an intimate relationship between phonology and syntax. Post-lexical phonological rules need to know many things about syntactic structure since, in languages as diverse as Ewe, Italian, Spanish and Luganda, certain rules only apply in specific syntactic environments (Clements 1978; Nespor and Vogel 1982, 1986; Hyman *et al.* 1987).

The two key issues are:

(a) What syntactic properties are post-lexical phonological rules sensitive to?
(b) In what form does phonology have access to those syntactic properties?

For different languages different syntactic properties have been shown to play a role in phonology[5]. Having recognised the relevance of syntactic information we could proceed to incorporate that information directly into the phonology using features like [+relative clause], [+impera-tive], etc. But as the same syntactic features tend to recur in rule after rule in a particular language such a solution would fail to capture any important generalisations – it would be as unrevealing as it would be repetitive.

That pitfall is avoided if we incorporate into phono-logical theory PROSODIC DOMAINS within which phonological rules apply. Post-lexical rules would then refer to prosodic domains and not directly to syntactic features which determine them.

In the case of English, Selkirk (1984: 26) suggests that the prosodic hierarchy includes at least the following categories:

[12.37]

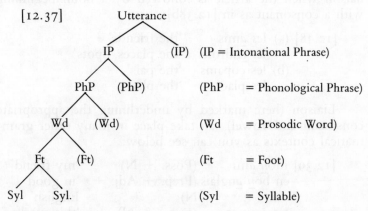

Prosodic domain theory makes the prediction that the domains are arranged in a hierarchy which is strictly adhered to. Domains never overlap. Lower domains are not allowed to include within them elements which belong to higher domains: lower domains form constituents of the higher ones, e.g. phonological phrases contain words; words contain feet; feet contain syllables. The reverse is not envisaged: syllables cannot contain feet, which in turn contain words, which contain phonological phrases.

An introductory book of this kind is not the place to explore the complex topic of prosodic domains in depth. All I shall do is to briefly air some of the issues at stake. I shall do so by outlining the role of syntactically determined phonological phrase domains in the application of liaison in French.

12.3.1 Prosodic domains and French liaison

The essential principles of liaison in French were introduced in Chapter 9 (page 184). Recall that liaison occurs when a word ending in a consonant is followed by another word which begins with a vowel. Re-syllabification takes place so that the consonant becomes the onset and the vowel the nucleus of the new syllable. The effect of this is to preserve open, CV syllable structure as in [12.38a] where the article is followed by a vowel-commencing noun. But there is no liaison when the article is followed by a noun beginning with a consonant as in [12.38b]:

[12.38] (a) le*s a*mis   'the friends'
            le*s e*ndroits   'the places, spots'
        (b) les copains   'the pals'
            les places   'the places'

Liaison (here marked by underlining the appropriate consonant and vowel) can take place in many other gram-matical contexts as you can see below:

[12.39] mo*n a*mi   (Poss. + N)   'my friend'
        en bo*n a*nglais (Prep. + Adj. +   'in good
                          N)   English'
        ce*t ou*vrier   (Dem. + N)   'this worker'
        il es*t a*llé   (Aux + V)   'he is gone'

It would be possible to formulate the rule in such a way that it makes direct reference to the relevant grammatical information, e.g. plural definite article followed by a noun, possessive followed by a noun, adjective followed by a noun etc. But that would miss the important generalisation that in all cases of liaison, the forms involved belong to the same phonological phrase (Selkirk 1978).

Interestingly, the domain of the phonological phrase is syntactically determined. It is governed by X-bar syntax.[6] Liaison only applies where the appropriate consonant and vowel belong to the same major syntactic constituent, such as a noun phrase or verb group, whose elements share the same head. In [12.39] where the constructions in question belong to the same phonological phrase liaison occurs but in [12.40] where the potential candidates for liaison (marked below by = under the consonant) belong to different phonological phrases, liaison fails to apply:

[12.40] Il part à six heures. 'He leaves at six o'clock'
Est-ce le matin ou le 'Is it morning or soir? evening?'
M. Dupont a deux 'Mr Dupont has two fils. sons'
Jean était ainsi occupé 'John was thus occupied'

French liaison is not a rule that applies blindly anywhere. In addition to requiring the right segmental phonological input, it also requires that the sounds belong to the same phonological phrase domain. Membership of a phonological domain is in turn determined by X-bar syntax. Clearly, the relationship between phonology and syntax is intimate.

12.4 Conclusion

This introduction to modern phonological theory has not been completely impartial. My selection of topics has been influenced to some extent by my own interests and to a greater degree by the emerging consensus among generative phonologists over the last twenty years. I have made no attempt to compare the merits of alternative phonological theories. Others have done that. There are already several excellent surveys of twentieth century phonology available (cf. Fischer-Jørgensen 1975; Sommerstein 1977; Anderson 1985).

My aim has not been to provide an encyclopedia of established phonological facts. The state of flux in which contemporary phonology finds itself precludes that. What I have attempted to do is to introduce you through the examination of a considerable amount of data from a wide range of languages, to one coherent model in which important phonological questions are being raised – and in a significant number of cases answered satisfactorily.

Exercises

1. Using the conventions of lexical phonology, show how the following inflectional processes could be dealt with:

	Singular	*plural*
(a)	addend*um*	addend*a*
	agend*um*	agend*a*
(b)	stimul*us*	stimul*i*
	cact*us*	cact*i*
(c)	m*ou*se	m*i*ce
	l*ou*se	l*i*ce
(b)	dog	dog*s*
	cat	cat*s*
	bitch	bitch*es*

2. Study the following data from Kimatumbi, a Bantu language of Tanzania (Odden 1987):

    (a) *long vowel* (shown by VV)   *short vowel* (shown by V)

kikól*oo*mbe	'cleaning shell'	kikól*o*mbe changu 'my cleaning shell'
mik*aá*te	'loaf'	mik*a*té mikúlu 'large loaves'
luk*aá*mba	'string'	luk*a*mbá lwalúpuwaaníké 'string which broke'
kit*úu*mbili	'monkey'	kit*ú*mbili ywaawiile 'monkey who died'
mb*oó*po	'machete'	mb*o*pó ye 'the machete'

(b) [kịkóloombél_{NP}   [chapúwaanịịke]_{VP}
    shell   broke
    'The shell broke'

    [naampéị   [kịkóloombe]_{NP}   [Mambóondo]_{NP}]_{VP}
    I-him-gave shell   Mamboondo
    'I gave Mamboondo the shell'

    [naakịbwéni [kikóloombe]_{NP}   lịịlị́] _{VP}
    I-it-saw   shell   NEG
    'I didn't see the shell'

(c) [naampéị [kịkólombe kịkúlú]_{NP}]_{VP}
    I-him-gave shell   large
    'I gave him a large shell'

    [naampéị   [kịkólombe]_{NP}   [Ø kikúlú]_{NP}]_{VP}
    I-him-gave shell   large
    'I gave the large (thing) a shell'

    [naampéị [kịkóloombe]_{NP} [cha [Ø[ywaángu]_{NP}]_{PP}]_{NP}]_{VP}
    I-him-gave shell   of   mine
    'I gave him the shell of my (human)'

(d) [kikólombe   kịkeéle   chaágu]_{NP}   'my red shell'
    shell   red   my
    *kịkólombe kịkelé chaángu

    [ịkólombe yaángu yanaanchịmá]_{NP} 'my many shells'
    shells   mine   many
    *ịkólombe yangú yanaanchịmá]_{NP}

        Note: NP = noun phrase, VP = verb phrase,
        PP = prepositional phrase

(a) At what point in a derivation does shortening apply?
(b) Referring to syntactic structure describe in detail the
     circumstances in which long vowels are:
     (i) shortened and (ii) not shortened.

3. Referring to the appropriate prosodic domain, state the
        rule that regulates glottalisation of /t/ so that it is
        realised as a glottal stop in nonstandard British English
        in the following data. Glottalisation is marked by
        underlining;
        Glottalisation of intervocalic /t/
          (i) Tom and his ca*t* a*t*e i*t*.
         (ii) I le*t* i*t* in.
        (iii) Tha*t* is the wa*t*er bo*tt*le in which the bu*tt*on fell..

Notes

1. The vowel alternation between e ~ o is a historical relic which goes back all the way to Proto-Indo-European. The name for it is ABLAUT. It is found in other languages of this family e.g. Greek *lego* 'I read' but *logos* 'word' and Latin *tegere* 'to cover' but *toga* 'toga i.e. outer garment'

2. Halle and Mohanan (1985) have relaxed this restriction and allowed 'looping back' from a later stratum to an earlier one in a derivation in certain circumstances.

3. If you can, now read Aronoff (1976: 7–17) for an elucidation of the concepts of 'word', 'morpheme' and 'productivity'.

4. The claim that level 1 affixes are always closer to the root than level 2 suffixes is probably too strong. There are cases where a level 2 affix is nearer to the root than a level 1 affix. For instance, in a word like *desirability*, the suffix *-abil-* which is a level 2 suffix (witness its semantic and phonological predictability) is closer to the root than *-ity* which is a level 1 suffix. We need to adopt a weaker position: in unmarked cases level 1 affixes are nearer the root than level 2 affixes.

5. The syntactic properties considered relevant to phonology have included X-bar categories, traces, c-command and labelled brackets carrying any syntactic features, e.g. definiteness, relative clause, past tense, which play a role in phonology (see Selkirk 1984, Hyman *et al.* 1987, Kaisse 1985, Nespor and Vogel 1982, 1986). Labelled brackets offer the most flexible and at the same time least constrained way of incorporating syntactic information. Ideally their use should be curtailed. The concept of X-bar which is the one we shall be using in this book is explained in the note below.

6. The phrasal categories within which liaison applies are known in syntax as X-bar domains. The head of any syntactic phrase (e.g. a noun phrase) is referred to as X. The phrasal category containing X (e.g. a noun) is called X̄ (or X'), the phrasal category containing X̄ is

in turn referred to as $\bar{\bar{X}}$ (or X''). An example will clarify this. A phrase like *a very clever idea* can be represented thus:

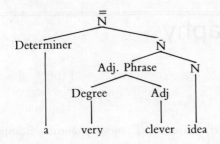

As you can see $\bar{\bar{X}}$ and $\bar{X}$ are 'projections' of X. By definition the head of a noun phrase must be N (a noun). There is an intermediate category $\bar{N}$ which is contained in the $\bar{\bar{N}}$ which corresponds to the noun phrase. The fact that features of X are projected throughout the phrasal domain of which it is head means that a language may not have a noun phrase which has a verb or preposition as its head. (See Radford 1981: 79–117 or Riemsdijk and Williams 1986: 39–54.)

Bibliography

Abercrombie, D. (1967) *Elements of general phonetics*. Edinburgh University Press.

Anderson, S. R. (1974) *The organization of phonology*. Academic Press, New York.

Anderson, S. R. (1985) *Phonology in the twentieth century: theories of rules and theories of representations*. University of Chicago Press, Chicago.

Archangeli, D. and Pulleyblank, D. (1986) *The content and structure of phonological representations*. MS, University of Arizona and University of Southern California.

Argyle, M. (1974) *Bodily communication*. Methuen, London.

Aronoff, M. (1976) *Word formation in generative grammar*. MIT Press, Cambridge, Mass.

Bell, A. and Hooper, J. B. (eds) (1978) *Syllables and segments*. North-Holland, Amsterdam.

Bendor-Samuel, J. (ed.) (1974) *Studies in Nigerian languages. No. 4: Ten Nigerian tone systems*. Institute of Linguistics, Jos and Centre for the Study of Nigerian Languages, Abdullahi Bayero College, Ahmadu Bello University, Kano, Nigeria.

Bloch, B. (1941) 'Phonemic overlapping'. *American speech* **16**, 278–84

Bloomfield, L. (1926) 'A set of postulates for the science of language'. *Language* **2**, 154–64

Bloomfield, L. (1933) *Language*. Holt, New York.

Bolinger, D. (1965a) *Forms of English: accent, morpheme, order*. Harvard University Press, Cambridge, Mass.

Bolinger, D. (1965b) 'Pitch accent and sentence rhythm'. In Bolinger 1965a.

Brown, G. (1972) *Phonological rules and dialect variation: a study of the phonology of Lumasaaba*. Cambridge University Press.

Brown, G. (1977) *Listening to spoken English*. Longman, London.

Chapman, W. H. (1966) *Introduction to practical phonetics*. 3rd edn 1978, Summer Institute of Linguistics. Horsleys Green, High Wycombe.

Chomsky, N. and Halle, M. (1968) *The Sound Pattern of English*. Harper and Row, New York. (This is normally cited as SPE.)

Clements, G. N. (1976) 'Vowel harmony in nonlinear generative phonology: an autosegmental model'. Indiana University Linguistics Club, Bloomington.

Clements, G. N. (1978) 'Tone and syntax in Ewe'. In Napoli D. J. (ed) *Elements of tone, stress and intonation*. Georgetown University Press, Washington, DC.

Clements, G. N. (1985) 'Akan vowel harmony: a nonlinear analysis'. In Goyvaerts, D. (ed) *African Linguistics: essays in memory of M. W. K. Semikenke*. John Benjamins. Amsterdam.

Clements, G. N. and Ford, K. C. (1979) 'Kikuyu tone shift and its synchronic consequences'. *Linguistic inquiry* 10, 179–210

Clements, G. N. and Goldsmith, J. (eds) (1984) *Autosegmental studies in Bantu tone*. Foris Publications, Dordrecht.

Clements, G. N. and Keyser S. J. (1983) *CV phonology*. MIT Press, Cambridge, Mass.

Cope, A. T. (1970) 'Zulu tonal phonology'. *Journal of African Languages* 9, 111–152

Crothers, J. (1971) 'On the abstractness controversy'. *Project on linguistic analysis* 11–12, CR1–CR2–29. University of California, Berkeley.

Cruttenden, A. (1986) *Intonation*. Cambridge University Press.

De Courtenay, B. (1894) *Versuch einer Theorie phonetischer Alternationen*. (German translation) Strassburg, 1895.

Dimmendaal, G. J. (1983) *The Turkana language*. Foris Publications, Dordrecht.

Dinnsen, D. A. (ed) (1979) *Current approaches to phonological theory*. Indiana University Press, Bloomington.

Dodds, R. W. (1977) *Malay*. Teach Yourself Books, Hodder and Stoughton.

Donaldson, T. (1980) *Ngiyambaa : Language of the Wangaaybuwan*. Studies in Linguistics, Cambridge University Press.

Donegan, P. J. and Stampe, D. (1979) 'The study of natural phonology'. In Dinnsen 1979.

Elimelech, B. (1976a) 'A tonal grammar of Etsako'. *UCLA working papers in phonetics* 35

Elimelech, B. (1976b) Noun tonology in Kombe. In Hyman, L. M. (ed) *Studies in Bantu tonology*. Southern California Occasional Publications in Linguistics 3. Department of Linguistics, University of Southern California, Los Angeles.

Firth, J. R. (1948) 'Sounds and Prosodies'. *Transactions of the Philological Society*. Reprinted in Palmer 1970.

Fischer–Jørgensen, E. (1975) *Trends in phonological theory: a historical introduction.* Akademisk Forlag, Copenhagen.

Fromkin, V. (1970) 'The concept of "naturalness" in a universal phonetic theory'. *Glossa* **4**, 29–45

Fromkin, V. (ed) (1978) *Tone a linguistic survey.* Academic Press, New York.

Fudge, E. C. (1969) 'Syllables'. *Journal of linguistics* **5**, 253–86

Fudge, E. C. (1984) *English word stress.* George Allen & Unwin.

Goldsmith, J. (1976) *Autosegmental phonology.* MIT doctoral dissertation. (Published by Garland, New York, 1979.)

Goldsmith, J. (1979) 'The aims of autosegmental phonology'. In Dinnsen 1979.

Grammont, M. (1961) *Traité pratique de prononciation française.* Nouvelle édition, Delagrave, Paris.

Halle, M. and Clements, G. N. (1983) *Problem book in phonology.* MIT Press, Cambridge, Mass.

Halle, M. and Mohanan, K. P. (1985) 'Segmental phonology of modern English'. *Linguistic inquiry* **16**, 57–116

Halle, M. and Vergnaud, J.-R. (1980) 'Three dimensional phonology'. *Journal of linguistic research* **1**, 83–105

Halliday, M. A. K. (1967) *Intonation and grammar in British English.* Mouton, The Hague.

Halliday, M. A. K. (1970) *A course in spoken English: intonation.* Oxford University Press, Oxford.

Harms, R. T. (1968) *Introduction to Phonological Theory.* Prentice-Hall, Englewood Cliffs, New Jersey.

Harris, J. W. (1969) *Spanish phonology.* MIT Press, Cambridge, Mass.

Harris J. W. (1983) *Syllable structure and stress in Spanish.* MIT Press, Cambridge, Mass.

Hayes, B. (1981) *A metrical theory of stress rules.* MIT doctoral dissertation. (Available from Indiana University Linguistics Club, Bloomington.)

Hayes, B. (1982) 'Extrametricality and English stress'. *Linguistic inquiry* **13**, 227–76

Hayes, B. (1983) 'A grid-based theory of English meter'. *Linguistic inquiry* **14**, 357–93

Hayes, B. (1984) 'The phonology of rhythm in English'. *Linguistic Inquiry* **15**, 33–74

Hayes, B. (1986) 'Assimilation as spreading in Toba Batak'. *Linguistic inquiry* **17**, 467–99

Herbert, R. K. (1974) 'Seven will get you five: Luganda vowels'. Paper presented at the fifth conference on African linguistics, Stanford University.

Hockett, C. F. (1947) 'Problems of morphemic analysis'. *Language* **23**, 321–47

Hockett, C. F. (1955) *Manual of phonology*. Indiana University Press, Bloomington.

Hoffmann, C. (1963) *A grammar of the Margi language*. Oxford University Press.

Hogg, R. and McCully, C. B. (1987) *Metrical phonology: a coursebook*. Cambridge University Press.

Hombert, J.-M. (1974) 'Universals of downdrift: their phonetic basis and significance for a theory of tone'. In Schuh, R. (1978) 'Tone rules'. In Fromkin (1978).

Hooper, J. B. (1972) 'The syllable in phonological theory'. *Language* **48**, 525–40

Hooper, J. B. (1976) *An introduction to natural generative phonology*. Academic Press, New York.

Hyman, L. M. (1970) 'How concrete is phonology?' *Language* **46**, 58–76

Hyman, L. M. (1973) 'The role of consonant types in natural tonal assimilations'. In Hyman, L. M. (ed) *Consonant types and tone*. Southern California Occasional Papers in Linguistics 1. Department of Linguistics, University of Southern California, Los Angeles.

Hyman, L. M. (1975) *Phonology: theory and analysis*. Holt Rinehart Winston, New York.

Hyman, L. M. (1985) *A theory of phonological weight*. Foris Publications, Dordrecht.

Hyman, L. M., Katamba, F. and Walusimbi, L. (1987) 'Luganda and the strict layer hypothesis'. *Phonology yearbook* **4**, 87–108

Hyman, L. M. and Pulleyblank, D. (1987) 'On feature copying: parameters of tone rules'. In Hyman, L. M. and Li, C. N. (eds) (1987) *Language Speech and Mind: studies in honor of Victoria A Fromkin*. Croom Helm.

Hyman, L. M. and Tadadjeu, M. (1976) 'Floating tones in Mbam-Nkam'. In Hyman, L. M. (ed) *Studies in Bantu tonology*. Southern California Occasional Papers in Linguistics 3. Department of Linguistics, University of Southern California, Los Angeles.

Introduction to Phonemic Analysis. 1980 Summer Institute of Linguistics. Horsleys Green, High Wycombe.

Jaeggli, O. (1980) 'Spanish diminutives'. In Nuessel, F. H., Jr (ed) *Contemporary studies in Romance languages*. Indiana University Linguistics Club, Bloomington.

Jakobson, R., Fant, G. and Halle, M. (1952) *Preliminaries to speech analysis: the distinctive features and their correlates*. MIT Acoustics Laboratory. 5th printing 1963, MIT Press, Cambridge Mass.

Jakobson, R. and Halle, M. (1956) *Fundamentals of language*. Mouton, The Hague.

Jones, D. (1931) 'On phonemes'. *Travaux du cercle linguistique de Prague* **4**, 74–9.

Joos, M. (1957) *Readings in Linguistics 1*. University of Chicago Press, Chicago.

Kahn, D. (1976) *Syllable-based generalizations in English phonology*. MIT doctoral dissertation. (Published by Garland, New York 1980.)

Kaisse, E. M. (1985) *Connected speech: the interaction of syntax and phonology*. Academic Press, New York.

Kaisse, E. M. and Shaw, P. A. (1985) 'On the theory of lexical phonology'. *Phonology Yearbook* **2**, 1–30

Kaye, J. D. (1971) 'Nasal harmony in Desano'. *Linguistic inquiry* **2**, 37–56

Kennedy, B. H. (1948) *The revised Latin primer*. Longmans, Green and Company, London.

Kenstowicz, M. and Kisseberth, C. (1977) *Topics in Phonological Theory*. Academic Press, New York.

Kenstowicz, M. and Kisseberth, C. (1979) *Generative Phonology*. Academic Press, New York.

Kiparsky, P. (1968) 'How abstract is phonology?' Indiana University Linguistic Club, Bloomington.

Kiparsky, P. (1973) 'Elsewhere in phonology'. In Anderson, S. R. and Kiparsky, P. (eds) *A festschrift for Morris Halle*. Holt Rinehart Winston, New York.

Kiparsky, P. (1979) 'Metrical structure assignment is cyclic'. *Linguistic inquiry* **10**, 421–41

Kiparsky, P. (1982a) 'From cyclic phonology to lexical phonology'. In van der Hulst H. and Smith, N. (eds) (1982a).

Kiparsky, P. (1982b) 'Lexical morphology and phonology'. In Yang, I-S (ed) *Linguistics in the morning calm*. Hanshin, Seoul.

Kiparsky, P. (1985) 'Some consequences of lexical phonology'. *Phonology Yearbook* **2**, 85–138

Knowles, G. (1987) *Patterns of spoken English*. Longman, London.

Koutsoudas, A., Sanders, G. and Noll, C. (1974) 'On the application of phonological rules'. *Language* **50**, 1–28

Ladd, D. R. (1980) *The Structure of intonational meaning*. Indiana University Press, Bloomington.

Ladefoged, P. (1971) *Preliminaries to linguistic phonetics*. University of Chicago Press, Chicago.

Ladefoged, P. (1975) *A course in phonetics*. 2nd edn1982. Harcourt Brace Jovanovich, New York.

Larsen, R. S. and Pike, E. V. (1949) 'Huasteco intonations and phonemes'. *Language* **2**, 268–277

Lass, R. (1984) *Phonology: an introduction to basic concepts*. Cambridge University Press.

Laver, J. (1980) *The phonetic description of voice quality*. Cambridge University Press.

Laver, J. and Hutcheson, S. (eds) (1972) *Face to face communication*. Penguin, Harmondsworth.

Leakey, L. S. B. (1959) *First Lessons in Kikuyu*. East African Literature Bureau, Nairobi.

Leben, W. (1973) *Suprasegmental phonology*. MIT doctoral dissertation. (Published by Garland, New York.)

Leben, W. (1978) 'The representation of tone'. In Fromkin 1978.

Liberman, M. and Prince, A. (1977) 'On stress and linguistic rhythm'. *Linguistic inquiry* **8**, 249–336

Lightfoot, D. (1982) *The language lottery*. MIT Press, Cambridge, Mass.

Lightner, T. M. (1965) 'On the description of vowel and consonant harmony'. *Word* **19**, 376–87

Lyons, J. (1977) *Semantics 1*. Cambridge University Press.

McCarthy, J. (1979) *Formal problems in semitic phonology and morphology*. MIT doctoral dissertation. (Available from Indiana University Linguistic Club, Bloomington.)

McCarthy, J. (1981) 'A prosodic theory of nonconcatenative morphology'. *Linguistic inquiry* **12**, 373–418

McCarthy, J (1982) 'Prosodic templates'. In van der Hulst and Smith (eds) (1982a).

McCarthy, J. (1986) 'OCP effects: gemination and anti-gemination'. *Linguistic inquiry* **17**, 207–63

McCawley, J. D. (1978) 'What is a tone language'. In Fromkin (1978).

Mohanan, K. P. (1982) *Lexical phonology*. MIT doctoral dissertation. (Available from Indiana University Linguistic Club, Bloomington.)

Mohanan, K. P. (1985) 'Syllable structure and lexical strata in English'. *Phonology Yearbook* **2**, 139–155

Mohanan, K. P. (1986) *The theory of lexical phonology*. Reidel, Dordrecht.

Nespor, M. and Vogel, I. (1982) 'Prosodic domains'. In van der Hulst and Smith (1982a).

Nespor, M. and Vogel, I. (1986) *Prosodic phonology*. Foris Publications, Dordrecht.

Newman, J. and Newman, B. (1974) 'Longunda'. In Bendor-Samuel (1974).

Odden, D. (1987) 'Kimatumbi phrasal phonology'. *Phonology yearbook* **4** 37–59

Okoth, D. O. (1979) *Dholuo morphophonemics in a generative framework*. Unpublished MA dissertation University of Nairobi, Kenya.

Palmer, F. R. (ed) (1970) *Prosodic analysis*. Oxford University Press.

Pierrehumbert, J. (1980) *The phonology and phonetics of English intonation*. Unpublished doctoral dissertation. MIT Press Cambridge, Mass.

Pike, K. (1947) *Phonemics: a technique for reducing language to writing.* University of Michigan Publications in Linguistics 3, Ann Arbor.

Pike, K. (1967) *Language in relation to a unified theory of human behaviour.* Mouton, The Hague.

Prince, A. (1983) 'Relating to the grid'. *Linguistic inquiry* 11, 19–100

Pulgram, E. (1970) *Syllable, word, nexus, cursus.* Mouton, The Hague.

Pulleyblank, D. (1986) *Tone in lexical phonology.* Reidel, Dordrecht.

Pullum, G. K. (1978) *Rule interaction and the organization of a grammar.* Garland, New York.

Radford, A. (1981) *Transformational syntax.* Cambridge University Press.

Riemsdijk, H. C. van and Williams, E. (1986) *Introduction to the theory of grammar.* MIT Press, Cambridge, Mass.

Ringen, C. O. (1972) 'On arguments for rule ordering'. *Foundations of language* 8, 266–73

Rubach, J. (1985) 'Lexical phonology: lexical and postlexical derivations'. *Phonology Yearbook* 2, 157–172

Sapir, E. (1925) 'Sound patterns in language'. *Language* 1, 37–51

Sapir, E. (1933) 'La réalité psychologique des phonèmes'. *Journal de psychologie normale et pathologique* 30, 247–65

Schachter, P. and Fromkin, V. A. (1968) 'A phonology of Akan: Akuapem, Asante, and Fante'. *UCLA working papers in phonetics* 9

Schane, S. A. (1968) *French phonology and morphology.* MIT Press, Cambridge, Mass.

Schane, S. A. (1973) *Generative phonology.* Prentice-Hall, Englewood Cliffs, New Jersey.

Schuh, R. (1978) 'Tone rules'. In Fromkin (1978).

Selkirk, E. O. (1978) 'On prosodic structure and its relation to syntactic structure'. Paper presented to the Conference on Mental Representation in Phonology. (Available from Indiana University Linguistics Club, Bloomington.)

Selkirk, E. O. (1980) 'The role of prosodic categories in English word stress'. *Linguistic inquiry* 11, 563–605

Selkirk, E. O. (1984) *Phonology and syntax: the relationship between sound and structure.* MIT Press, Cambridge, Mass.

Sommerstein, A. (1977) *Modern Phonology.* Arnold.

Stampe, D. (1973) *A dissertation on natural phonology.* Unpublished doctoral dissertation, University of Chicago.

Steriade, D. (1982) *Greek prosodies and the nature of syllabification.* Unpublished doctoral dissertation, MIT, Cambridge, Mass.

Thomas, E. (1974) 'Engenni'. In Bendor–Samuel (1974).

Toweett, T. (1975) *Kalenjin nouns and their classification*. Unpublished MA dissertation. University of Nairobi, Kenya.

Trager, G. L. and Smith H. L. (1951) *An outline of English structure*. *Studies in linguistics occasional paper 3*. Battenburg Press, Norman, Oklahama.

Trubetzkoy, N. S. (1939) *Grundzüge der phonologie*, trans. by Baltaxe, C. (1969) *Principles of phonology*. University of California Press, Berkeley.

Twaddell, W. F. (1935) 'On defining the phoneme'. *Language monographs 16*. Reprinted in Joos (1957).

van der Hulst, H. and Smith, N. (1982a) *The structure of phonological representations (Part I)*. Foris Publications, Dordrecht.

van der Hulst, H. and Smith, N. (1982b) *The structure of phonological representations (Part I)*. Foris Publications, Dordrecht.

Vennemann, T. (1972) 'On the theory of syllabic phonology'. *Linguistiche Berichte* 18, 1–18

Vennemann, T. (1974a) 'Phonological concreteness in natural generative grammar'. In Shuy, R. and Bailey, C. J. (eds) (1974) *Toward tomorrow's linguistics*. Georgetown University Press, Washington, D.C.

Vennemann, T. (1974b) 'Words and syllables in natural generative grammar'. *Natural phonology parassession*. Chicago Linguistic Society, Chicago Linguistic Society, Chicago.

Welmers, W. (1973) *African language structures*. University of California Press, Berkeley and Los Angeles.

Whiteley, W. H. and Muli, M. G. (1962) *Practical introduction to Kamba*. Oxford University Press.

Suggested answers to exercises

Some of the questions have more than one 'correct' answer. A solution different from the one suggested below may also be valid. The answer I suggest need not always be regarded as the definitive solution.

Chapter 1

1. (a) Phonetics is the study of SPEECH SOUNDS which humans can produce.
   (b) The three main branches of phonetics are acoustic phonetics, auditory phonetics and articulatory phonetics.
   (c) (i) (a) airstream mechanisms
            (b) production of voicing (technically called PHONATION)
            (c) place of articulation
            (d) manner of articulation
        (ii) (a) lip rounding
             (b) tongue height
             (c) location of the highest point of the tongue at the front, centre or back of the mouth.
        (iii) (a) monophthongs like [e] in *bet*
              (b) diphthongs like [eɪ] in *bait*

2. (i) [l] *l*aw   (ii) [s] *s*aw   (iii) [n] *n*ew   (iv) [h] *h*e
    (v) [b] *b*ee   (vi) [p] *p*ea   (vii) [ŋ] lo*ng*er
    (viii) [ð] *th*en   (ix) [ʃ] *sh*e   (x) [dʒ] *j*et

3. (i) a high front vowel
        f**ee**t fell pat wet full p**ea**t
    (ii) a low front vowel
         what b**a**d c**a**t saw these eggs

(iii) a high back vowel
women suit pool fool blood flood
(In popular North of England speech [blʊd]
blood and [flʊd] *flood* also have a high back vowel.)
(iv) a front vowel
weed word when hat card hit
(v) a back vowel
hut call guard sell soot mist
(vi) a central vowel
skin her winter pertain doctor sir
(In American, Scottish and South-West of
England accents there is considerable R-
COLOURING of the central vowel.)
(vii) a rounded vowel
her good dumb ball pod cart
(In North of England accents [dʊm] *dumb*
would also have a rounded vowel.)
(viii) a high vowel
we do see ten pan bin
(ix) a mid vowel
send card keys school hall you
(x) a low vowel
man moon art cup knot teeth
(xi) a diphthong
why he may boy tar house bird

Chapter 2

1. | *word initially* | | *word finally* | |
    |---|---|---|---|
    | bet | met | cub | come |
    | tell | sell | hit | hiss |
    | zoo | sue | his | hiss |
    | pail | tail | harp | heart |
    | debt | net | maid | main |
    | call | gall | back | bag |
    | see | she | bass | bash |
    | chest | zest | watch | was |
    | char | jar | batch | badge |
    | lad | dad | feel | feed |

2. Voiceless [m̥ l̥ r̥] occur word finally following a voiceless consonant. Voiced [m l r] occur elsewhere.

Chapter 3

1. The segments with the specified feature are circled:

    (i) [+syll]   w p ⓘ ⓔ m h ⓤ g v ⓐ
    (ii) [+ant]   ⓓ ⓩ ʔ ⓟ ⓑ ⓝ N ⓢ ⓞ ⓣ
    (iii) [−cons]   ⓐ f v l r h ⓞ ⓙ x ⓤ
    (iv) [+cor]   v ⓣ ⓡ ⓝ ⓙ ⓛ ŋ x ⓓ k
    (v) [+round]   ⓦ t i ⓤ ⓞ ⓨ ⓞ e l æ
    (vi) [−voice]   o w ⓢ ⓟ l ⓣ g m i ⓠ

2.

	Original segment	Feature value changed		New segment
(i)	i	[+syll]	j	[−syll]
(ii)	u	[+back]	y	[−back]
(iii)	b	[−nasal]	m	[+nasal]
(iv)	e	[−round]	ø	[+round]
(v)	d	[+voice]	t	[−voice]
(vi)	g	[−nasal]	ŋ	[+nasal]

3. (a) The phonetic symbols for the initial segment of each one of the words below are:

that	_cat_	_band_	_wet_	_write_
[ð]	[k]	[b]	[w]	[r]

philosophy	_shy_	_June_	_knee_	_tea_
[f]	[ʃ]	[dʒ]	[n]	[t]

(b)

	ð	k	b	w	r	f	ʃ	dʒ	n	t
cons	+	+	+	−	+	+	+	+	+	+
son	−	−	−	+	+	−	−	−	+	−
syll	−	−	−	−	−	−	−	−	−	−
voice	+	−	+	+	+	−	−	+	+	−
cont	+	−	−	+	+	+	+	−	−	−
nas	−	−	−	−	−	−	−	−	+	−
ant	+	−	+	−	+	+	−	−	+	+
cor	+	−	−	−	+	−	+	+	+	+
lab	−	−	+	+	−	+	−	−	−	−
back	−	+	−	+	−	−	−	−	−	−
high	−	+	−	+	−	−	+	+	−	−

Chapter 4

1. The words which you were asked to read aloud are:
   (i) *den* [den]   (vi) *linguistics* [lɪŋgwɪstɪks]
   (ii) *pan* [pæn]   (vii) *house-breakers* [haʊsbreɪkəz]
   (iii) *science* [saɪəns]   (viii) *individual* [ɪndɪvɪdjʊəl]
   (iv) *sixteen* [sɪkstin]   (ix) *knighthood* [naɪthʊd]
   (v) *angle* [æŋgl̩]   (x) *profusion* [prəfjuʒn̩]

2. (a) full   fool   foot   coot   cut
      /fʊl/   /ful/   /fʊt/   /kut/   /kʌt/
      but   boot   tuck   took
      /bʌt/   /but/   /tʌk/   /tʊk/
      (In the north of England usually standard English /ʌ/
      corresponds to /ʊ/. Hence *cut, but* and *tuck* are realised
      as /kʊt/, /bʊt/ and /tʊk/ respectively.)
   (b) glass   path   mast   plastic   bath   last   laugh
      /glɑs/   /pɑθ/   /mɑst/ /plæstɪk/ /bɑθ/   /lɑst/ /lɑf/
      (In northern English accents standard English /ɑ/
      usually corresponds to /æ/ when it is followed by a
      fricative. The above words are rendered as /glæs/,
      /pæθ/, /mæst/, /plæstɪk/, /bæθ/, /læst/ and /læf/.
   (c) stair   stare   fare   rare   fair
      /steə/   /steə/   /feə/   /reə/   /feə/
      fur   where   wear   were
      /fɜ/   /weə/   /weə/   /wɜ/
   (d) philosophy   finish   enough fish   caution
      /fɪlɒsəfɪ/   /fɪnɪʃ/   /ɪnʌf/ /fɪʃ/ /kɔʃn/
   (e) ringing   wringing bringing   longer   long
      /rɪŋɪŋ/   /rɪŋɪŋ/   /brɪŋɪŋ/   /lɒŋgə/   /lɒŋ/

3. (a) apart   attention   atmosphere
      [əpʰatº]   [ətʰenʃn̩]   [ætmɒsfɪə]
   (b) button   cotton   bottom bacon   baking
      [bʌtn̩]   [kɒtn̩]   [bɒtm̩] [beɪkn̩] [beɪkɪŋ]
   (c) kettle   little   medal metal
      [kʰetɫ]   [lɪtɫ]   [medɫ] [metɫ]
   (d) drain   train   strain   play
      [dreɪn]   [tʰr̥eɪn] [str̥eɪn] [pʰl̥eɪ]
      splay   sweep   scream
      [spl̥eɪ] [swip]   [skr̥im]

Chapter 5

1.(a) A broad phonetic transcription of the English data in example [5.1] above is given below:

A		B		C	
Singular	Plural	Singular	Plural	Singular	Plural
dog	*dogs*	*dock*	*docks*	*witch*	*witches*
/dɒg/	/dɒgz/	/dɒk/	/dɒks/	/wɪtʃ/	/wɪtʃɪz/
bid	*bids*	*bit*	*bits*	*nose*	*noses*
/bɪd/	/bɪdz/	/bɪt/	/bɪts/	/nəʊz/	/nəʊzɪz/
rib	*ribs*	*tip*	*tips*	*marsh*	*marshes*
/rɪb/	/rɪbz/	/tɪp/	/tɪps/	/maʃ/	/maʃɪz/
love	*loves*	*giraffe*	*giraffes*	*badge*	*badges*
/lʌv/	/lʌvz/	/dʒɪraf/	/dʒɪrafs/	/bædʒ/	/bædʒɪz/
sea	*seas*	*moth*	*moths*	*bus*	*buses*
/si/	/siz/	/mɒθ/	/mɒθs/	/bʌs/	/bʌsɪz/

(b) The genitive ending has the same shape as the plural ending. The rule which predicts the shape of the plural ending also applies to the genitive. It is realised as:

    (i) [−z] after words ending in a voiced segment (see column A).

    (ii) [−s] after words ending in a voiceless segment (see column B).

    (iii) [−ɪz] after words ending in a sibilant (i.e. a shrill fricative like /s z ʃ ʒ/ or a shrill affricate like /tʃ/ or /dʒ/) (see column C).

2.(a) A broad phonetic transcription of the data:

present	past	present	past
walk	*walked*	*paint*	*painted*
/wɔk/	/wɔkt/	/peɪnt/	/peɪntɪd/
look	*looked*	*want*	*wanted*
/lʊk/	/lʊkt/	/wɒnt/	/wɒntɪd/
trap	*trapped*	*part*	*parted*
/træp/	/træpt/	/pat/	/patɪd/
wish	*wished*	*fit*	*fitted*
/wɪʃ/	/wɪʃt/	/fɪt/	/fɪtɪd/
laugh	*laughed*	*court*	*courted*
/laf/	/laft/	/kɔt/	/kɔtɪd/
watch	*watched*	*land*	*landed*
/wɒtʃ/	/wɒtʃt/	/lænd/	/lændɪd/

launder	*laundered*	*sound*	*sounded*
/lɔndə/	/lɔndəd/	/saʊnd/	/saʊndɪd/
arm	*armed*	*fade*	*faded*
/ɑm/	/ɑmd/	/feɪd/	/feɪdɪd/
warn	*warned*	*pad*	*padded*
/wɔn/	/wɔnd/	/pæd/	/pædɪd/
sue	*sued*	*row*	*rowed*
/su/	/sud/	/rəʊ/	/rəʊd/

(b) The regular past tense is realised as:
  (i) /−ɪd/ after a verb ending in /t/ or /d/
  (ii) /−t/ after a verb ending in any voiceless segment except /t/
  (iii) /−d/ elsewhere (i.e. after any voiced segment except /d/)
  (Note that this rule also applies to regular past participles
  e.g. *a fitted* ([fɪtɪd]) *carpet*
      a padded ([pædɪd]) *anorak*
      armed ([ɑmd]) *forces*
      a trapped ([træpt]) *animal*).

(c) Both the past tense and the plural endings are subject to the same basic phonological principle of voice assimilation. In the case of the plural, an underlying alveolar fricative agrees in voicing with the last segment of the noun. In the case of the past tense suffix, the underlying alveolar stop agrees in voicing with the last segment of the verb.

However, where the suffix is too similar to the root to which it is attached, a vowel ([ɪ] or [ə]) is inserted to separate the consonant of the suffix from that of the root. This happens when an alveolar sibilant ([z] or [s]) representing the plural suffix (or the genitive suffix or the third person singular present tense marker) would be adjacent to another sibilant as in *buses* [bʌs-ɪz] (not *[bʌs-s]) or *noses* [nəʊz-ɪz] (not *[nəʊz-z]). It also happens where an alveolar stop of the past tense (or past participle) ending would be next to another alveolar stop as in *painted* [peɪntɪd/ (not *[peɪnt-t]) or *padded* [pæd-ɪd/ (not *[pæd-d]).

Chapter 6

1. (a) r l m Ⓚ   *example* Ⓚ is an obstruent but r l m are sonorants

(b) p t x Ⓖ k s f   Ⓖ is voiced, unlike the other consonants

(c) l r n ɲ d w j Ⓣ   Ⓣ is the only voiceless sound in the group

(d) f ʃ t p Ⓖ b θ   Ⓖ is the only nonanterior consonant

(e) s z f v x ʃ Ⓣ   Ⓣ is a stop; the rest are fricatives

(f) pf Ⓓ ts tʃ bv dʒ   Ⓓ is a stop; the rest are affricates

(g) ã õ Ⓘ ũ ỹ   Ⓘ is oral; the rest are nasal

(h) p Ⓜ t s b d   Ⓜ is nasal; the other consonants are oral

(i) b Ⓓ g d   Ⓓ is implosive; the other stops are plosives

(j) e i ɛ Ⓞ̷   Ⓞ̷ is the only front rounded vowel

2. Tairora (Papua New Guinea) (SIL: 1980: 39)

(a) The sounds [l] and [ɾ] are not distinct phonemes. They occur in complementary distribution and are allophones of the same phoneme:
   (i) [l] occurs before the back rounded vowels [u] and [o] (as in [bi'lo], ['bulo], [aluke'loma] and ['biri 'timilo]).
   (ii) [ɾ] occurs elsewhere i.e. before any other vowel (as in [biɾeße], ['iria] [bi'ɾeɾaße ti'lo]).

(b) [b] occurs word-initially and [ß] between vowels within a word (as in [bi'ßa] and [bu'aaßa]).

(c) Intervocalic position tends to be a weak position. In many languages consonants occurring in that environ-ment are moved lower down the strength hierarchy. When flanked by vowels, stops often become fricatives. The phonetic basis of this phonomenon is simple: as vowels are made without obstructing the airstream in the oral tract, in order to minimise articulatory effort in the articulation of a consonant in inter-vocalic position (like the stop [b] in our example), it makes sense for a speaker not to form a strong obstruction of the airstream (which would have to be undone a few milliseconds later). Thus Tairora speakers will produce the bilabial fricative [ß] in between vowels instead of the bilabial stop [b].

3. The addition of the genitive suffix has no effect on the final consonant of the noun. As here the genitive ending is attached to a root ending in a voiceless consonant, the allomorph of genitive morpheme selected is /–s/. This ensures agreement in voicelessness between the suffix and the final root consonant. (The rule accounting for regular plural endings which was worked out on page 300, in the answer to question 1 in Chapter 5, applies here as well.)

In the plural, however, something unusual happens. The final labiodental fricative which is realised as voiceless [f] elsewhere in words like *wife* is realised as voiced [v] in *wives* and other words off this ilk. The form of the plural suffix selected in this case is predictably /–z/. This ensures agreement with the voiced final consonant of the noun root.

The process described above is not purely phonological. Two suffixes which appear to be phonologically identical /–s/ trigger off different phonological alternations. In order to predict the behaviour of these suffixes it is necessary to take into account morphological information as I have done above. The voicing of final fricatives before /–s/ is an idiosyncratic property of the plural morpheme. It is not an automatic, natural phonological alternation.

Chapter 7

1.(a) The rules needed are:
(i) /d/ DELETION: d → ø / — C
(In these compounds the final /d/ of the first word is deleted when the second part of the compound word begins with a consonant.)
(ii) HOMORGANIC NASAL ASSIMILATION
The nasal acquires the place of articulation of the following consonant: alveolar /n/ is realised as bilabial [m] to match the bilabial [b] that comes next.
(The homorganic nasal assimilation rule is written formally in the answer to the next question.)

(b) The first rule feeds the second one. If we assume extrinsic linear ordering, the deletion of /d/ must apply first, creating the input to homorganic nasal assimilation rule.

However, it is possible to handle this rule interaction without insisting on extrinsic linear ordering. Observe that until rule (i) has applied deleting /d/, the nasal is not adjacent to the initial consonant of the second word and cannot therefore assimilate to it. For both /d/ deletion and homorganic nasal assimilation to apply, universal principles require that /d/ deletion precedes homorganic nasal assimilation since a rule cannot apply until its structural description is met. A feeding rule must apply before the rule whose application it facilitates. No explicit linear ordering statement is required.

2.(a) Generative phonologists claim that differences between dialects of the same language can be attributed either,

(i) to innovations in the rule system of one dialect which are not shared by other dialects or to the loss of a particular rule in some dialects,

or

(ii) to a change in the order in which the same rules are applied to the same underlying representations in different dialects.

Any one of these factors will result in differences in the phonetic representation (Kiparsky 1968).

The Lumasaaba data exemplify innovation in the rule system. We can set up /iN-/ as the underlying representation of the noun class prefix. The same form would also serve as the underlying representation of the first person singular personal pronoun. The differences in the phonetic manifestation of the prefixes are due to the rules stated below:

(b) (i) HOMORGANIC NASAL ASSIMILATION

$$\begin{bmatrix} C \\ [+\text{nasal}] \end{bmatrix} \longrightarrow \begin{bmatrix} \alpha\text{ant} \\ \beta\text{cor} \\ \gamma\text{back} \end{bmatrix} / \underline{\quad} \begin{bmatrix} \alpha\text{ant} \\ \beta\text{cor} \\ \gamma\text{back} \end{bmatrix}$$

(This rule was introduced in [7.16] and [7.17] on page 125.)

In dialect A the underlying nasal shares the place of articulation of the following consonant (see *impiso, intemu, iɲcese* and *iŋkafu*).

Dialect B as well has the homorganic nasal assimilation rule. Its effects can be seen where the root begins with a voiced consonant (see [*imbeba, iŋgwe, indima*]).

However, in dialect B, if the root begins with a voiceless consonant (as in [*iːtemu, iːfula, iːkuba*]) two additional rules come into play. They are nasal deletion and compensatory lengthening of the vowel preceding the deleted nasal.

(ii) COMPENSATORY LENGTHENING

$$V \longrightarrow [+long] /\_\_ N \begin{bmatrix} +cons \\ -voice \end{bmatrix}$$

(iii) NASAL DELETION

$$N \longrightarrow \emptyset /\_\_\_ \begin{bmatrix} +cons \\ -voice \end{bmatrix}$$

Rules (ii) and (iii) are an innovation in dialect B. They are absent from dialect A.

(c) First, observe that rule (iii) bleeds rule (i) in dialect B. Nasals are deleted before voiceless consonants. This deprives the homorganic nasal assimilation rule of some of its input. As we have already seen, in this dialect homorganic nasal assimilation is restricted to roots commencing with voiced consonants

Secondly, if extrinsic ordering is assumed, rule (iii) cannot apply before rule (ii) because, if it did, it would remove the nasal whose presence is required by the compensatory lengthening rule.

But extrinsic ordering of these last two rules is not essential. If we stipulate that rules apply at the earliest opportunity when their structural description is satisfied, both (ii) and (iii) can apply directly and simultaneously to the underlying representation since at that point the structural description of both rules is satisfied.

Chapter 8

1.(a) The plural morpheme has the shapes [i], [e] and [ɛ].
(b) The underlying representations of the noun roots are:

    (a) alɔd   'vegetable'
        luð   'stick'
        gɔd   'hill'
        kɔð   'rain'
        guog   'dog'
    (b) lɛp   'tongue'
        lak   'tooth'
        adit   'basket'

    I have posited as underlying the consonants that appear in the plural form of the noun rather than those which occur in the singular form because this allows us greater generality. The solution I am suggesting requires an obstruent devoicing rule which changes underlying voiced obstruents into voiceless obstruents in the data in (a). Obviously, the devoicing rule has no effect on the underlying voiceless obstruents in (b).

    If, instead, we assumed that the words in 1.(a) end in a voiceless obstruent which becomes voiced when it occurs between vowels as a result of the addition of the plural ending, we would be unable to explain why our voicing rule fails to apply to the words in (b). They would have to be marked as exceptions. This solution is to be rejected in favour of the more general first alternative.

(c) The devoicing rule which I propose can be written thus:

$$\begin{bmatrix} +\text{cons} \\ -\text{son} \\ +\text{voice} \end{bmatrix} \rightarrow [-\text{voice}] \, / \, \underline{\quad}\#$$

The voicing rule which I reject would be written thus:

$$\begin{bmatrix} +\text{cons} \\ -\text{son} \\ +\text{voice} \end{bmatrix} \rightarrow [+\text{voice}] \, / \text{V} \, \underline{\quad}\text{V}$$

(d) In the first solution I suggest that underlying voiced obstruents are devoiced word finally (in the singular form). They become indistinguishable from underlying voiceless obstruents like those in (b). In other words, the opposition between voiced and voiceless obstruents is NEUTRALISED (i.e. SUSPENDED) in word final position. For a better known example of the neutralisation of the voicing opposition see the Turkish data in [6.7] on page 103.

2. (a) The only allomorph of the class 12 prefix is /xa-/. The class 9 prefix has these allomorphs:
  [m] before roots commencing with labials
  [n] before roots commencing with alveolars
  [ɲ] before roots commencing with palatals
  [ŋ] before roots commencing with velars
(b) [mbusi], [ndeße]
(c) The rule in question is homorganic nasal assimilation. Proposing a rule is preferable to making a list because it allows us to capture the generalisation that in Luyia nasals assimilate to the place of articulation of the following consonant.
(d) HOMORGANIC NASAL ASSIMILATION

$$C \atop [+\text{nasal}] \rightarrow \begin{bmatrix} \alpha\text{ant} \\ \beta\text{cor} \\ \gamma\text{back} \end{bmatrix} \Big/ \underline{\quad} \begin{bmatrix} \alpha\text{ant} \\ \beta\text{cor} \\ \gamma\text{back} \end{bmatrix}$$

(e) CONTINUANT STRENGTHENING
  The continuants [ß r j] become the stops [b d ɟ] respectively when a nasal prefix is present:
  'hoe'   [xaßako]   ~   [mbako]
  'snake'   [xaremu]   ~   [ndemu]
  'jackal' [xajusi]   ~   [ɲɟusi]
  VOICE ASSIMILATION:
  [t] becomes [d] after a nasal as in 'lemon' e.g. [xatimu] ~ [ndimu]
  PALATAL SONORANT DELETION
  The palatal glide [j] is deleted following a nasal when the next syllable also begins with a nasal as in 'house' /N+jumba/ → /ɲ+jumba/ → [ɲumba]. The same happens to the palatal nasal [ɲ] when the next syllable also contains a nasal as in 'meat' /N+ɲama/ → /ɲ + ɲama/ → [ɲama].
(f) CONTINUANT STRENGTHENING
  [+cont] $\longrightarrow$ [−cont] / [+nasal] $\underline{\quad\quad}$

VOICE ASSIMILATION:

$$\begin{bmatrix} -\text{voice} \\ -\text{cont} \end{bmatrix} \rightarrow [+\text{voice}] \: / \: [+\text{nasal}] \underline{\hspace{2em}}$$

PALATAL SONORANT DELETION

$$\begin{bmatrix} +\text{cor} \\ +\text{high} \\ +\text{sonorant} \end{bmatrix} \rightarrow \emptyset \: /N \underline{\hspace{1em}} VN$$

(g) All the rules above except one are mutually non-affecting. The order in which they apply makes no difference. The only case where the order is relevant is the last two examples.

Since the nasal prefix surfaces as a palatal nasal although the initial nasal of the root is absent from the phonetic representation in class 9, we can assume that the rule of homorganic assimilation applies when the palatal sonorants /j/ and /ɲ/ are still present. The deletion of /j/ and /ɲ/ must apply after homorganic nasal assimilation. If we tried to apply palatal sonorant deletion before homorganic nasal assimilation, the derivation would abort because the palatal nasal which conditions the homorganic nasal assimilation rule would be missing.

3. Hyman (1970) suggests this solution:

(a) A rule palatalising consonants before front vowels applies to the data in (a).

$$[+\text{cons}] \rightarrow [+\text{high}] \: / \underline{\hspace{1em}} \overset{V}{[-\text{back}]}$$

(b) A rule labialising consonants before round vowels applies to the data in (b).

$$[+\text{cons}] \rightarrow [+\text{round}] \: / \underline{\hspace{1em}} \overset{V}{[+\text{round}]}$$

(c) Nothing happens to consonants followed by /a/ which is neither front nor round.

(d) The surface [a] in these words is derived from an underlying /ɛ/ which never occurs phonetically because it is absolutely neutralised with [a]. This derivation is assumed:

(i) UR /egɛ/

(ii) Palatalisation before the underlying front vowel
(by rule a) /egɛ/ → /egʲɛ/
(iii) Lowering: underlying /ɛ/ → [a]
/egʲɛ/ → [egʲa]

(e) The surface [a] in these words is derived from an underlying [ɔ/ which never occurs phonetically because it too is absolutely neutralised with [a]. This derivation is assumed:
  (i) UR /egɔ/
  (ii) Labialisation before the underlying round vowel
  (by rule b) /egɔ/ → /egʷɔ/
  (iii) Lowering: underlying /ɔ/ → [a]
  /egʷɔ/ → [egʷa]

Chapter 9

1.(a) Make a broad transcription of the data below.

met	*fright*	*sphere*
/met/	/fraɪt/	/sfɪə/
strict	*laughed*	*scratched*
/strɪkt/	/lɑft/	/skrætʃt/
juxtapose	*Knesset*	*Gdańsk*
/dʒʌkstəpəʊz/	/kneset/	/gdæɲsk/

(b) Divide the words in syllables using the syllabification convention in [9.10[.

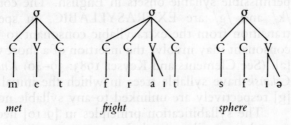

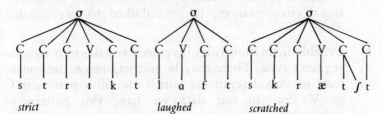

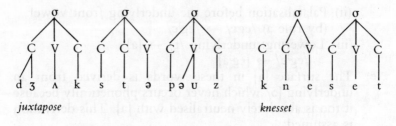

juxtapose   *knesset*

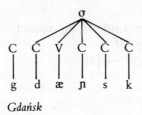

Gdańsk

Remarks:
(a) Diphthongs and affricates are complex elements. In a diphthong (e.g. /aɪ/ as in *fright*) two segments with different phonetic properties occupy a single V slot. Likewise, with affricates like /dʒ/ in *juxtapose* a single C slot is occupied by two consonantal segments.

(b) *Knesset* and *Gdansk* are foreign words which have an initial consonant sequence that does not fit in the English syllable template: /kn/ and /gd/ are not permissible syllable onsets in English. The consonants /k/ and /g/ are EXTRASYLLABIC. In speech the transition from the extrasyllabic consonant to the next consonant may involve the insertion of a short voiceless [ə]. (See Clements and Keyser 1983: 39–40) *Knesset* and *Gdansk* have syllable trees in which the initial [k] and [g] respectively are unlinked to any syllable node.

The syllabification principles in [9.10] need to be amended to allow underlying consonants, in exceptional circumstances, to be unlinked to any syllable node.

2. Syllable formation rules may need to take into account segment type. There may be restrictions on the consonant or vowel segments which can fill a particular C or V slot. In our data we have this pattern of restrictions:

Column A: lax vowels may occur in STRESSED CLOSED syllables

Column B: tense vowels may occur in STRESSED CLOSED syllables

Column C: only tense vowels occur in STRESSED OPEN syllables in monosyllabic words

Column D: only lax vowels can precede /ŋ/.

3. The plural definite article /lez/ contains an underlying final /z/ which only surfaces when it is followed by a vowel (as in *les animaux* [lez animo]) and is deleted in preconsonantal position (as in *les dames* [le dam]). We can assume that this consonant is underlyingly EXTRAMETRICAL. It cannot be pronounced unless it gets associated to a syllable node during a derivation. French being a language which generally prefers open syllables, in cases where the extrasyllabic consonant is followed by a consonant it is deleted:

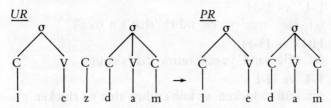

But when the extrasyllabic consonant is followed by a vowel it is preserved. It is linked by the liaison rule to the syllable node to its right and functions as a syllable onset. This is shown by the broken line drawn between /z/ and the syllable node dominating /a/:

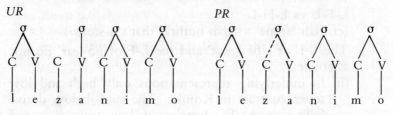

les animux

Chapter 10

1.(a) In the Bekwarra data tone has a lexical function. There are no minimal pairs distinguished solely by pitch but at the same time it would not be possible to predict the pitch that occurs in a given position in a word. The examples contain many near minimal pairs. We can recognise high (′), mid (—) and low (‵) tone as phonemic using the principle of contrast in analogous environments on the basis of pairs like:

[ókú] ~ [úkò], [īgē] ~ [ījè] [īdē] ~ [īnē]
[ùbú] ~ [ùpù] [ápì] ~ [àbì] [ūbì/ ~ [ābì]

(b) The data shows that Bekwarra is a register tone language. All the tones have level high, mid or low pitch. There are no rising or falling contour tones.

2. (i) The following tonal alternations are observed (based on Elimelech 1976[b]):

L-L° vs L-H
(cf. èlè° 'tree' vs èlé ndirà 'that's a tree')

H-D vs H-H
(cf. célè 'sand' vs célé ndîrà 'that's sand')

F-L vs H-L
(cf. kûɓà 'chicken' vs kúɓà ndírà 'that's a chicken')

H-F-L vs L-L-L
(cf. íbûmù 'belly' vs ìbùmù ndiɟirà 'that's a belly')

L-L-L° vs L-L-H
(cf. ßiɲɔ̀nì° 'bird' vs ßìɲɔ̀ní ndíßírà 'that's a bird')

L-H-D vs L-H-H
(cf. ikáyì 'leaf' vs ikáyi ndijirà 'that's a leaf')

L-F-L vs L-H-L
(cf. ilâlì 'stone' vs ìláli ndíɟirà 'that's a stone')

The L-L of tàɓà 'goat' and the L-F of ilɔ̂ 'ear' do not alternate.

(ii) In underlying representations only high and low tones contrast in Kombe. The rules below derive falling tone (F), unreleased low tone (L°) and downstep high tone (D).

Falling tone
The F occurs in penultimate position before a L tone followed by a pause as in:

kûbà 'chicken' à tóyèndì 'he saw a chicken'
              kûɓà
ìlâlì 'stone' à tóyèndì 'he saw a stone'
            ìlâlì

Where these nouns occur phrase medially the F tone is simplified to H. This is the case in the identification construction:

kûɓà 'chicken' kúɓà ndirà 'that's a chicken'
ìlâlì 'stone' ìláli ndíɟìrà 'that's a stone'

Falling tones are derived from underlying high tones by a rule which spreads the L tone in pre-pausal position to the preceding vowel:

As a result of this rule, the first vowel is simultaneously associated with a high and a low tone. This makes it a falling tone.

Unreleased low tone (L°)
L° occurs word finally after a L and followed by a pause:

èlè° 'tree' à tóyèndì èlè° 'he saw a tree'
ɓìɲɔnì° 'bird' à tóyèndì ɓiɲɔni° 'he saw a bird'

But when the relevant nouns occur in phrase medial position, instead of L° we find a H tone:

èlè° 'tree' èlé ndìrà 'that's a tree'
ɓìɲɔnì° 'bird' ɓìɲɔní ndíɓìrà 'that's a bird'

We shall therefore assume that L° tone is derived from an underlying H. A high tone is lowered to L° when preceded by L and followed by a pause.

The L tone spreads from the first vowel to the second. Interestingly, in the phonetic representation the language distinguishes these derived unreleased (non-falling) low tones from falling low tones which come from underlying low tones (see *tàɓà*).

Downstep tone

Downstep is restricted to final syllables of nouns:

cɛ́lɛ̀ 'sand' à tóyèndì cɛ́lɛ̀ 'he saw sand'
ikáyì 'leaf' à tóyèndì ikáyì 'he saw a leaf'

Always D is preceded by H and followed by a pause. D does not occur when a noun is inside a phrase:

cɛ́lɛ̀ 'sand' cɛ́lé ndîrà 'that's sand'
ikáyì 'leaf' ikáyí ndîjîrà 'that's a leaf'

The rule stating that underlying H becomes D when it is preceded by H and followed by a pause is given below (with # # marking a phrase boundary):

$$
\begin{bmatrix} H & H \\ | & | \\ V & V & \# \# \end{bmatrix} \rightarrow \begin{bmatrix} H & H & D \\ | & | & \nearrow \\ V & V & \# \# \end{bmatrix}
$$

These data foreshadow the problem of PHON-OLOGICAL DOMAINS which is explored in the final chapter: certain rules only apply within a syllable, other rules only apply within a word or even only within words of a particular category and other rules only apply within a phonological phrase.

Chapter 11

1.(a) Stress placement in Arabic is sensitive to syllable weight. A syllable with a short vowel (CV) followed by nothing is light. But a syllable containing a long vowel (CV:) or a short vowel followed by at least one consonant (CVC) is heavy. Furthermore, a word final consonant is extrametrical and does not contribute anything to the weight of a syllable. So, CVC syllables in word final position are light. In that position only CVCC syllables and syllables with long vowels count as heavy.

The Arabic stress rule is reminiscent of the Latin

stress rule: stress falls on the first heavy syllable, counting from the right-hand end of the word. In a disyllabic word with no heavy syllables stress goes on the initial (penultimate) syllable. In longer words with no heavy syllable stress goes on the antepenultimate syllable. The operation of this rule is shown below in (b).

(b) Metrical trees to show where stress falls in the words: *kátab, kátabu, kátabit, katábt, katábti, lamúuna* and *lamunáat* are shown below. (Note that it makes no difference whether trees are drawn above the words as I did in the text of Chapter 9 or below the word as I have done here.)

(a) ká - ta(b)   The final consonant is extrametrical.
     s   w   Therefore the final syllable is light
      \   /   although it ends in a consonant. It
       \   /   is skipped over. Stress goes on the
        \ /   first syllable.

(b) ká - ta - bi(t)   Final /t/ is extrametrical. In a word
    ká - ta - bu   of more than two syllables, where
     s   w   w   as here, none of the syllables is
      \ | /   heavy, stress goes on the antepenul-
       \ | /   timate syllable.
        \   s/
          s

(c) ka - táb - ti   Stress is on the heavy CVC or CV:
    la - múu - na   syllable in penultimate position.
     w   s   w
      \ | /
       \ | /
        \   s/
          s

(d) la - mu - náa(t)   Even though the final /t/ is extra-
     w   w   s   metrical, the last syllable is still
      \ | /   heavy (CV:). As it contains a long
       \ | /   vowel it receives the stress.
         s

2. Ngiyamba (Australia) (Based on Donaldson 1980)
(a) The most salient characteristics of Ngiyamba stress are summarised in this section.
    (i) This language has a quantity sensitive metrical structure, with the left-hand dominant. Primary stress falls on the initial syllable if a word contains no long vowels or on the heavy syllable (with a

long vowel) nearest to the beginning of a word, if there is one.

(ii) The assignment of secondary stress is subject to a rhythm rule requiring an alternating stress pattern. On the one hand, adjacent syllables cannot receive stress even where they otherwise qualify to bear it, and on the other hand, no more than two unstressed syllables can occur in a sequence.

(iii) Any word–final syllable is extrametrical. It is 'invisible' to stress rules – unless it contains a long vowel.

(b) The following analysis, based on Donaldson (1980: 42) informally exemplifies Ngiyamba stress rules:

STRESS RULE 1: PRIMARY STRESS IN ROOTS

(i) If a root contains no heavy syllable (with a long vowel), primary word stress falls on the first
$$\overset{\text{I}}{}$$
syllable (as in *girala*).

(ii) If a word contains a heavy syllable, primary word stress falls on the first heavy syllable, i.e. the
$$\overset{3}{}\quad\overset{\text{I}}{}$$
syllable containing a long vowel (as in *gabadaː-ga,*
$$\overset{3}{}\ \overset{\text{I}}{}\qquad\overset{3}{}\qquad\overset{\text{I}}{}$$
gabadaː-bidi and *binjdju-binjdjuːri-nji*).

(iii) In a trisyllabic root without long vowels, if the final syllable is open and a monosyllabic final suffix with a short vowel follows, primary stress
$$\overset{\text{I}}{}$$
falls on the second syllable, as in *girbadja-gu* and
$$\overset{\text{I}}{}$$
bayirga-gu.

STRESS RULE 2: SECONDARY STRESS IN SUFFIXES

(i) Secondary stress falls on each (heavy) syllable containing a long vowel in each suffix so long as no adjacent syllables are stressed.

(ii) If a suffix has no long vowel, and has more than one syllable, stress falls on the first syllable. This is an ITERATIVE rule. It applies to each suffix in turn, starting with the first to be affixed to the root, provided that none of the general constraints mentioned above is violated. For instance, the rule does not apply in cases where it would otherwise place a secondary stress adjacent to a root-final syll-

able with primary stress as in gabadaː-_bidi_, or to a suffix-final syllable with secondary stress, as in

yana-wa-gaː-giri.

STRESS RULE 3: SECONDARY STRESS IN ROOTS

(i) Secondary stress falls on the first syllable of a root if primary stress falls on some other syllable than the first or second (adjacent) syllable, as in gabadaː- ga, gabadaː-bidi and binjdju-binjdjuːri-nji.

(ii) Secondary stress falls on alternate syllables of the root to the right of the syllable carrying primary stress, as in giralan-ga unless this would result in two adjacent syllables being stressed. The effect of this constraint can be seen in giralam-bidi and girbadja-bidi.

STRESS RULE 4: SECONDARY STRESS IN MONOSYLLABIC SUFFIXES WITH SHORT VOWELS

Secondary stress falls on monosyllabic suffixes with short vowels which are adjacent to unstressed syllables, as in yana-wa-y-garaː-dha and yana-buna-wa-dha.

Chapter 12

1. We assume that the irregular plural formation processes in (a)–(c) take place at level 1. In order to qualify for any one of these ways of forming the plural, a noun must be expressly marked [+ rule a] to show that it undergoes the rule which 'replaces' the singular ending -um with the plural ending -a, or [+ rule b] which 'replaces' the singular ending -us with the plural ending -i or [+ rule c] which causes the internal vowel change

/aʊ/ → /aɪ/. Any of these level 1 rules BLOCKS the application of the later level 2 regular plural formation rule exemplified in (d). Having been already inflected for plural at level 1, the forms in (a)–(c) cannot subsequently undergo the regular level 2 rule.

2. Kimatumbi (Based on Odden 1987)
(a) Shortening is a POST-LEXICAL rule. It applies after words have been put together by the syntax to form phrases.
(b) Shortening in Kimatumbi only applies within a single X̄-bar domain.
  (i) A long vowel in a noun stem is shortened if the stem is the head of the noun phrase and occurs in phrase medial position. This is illustrated by the data in (a).
  (ii) Shortening fails to apply if the noun is not immediately followed by a modifier within the noun phrase of which it is the head.
    Thus in (b) shortening fails because the noun is followed by a verb phrase (*chaapúwaaniike*) or by a noun which is not in the same NP (*Mamboondo*).
    Likewise, in (c) the long vowel is shortened in the first example where [kị̄kólombe kikúlú]ₙₚ is a single noun phrase whose head is [kị̄kóloombe] but shortening is blocked in the second example where the same words are adjacent to each other but do not belong to the same noun phrase: [kị̄kóloombe]ₙₚ [Økikulu]ₙₚ. This shows that it is constituent structure rather than lexical category or grammatical agreement that determines the applicability of the shortening rule.
    Finally, in (d) we can see that shortening only applies to a noun which is the head of a noun phrase. Thus, the long vowels of the adjective *kikeéle* and the possessive *yaángu* fail to shorten when they occur in phrase medial position.

3. The English glottalisation rule applies to /t/ when it is initial in an unstressed syllable and occurs either

between vowels or between a vowel and a sonorant like /l/ or /n/:

$$t \rightarrow ? \, / \, V \, \underline{\hspace{2cm}} \begin{bmatrix} -\text{stress} \\ -\text{consonant} \\ +\text{sonorant} \end{bmatrix}$$

This rule applies both lexically as in *wat̲er*, *bot̲tle* and *but̲ton* and post-lexically as in *let̲ it̲ in*.

Language Index

Subject Index